Acknowledgments

Since its initial appearance as a guide to Notes 3, this book has been through countless phases of updating and revision. The advice and encouragement of many people has made sure that it covers what you, the reader, need to know.

First, thanks to Miriam for again performing the labors of Hercules while I closeted myself away with disks and manuals. Without her months of good-natured support and counsel, this book would not have come together.

A large cast of people at Sybex worked on this book, all with great professionalism, but several deserve particular thanks. Jim Sumser, my original developmental editor, gets credit for everything from the initial idea to making sure the first edition kept on schedule (or close to it). My thanks go also to Suzanne Rotondo for her friendly assistance on the second edition.

For this edition, developmental editor Neil Edde provided rock-solid direction and unfailing assistance. Project editor Brenda Frink skillfully managed production schedules to keep the book on track.

Anamary Ehlen edited the manuscript with good humor and aplomb. You should thank her each time the step-by-step directions help you to successfully accomplish a task in Notes. Chris Kirby scrupulously checked the descriptions of Notes procedures and gave sage technical advice.

I also want to thank Anton Reut, Bob Bihlmayer, Alissa Feinberg, Kate Kaminski, Jennifer Metzger, Theresa Gonzalez, Ronn Jost, and Patrick Dintino from the production team.

Finally, I'd like to thank Michael Miller, who gave me the opportunity to learn about Notes in the first place.

Contents at a Glance

27.59.

Waterford Institute of Technology
Libraries
Cork Road, Waterford, Ireland.
Tel: (051) 302616

The ABCs of
Lotus® Notes® 4.5

Rupert Clayton

SYBEX®

San Francisco - Paris - Düsseldorf - Soest

Associate Publisher: Amy Romanoff
Acquisitions Manager: Kristine Plachy
Acquisitions & Developmental Editor: Neil Edde
Editor: Anamary Ehlen
Project Editor: Brenda Frink
Technical Editor: Chris Kirby
Book Designer: Catalin Dulfu
Graphic Illustrator: Patrick Dintino
Electronic Publishing Specialists: Bob Bihlmayer, Kate Kaminski, and Alissa Feinberg
Production Coordinator: Anton Reut
Proofreaders: Jennifer Metzger, Theresa Gonzalez
Indexer: Ted Laux
Cover Designer: Design Site
Cover Illustrator/Photographer: Mark Johann

Screen reproductions produced with Collage Complete.

Collage Complete is a trademark of Inner Media Inc.

SYBEX is a registered trademark of SYBEX Inc.

Earlier versions of this book were published under the titles *Lotus Notes Plain & Simple* ©1995 SYBEX Inc. and *Lotus Notes 4 Plain & Simple* ©1996 SYBEX Inc.

Library of Congress Card Number: 97-66373
ISBN: 0-7821-2085-7

Manufactured in the United States of America

10 9 8 7 6 5 4 3 2 1

Table of Contents

PART 2: WORKING WITH NOTES DOCUMENTS 73

Chapter 5: Finding Your Way around in Notes 74

Chapter 6: Building a Better Memo 90

Chapter 10: Standard Notes Databases 190

Chapter 11: Using the Web Navigator 208

PART 4: ADVANCED NOTES FEATURES 277

Chapter 14: Notes Tools 278

Introduction

Welcome to Lotus Notes 4.5, the foremost software for workgroups. Notes offers a variety of new ways to collaborate with coworkers and to find information. Although the range of things you can do in Notes is very broad, learning how to use the program is very easy. With the help of this book, you'll soon find that Notes is an efficient addition to the tools you use to do your job.

This book can help you learn about Notes whether:

- You've never used Notes before (and maybe you're not even too sure what Notes does).
- You've been using Notes for a while, but would like to make Notes work more effectively for you.
- You're upgrading to Notes 4.5 from an earlier version and want to learn how to use Notes' new features.

What Is Notes?

Notes is the most successful example of a new type of software called *workgroup software,* or *groupware*. Not all groupware does precisely the same thing, but its general aim is to help a group of computer users, from a few people up to a multinational company, exchange information via a computer network.

Notes' particular strength is that it lets you exchange almost any type of information with a virtually unlimited number of colleagues anywhere in the world. In practice, Notes allows you to do three main things:

Electronic mail You can send electronic mail to coworkers through Notes. By pressing a few keys, you can send a message to someone on the floor above or on the other side of the globe. Electronic mail, or e-mail, is a core part of Notes, and it's what we concentrate on in the first part of this book.

Shared databases You can share information with colleagues via shared databases. Understanding what this means and why it is useful takes a little time. The best way is to learn how to use Notes e-mail first. Once you are comfortable with e-mail, using Notes' information-sharing capabilities becomes more intuitive.

Workflow management You can use Notes to simplify and speed up many "paper shuffling" processes. Notes can route requests, requisitions, orders, and customer complaints efficiently through an organization. Although each company has different needs and procedures, the skills you learn from using Notes e-mail are the main key to using a Notes workflow system.

Just to pique your interest, here are some of the ways that Notes lets people share information. *Discussion databases* let colleagues present suggestions and comment on others' ideas. *Document libraries* can replace all sorts of paper records, from product catalogs to legal contracts. *Workflow databases* can automate corporate processes, such as compiling and approving employees' performance reviews or fielding product support calls. Notes' *Web Navigator* gives you complete access to the Internet and lets you combine World Wide Web information into Notes databases. In fact, Notes databases can manage most kinds of information that you would want to share with coworkers.

What's New in Notes 4.5?

If you've used Notes before, you'll find that version 4.5 is both easier to use and more powerful. That might seem to be what every new or improved software package claims, but it really is true with Notes 4.5. Version 4.5 offers two main improvements on Notes 4: It integrates full scheduling and calendar capabilities into Notes, and it gives you wider access to the World Wide Web. Notes 4 itself made many radical improvements to Notes' capabilities.

Of course, it may take you a short while to get used to some of the new ways things are presented in Notes. Throughout this book, I'll tell you when Notes 4.5 does something differently than earlier versions.

If you're completely new to Notes, don't worry that the list of new features in Notes 4.5 seems a bit intimidating. The basic way that Notes works is more straightforward than ever before, and you have the advantage over experienced Notes users in that you don't have to "unlearn" any old techniques.

Here are some of the main changes you will notice if you are upgrading to Notes 4.5 from Notes 4 or 4.1:

- A complete range of **calendar functions** lets you manage your schedule and coordinate it with other people's. You can invite Notes-using colleagues to meetings, check their availability, and book rooms and equipment.
- A new **Personal Web Navigator** lets you browse the Web without the need to connect to an InterNotes Server.
- You can track changes to Web pages with **Page Minder** and preload links with **Web Ahead**.
- New **table formatting** options include the ability to merge and split cells, add fancy borders, and change the background color.
- You can use one of three new **text special effects**.
- Mobile users can dial a **hunt group** to connect to any of several servers via a single phone number.

If You Have Been Using Notes 3

If you are upgrading to Notes 4.5 from Notes 3.x, you will also notice these major new features:

- A new **three-pane window** interface makes it a lot easier to work your way through your mailbox and other Notes databases.
- **Folders** let you sort documents yourself.
- **Navigators** give you a graphical means of finding your way through databases. Now you can click on a city on a map and have Notes show you your suppliers or customers in that city.
- **Agents** provide an easy way to automate repetitive tasks. An agent could track down all the customer complaints about a particular new product and mail these customers an explanation of what you're doing to solve the problem.
- **Text-editing** is a lot less frustrating, with better control over tables, lists, and paragraph styles, and the addition of **InfoBoxes** lets you change things like fonts and tabs without poking through menus.

Mobile users upgrading from Notes 3.x also get some major improvements:

- A new **Replicator Tab** in the workspace gives you a point-and-click way to keep your Notes information up to date.

- New **named locations** let you tell Notes how you want to connect at each place you use the program (Home, Head Office, Milwaukee Office, Hotel, etc.).
- **Stacked Replicas** clear up the desktop clutter of having to find homes for multiple replicas of each database you use. As a bonus, Notes will remember which one you prefer to use in which location.
- **Field-level replication** is a behind-the-scenes improvement that dramatically reduces the amount of time most remote Notes users need to spend connected to a server to update their databases.
- **Server Passthru** frees remote Notes users to work with databases on Notes servers beyond just the one they dial into.

Even if the names sound complicated, this stuff will actually make being a mobile Notes user easier.

What Are Notes Mail and Notes Desktop?

Lotus Notes Mail and Lotus Notes Desktop are less expensive versions of Notes. Notes Desktop is a little more expensive than Notes Mail and a little less expensive than regular Notes. As you might expect, its capabilities also fall somewhere between the two.

Both Notes Mail and Notes Desktop users can use Notes' mail functions in exactly the same way as regular Notes users.

Confusingly, Lotus also uses the words "Notes mail" for e-mail that you create or receive in Notes. In this book I have used Notes Mail (with a capital M) on the few occasions I have needed to refer specifically to the Lotus Notes Mail software. All the other times you see Notes mail (not capitalized), the words refer to the general process of sending messages back and forth in Notes.

Notes Desktop users can use any Notes database that a regular user can. Notes Mail users can use only seven main types of databases: discussions, document libraries, personal and company address books, Notes' Web Navigator, resource reservations databases, and personal journals. Neither Notes Desktop nor Notes Mail users can design their own databases.

Most of this book applies as much to Notes Mail and Notes Desktop users as it does to users of the full Notes software.

What Is Domino?

There's been a great deal of publicity about something called *Domino*, which you may have gathered is somehow related to Notes. Like most new types of software, at first it's a little difficult to understand just what Domino does. In a sentence, Domino is software that automatically converts Notes information into Web pages and vice versa.

Domino gives companies an easy way to create a Web site that contains real information (not just dull promotional material), while using Notes' strict security to control who can see and change which parts of that information. It's a great way to extend the powers of Notes to people who aren't using Notes themselves.

> **NOTE** **Domino server** is Lotus' new name for what was called the **Notes server** in Notes 4 and earlier versions. You can find a more detailed discussion of Domino and Domino server in Chapter 9.

Why You Probably Don't Need to Use Domino

Domino sounds great—why shouldn't I use it? Well, there are two ways to use Domino: as an information user or an information producer.

Information users view and interact with the Web pages that Domino produces. Domino-produced Web pages are very similar to all the others out there, so you don't need any special knowledge. Anyway, as a Notes user yourself, you are likely to already have access in Notes format to any information your company chooses to publish with Domino.

Information producers use Domino to make Notes-based information available on the Web. You may need these skills eventually, but this area is the province of Notes database developers rather than Notes users. Domino *is* a much easier and better organized way to put information on the Web than most alternatives. However, if you plan to produce Web pages with Domino, you will first need to learn many of the core Notes skills that this book covers. Then, with some practice in database development, you will be ready to use Domino.

What You Need to Know about Computers before You Start

You don't need to know much about computers to start running Notes. You don't have to be a computer genius, because a lot of the effort that went into Notes was spent on making things work the way you would expect them to. Because this is a book about Notes, not about computers in general, and because Notes runs on several different types of computers, this book makes a few assumptions about what you know.

You need to know how to start your computer. On some computers (often with Windows 3.1), you may also need to know how to get your operating system running. On many others (such as on a Macintosh), the operating system starts up of its own accord.

It will also help you if you have used one or two other programs on your computer already. General conventions, such as how to use the mouse to select text, aren't explained in great detail in this book.

Mouse Terminology

If you have a mouse (and it is a lot easier to use Notes if you do), you should be familiar with how to use it with your computer. Here is some mouse terminology you should know to use your computer's mouse with Notes:

Term	What It Means
click on	Use the mouse to move the cursor onto the item described and press and release the left mouse button once. Clicking selects an object, item, or menu choice.
double-click on	Like clicking, but press and release the left mouse button twice in quick succession. Double-clicking opens an object.
Shift+click	Hold down the Shift key on the keyboard while you press the left mouse button. Shift+clicking selects multiple items.
highlight	Click on the item with the mouse. The background changes color or a frame appears around the item to show you which item you have selected. Clicking again usually removes the highlighting.

Term	What It Means
drag	To move an item by dragging, move the cursor onto the item. Hold down the left mouse button and move the mouse. Release the left mouse button when the item is in the correct new position. To select text by dragging, move the cursor to either end of the text. Hold down the left mouse button and move the mouse. The text is highlighted as you move the mouse. Release the mouse button when the correct portion of text is highlighted.
right-click	Press and release the right mouse button (Macintosh mice have only one button).
double-right-click	Press and release the right mouse button twice in quick succession (again, this isn't available on the Macintosh).

Notes on Different Computers

One reason Notes is so successful is that you can use it across most computer platforms. Obviously, software that is supposed to let people share information shouldn't require its users to all have the same type of computer. Specifically, Notes works on these computers:

- PCs using the Windows 3.1, Windows 95, Windows for Workgroups 3.11, and Windows NT 3.51 and 4.0 operating systems
- PCs using the OS/2 Warp version 3 and OS/2 Warp Connect version 3 operating systems
- Apple Macintoshes using System 7.5 or a later version
- IBM RS/6000 workstations running IBM AIX 4.1.4 or 4.2
- HP 9000 workstations running HP-UX 10.01
- Sun SPARC workstations running Sun Solaris 2.5 or 2.5.1
- PCs running Sun Solaris Intel Edition 2.5

Most things in Notes work the same way no matter what computer you are using. However, some things do vary from one type of computer to the next. In this book, if a procedure is different on different computers, the procedure for using Windows 95 is explained first, and any differences between Notes for Windows 95 and Notes for the other operating systems are explained in detail.

How This Book Is Organized

There are two guiding principles behind this book: to teach you practical Notes skills that you can use in your daily work, and to gradually introduce the concepts behind Notes so that you develop confidence in your ability to make Notes work for you.

Many of the skills that you develop in the first part of this book, "The Essentials of Notes Mail," will help you use Notes later on. Because we concentrate on learning how to use Notes mail and the calendar first, a number of items on the screen aren't explained until later. Don't be afraid to try out an item that intrigues you. If you need assistance, use the index to find specific information.

Part Two, "Working with Notes Documents," looks at some of the things that make Notes mail more flexible than most other e-mail software. You'll see how Notes lets you communicate in detailed, formatted documents rather than the ticker-tape style of plain-text e-mail. You'll also start to see how Notes can work with the other software you use.

In Part Three, "Sharing Information," you'll take the skills you honed while working with Notes mail and apply them to Notes' shared databases. You'll see how to engage in electronic discussions, look up policies and phone numbers, and track customer comments. You'll learn to use Notes' Web Navigator to find information on the Internet.

Once Notes has become an important tool in your work, Part Four, "Advanced Notes Features," shows you how to use Notes mail and the calendar more efficiently. You'll find out how to check whether your messages have been received, how to send mail to people on the Internet, and how to keep your mailbox free from clutter. We'll also look at Notes' powerful full-text searching capabilities and discover how you can get Notes agents to do your job for you!

Conventions Used in This Book

In this book, menu choices are shown in the form "Create ➤ Memo." This means to pull down the Create menu and select the item Memo. "Select File ➤ Mobile ➤ Choose Current Location," for example, means to pull down the File menu, select the item Mobile, and then select the item Choose Current Location from the submenu. *Italics* are used to highlight new terms when they appear, while text that you should type yourself is shown in **boldface**.

Throughout this book, you will see tips, notes, and warnings that stand out from the rest of the text. Each is a way to highlight a particular type of information.

TIP

Tips are just little tidbits of information that relate to the main point of the section. Sometimes tips give advice on a shortcut or a way to accomplish a particular task. Sometimes they tell you when Notes does things a little differently on one type of computer.

NOTE

Notes (not the Lotus sort) refer to information found elsewhere in this book. They're also used to point out where Notes 4.5 differs from earlier versions. Occasionally, they refer to other information resources you might consult, such as Lotus Notes' own electronic and printed documentation.

WARNING

Warnings are notifications of what *not* to do. When a potentially hazardous option is available, I alert you with a warning.

Part 1

The Essentials of Notes Mail

Chapter

1

BASIC NOTES MAIL

- **Starting and closing Notes**
- **Writing, addressing, and sending e-mail**
- **Reading and organizing e-mail**
- **Replying to and forwarding messages**
- **Switching to and from other programs**

Lotus Notes lets you exchange information and collaborate with your coworkers in many ways, but it can be hard to understand what Notes is until you use it. Instead of starting off by memorizing the formal terms for each Notes component, the easiest way to understand Notes is to build some practical knowledge of how to use it to do what you want.

This first chapter will get you comfortable with the most central part of using Notes: sending and receiving e-mail. By the end of this chapter, you will be able to send electronic messages to your coworkers and read the messages they send you.

As you try your hand at working with e-mail messages, you'll probably glimpse a number of other parts of Notes that will seem confusing. I'm not going to confuse matters further by explaining these parts of the program in this chapter. However, feel free to try out anything that takes your interest—it's difficult to wreak any major havoc in Notes.

Starting Lotus Notes

You start Notes the same way you start other programs on your computer: by double-clicking on the appropriate icon, which should resemble the one shown here. The icon is probably in a folder or group named Lotus Applications or Lotus Notes.

When you double-click on the icon, Notes briefly displays the "splash screen" in Figure 1.1. This tells you such things as which version of Notes you are using.

FIGURE 1.1: The Notes splash screen

TIP   In Unix, you can start Notes by typing **notes &** at the Unix prompt.

Then your Notes *workspace* appears. It probably looks something like Figure 1.2.

Your Notes Workspace

Every time you start Notes you'll find yourself at the workspace. It's your jumping-off point for dealing with e-mail, for contributing to online discussions, and for working with any special Notes applications your company uses. For this reason, the workspace is sometimes also called the *desktop*.

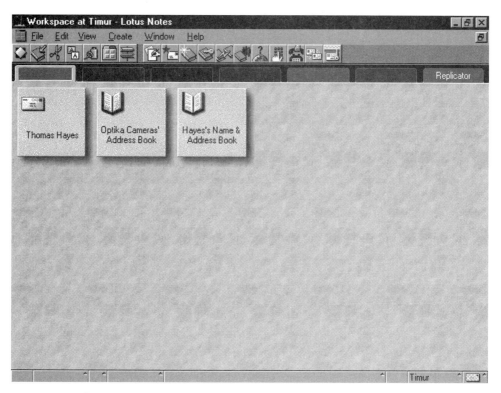

FIGURE 1.2: The Notes workspace

Probably one of the first things you will notice about the workspace is the presence of several rectangular slabs or icons. In Figure 1.2 they are labeled "Thomas Hayes," "Optika Cameras' Address Book," and "Hayes's Name & Address Book." Each icon can show a variety of things, but at a minimum there will be some sort of graphic and a description. Each icon corresponds to a particular Notes application—that is, a particular thing you can do with Notes.

Opening Your Notes Mailbox

The envelope icon in Figure 1.2 labeled "Thomas Hayes" is Thomas Hayes' Notes mailbox. On your own desktop, there should be a similar icon with your name on it. Double-click on this icon to open your mailbox.

> **NOTE**
>
> Most companies that use Notes use its e-mail functions. However, it is possible to use Notes' workgroup functions but use a different program for e-mail. If your company has chosen this option, then you won't see the mailbox icon on your desktop. If you use cc:Mail or another mail system that complies with the VIM or MAPI standards, you can use the Open, Forward, and Send commands on the Create ➤ Mail menu to have your e-mail software mail Notes documents to coworkers. If you use a mail system that doesn't comply with the VIM or MAPI standards, you cannot mail Notes documents directly. In either case, if you don't use Notes mail, you should still read the chapters of this book that deal with Notes' mail functions, because they introduce concepts that you will use in other parts of the program. However, you may want to skim Chapters 1–4 and 17–18.

Once you double-click on the icon for your mailbox, Notes asks for your Notes password, as in Figure 1.3. It needs your password to keep your mail file secure: You wouldn't be very happy if Notes let everyone browse through your mail!

The password that Notes is asking you for is specific to Notes. It is unlikely to be the same as other passwords you might already use to access your company's computer

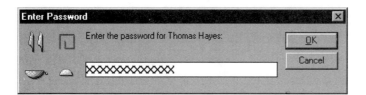

FIGURE 1.3:
You need to enter a password to view your Notes mail.

network or other programs. The person who installs Notes for you should tell you what your password is or show you how to set it. If you don't know your password, ask your Notes administrator.

> **NOTE**   If you are using Notes 4.5 for Windows NT, you may find that you only need to enter one password for both Windows NT and Notes.

The *X*s that appear as you type are Notes' way of stopping prying eyes from reading your password. Keep in mind that Notes passwords are *case-sensitive*. This means that if your password is **Grumpy**, for example, Notes will not allow you to type in **grumpy** or **GRUMPY**. You have to type the right combination of uppercase and lowercase characters. Once you have typed your password, press Enter.

When Notes accepts your password, you should be presented with a screen that looks like Figure 1.4. This is a Notes folder. In this case, it's Thomas Hayes' Inbox folder. Each line on the right-hand side of the screen in Figure 1.4 corresponds to a message that Thomas Hayes has received recently.

We'll leave the labeled icons on the left of the screen until Chapter 2, although you can probably guess the functions of some of them.

Don't worry if the Inbox on your screen is empty; it will soon have at least one item in it, because you're going to send yourself a message.

> **NOTE**   You may find that Notes asks you at this point to configure certain calendar options. If you want, you can leave these settings until later; setting your Calendar Profile is covered in detail in Chapter 17.

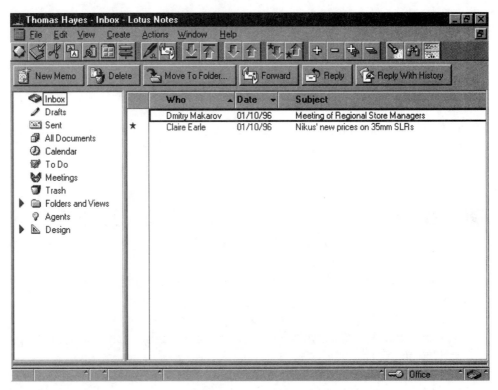

FIGURE 1.4: The Inbox folder shows messages that Thomas Hayes has received recently.

Sending an E-Mail Message

Sending a Notes mail message is in fact a two-step process: First you write the message (which takes most of the time), and then you send it (which happens very quickly).

Above your Inbox is a row of large, captioned buttons. Click on the one labeled New Memo, and Notes will open a blank memo document like the one in Figure 1.5 for you to start writing your message. Another way to start a new memo is to choose Create ➤ New Memo.

Notice that Notes has automatically filled in your name and the current date and time on the line at the top. If the memo you see is a little different, that's probably because you're using a different letterhead. Letterheads are just a way to change the graphic at the top of your message; you can find out more about them in Chapter 18.

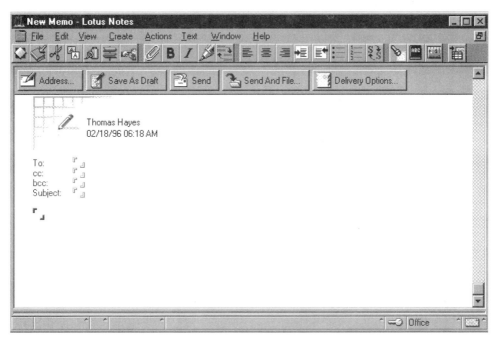

FIGURE 1.5: A blank memo document ready for you to write a new message

It could also be that someone at your company has modified the standard mail memo that Notes uses. Whatever your memo looks like, it will work in basically the same way.

NOTE The row of captioned buttons is new in Notes 4.x. It's called the Action Bar and is meant to give you quick access to the things you're most likely to want to do in any situation in Notes.

Addressing Your Message

Notes starts off your memo with the *insertion point* (the flashing vertical line that tells you where letters appear when you type) next to the word "To." Notice the L-shaped brackets to the top left and bottom right of the insertion point and the several other pairs of these brackets at other points on the screen. These brackets mark *fields,* which are the places on the screen where you can type information.

Pressing the Tab key moves you to the next field and pressing Shift+Tab moves you back again. You can also get around between fields by using the arrow keys or by clicking next to or inside a field.

In the To field, type the first and last name of someone else at your company who has Notes, preferably someone who won't mind receiving a trial message from you. You can type more than one person's name here, so long as you separate the names with commas. Names you type in the To field should be the primary recipients of your memo—the main people to whom you are writing your message.

As you type, Notes scans the list of Notes users at your company. It tries to work out who you want to send your memo to and fills in the person's name. Figure 1.6 shows how Notes can complete the recipient's name as you type.

Don't worry too much if Notes tells you it can't find the person whose name you have typed. If you're not sure of how the name is spelled, try an alternative spelling and see if Notes recognizes it. If that doesn't work, several other ways to track down

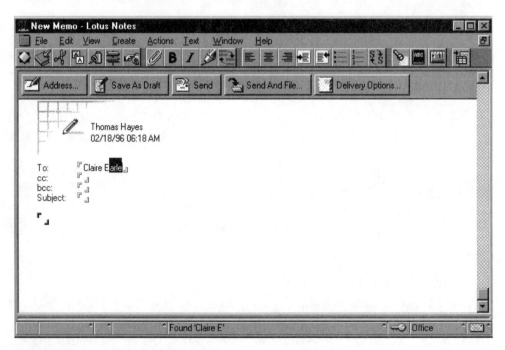

FIGURE 1.6: You type the beginning of the name and Notes fills in the rest.

the person you want are described in Chapter 3, but for now you might want to choose a different Notes user at your company.

Move to the cc field and type your own name here. If you type other people's names in the cc field, they also get a copy of the memo, but they will understand that they're only getting a courtesy copy, or carbon copy (hence the "cc"). You wouldn't normally type your own name here, but at the moment you want to learn how to read Notes mail as well as send it, and so you're going to send a copy of this message to yourself.

The bcc field stands for "blind courtesy copy," or "blind carbon copy." If you type someone's name here, that person gets a copy of the memo, but the other recipients don't know about it.

Writing and Sending Your Message

Move to the Subject field and type in a title for your memo. Write something like **A test message from Thomas**. It might seem superfluous to give a title to your message, especially if it's very short. The real reason to care about the Subject field is that Notes uses whatever is written here to identify messages in mailbox views and folders. The information in the Subject column in the view in Figure 1.4 came from the Subject field of each message.

Next, move down to the Body field, the unlabeled pair of red, L-shaped brackets below the Subject field. This is where you put the substance of your message. You can send all sorts of information through Notes mail, and later you'll learn how. For the moment, type a few sentences to tell the person or people you're sending your message to what it's about. Tell them you just got Notes and you're learning to use Notes mail. Ask them to send you a message so that you can practice reading mail as well as sending messages. When you are done, the screen should look like Figure 1.7.

When you are comfortable with the message you want to send, you have three options:

- You can click on the button marked Send and File to have Notes send the memo to the people in the To, cc, and bcc fields and also store a copy in a folder for yourself. Often this will be the option you choose, as it's good practice to file your mail straight away. Using and creating folders is explained in Chapter 2.

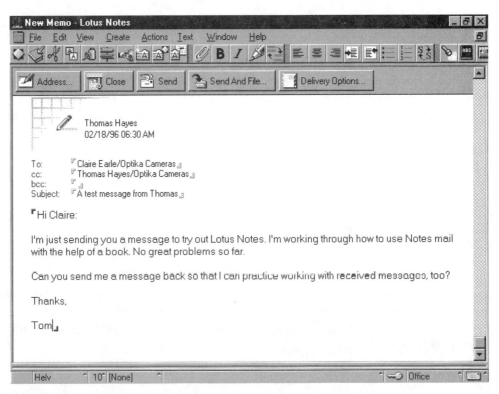

FIGURE 1.7: A completed message, ready to send

- You can click on the button marked Send to have Notes deliver your message to the recipient. Normally, Notes will also keep a copy for you (although it won't be stored in any special folder). If you want Notes to ask you whether to keep a copy, or never to keep a copy, read Chapter 14. Send differs from Send and File in that, if you do choose to keep a copy, Notes does not automatically prompt you for a folder in which to file it.
- You can click on the button marked Save As Draft to store the memo but not send it yet. You might choose to save without mailing if you were part-way through drafting a complicated message.

Choose Send for the memo you just wrote. Once you click on the button, Notes saves your message and sends off a copy to each of the people you listed. Then it returns you to your Inbox.

At this point, you might want to check to see that Notes actually filed your message as you expected it to do. Of course, your Inbox isn't going to be the place to look—Notes only puts messages you *received* in there.

Click on the icon marked All Documents in the left-hand pane on your screen and Notes will show you a screen like Figure 1.8. The All Documents view looks a lot like your Inbox, but it shows messages you've sent and drafts as well as messages you've received. The last item in the list of messages should be the message you just wrote. This is the copy that you saved for yourself. If you ever needed to refer to this message, you could go back to it and see what you wrote.

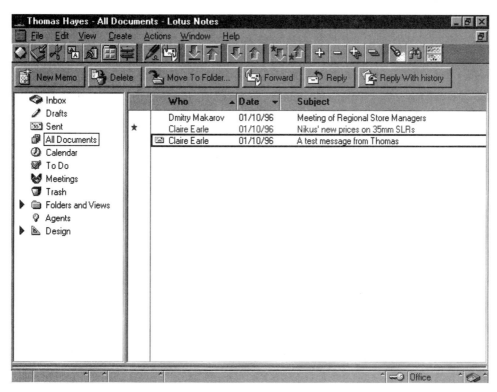

FIGURE 1.8: The All Documents view of your mailbox

Reading Messages You Receive

To choose a message to read, you need to know which messages listed in your mailbox are new. Generally, unread messages are marked by a star in the far left column and are listed in red. The saved copy of the message that you just wrote is listed in black. Notes knows that you already saw this message.

Notes is usually set up to look for new mail automatically every 15 minutes. If Notes finds that you have new mail, it beeps and changes the icon at the bottom right of the screen from a little envelope to a little Inbox.

When you receive new mail, Choose View ➤ Refresh (or press F9) to update the view of your mailbox to display the new messages. Among your new mail should be the copy of the message that you sent to yourself. This message will be listed in red, because as far as Notes is concerned the message is new and you haven't read it.

> **NOTE**
>
> If your computer is not permanently connected to a network (say you're a salesperson who uses Notes on a notebook computer), Notes stores your outgoing mail until you do connect to the network. Try connecting to your company's Notes network now to test sending and receiving mail. Chapter 13 covers using Notes remotely and can help you get connected. Alternatively, you can use the saved copy of the message you just wrote to practice reading a message.

Opening and Reading a Message

To open the message that you sent yourself (or to open any other message in your mailbox), use either of these methods:

- Press the ↑ or ↓ key to highlight the message you want to open and then press Enter to open it.
- Double-click on the row of the message you want to open.

When you open the message, it should look something like Figure 1.9. Notice that the angle brackets that showed you where to type when you wrote this message are no longer visible. That's because you're reading this message and can't change the

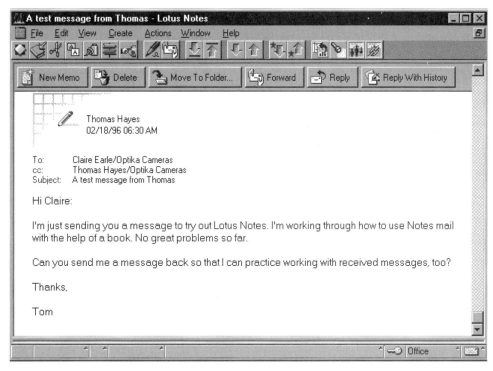

FIGURE 1.9: It's not surprising that the messages you receive look much like those you send.

information in it. Except for the angle brackets, the message looks very close to the one you created (which should be reassuring).

Closing a Message

Once you have finished reading a message, you may well want to close it and go back to your mailbox to read or write another message. Closing a message you've been reading leaves it exactly as it was (though no longer marked unread) so that you can come back to it later.

You can use any of the following methods to close a message or any other window in Notes:

- Choose File ➤ Close.
- Press Esc.
- Press Ctrl+W.
- On the Macintosh, click on the window's close box.
- In Windows or OS/2, press Ctrl+F4.

> **NOTE**
>
> If your mouse has two buttons (not Macintosh mice) you can also set up Notes to close the current window when you double-click the right mouse button. See Chapter 14 for information on how to set up Notes to do this.

If you were just reading the message, Notes will return you straight to your mailbox. However, if you have edited the message, Notes will ask you how it should deal with it. This might be the case with a draft message to which you have added some more information. If you have altered the message, Notes will present the dialog box in Figure 1.10.

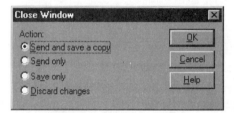

FIGURE 1.10: Notes uses the Close Window dialog box to ask you how to deal with a message you have altered.

The first three options let you send the message and keep a copy, send the message without saving a copy, or save the message for later use without sending it. Your remaining option is to discard any changes. If you were editing a message you saved earlier, this lets you abandon any changes you made since you last saved it. If you were working on a new message, this abandons it entirely.

It's a matter of personal preference whether you use the buttons at the top of your screen to save and send messages, or whether you close the message window and choose an option in the Close Window dialog box.

Replying to a Message

Often when you receive a message, you'll want to send a reply to whomever sent it. Maybe you have comments or need more information; maybe you just want to say thanks.

Notes makes sending a reply easy. Click on the button marked Reply at the top of the message and Notes creates a new message for you. Like the one shown in Figure 1.11, the new message is addressed to the sender of the original one and references the original subject. Another way to start a reply is to choose Create ➤ Reply.

Once you have written the text of your reply, you can send it, file it, or do both, just as you would a regular Notes message.

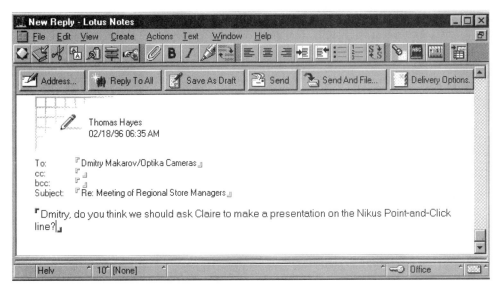

FIGURE 1.11: Notes can automatically fill in the addressee and title information for replies.

Replying to All

One convenience of e-mail is that you can send a message to a number of people almost as easily as to just one person. However, if you receive a message that was sent to several people and press Reply, your response is addressed only to the original author. Sometimes that's what you want, but there are times you would like to be able to reply to the author *and* everyone else who received the message.

At any time when you are writing your reply, you can click on the button marked Reply to All or choose Actions ➤ Reply to All, and Notes will add in the names of all the other addressees from the original message. If you want to send your reply to some other people too, or to exclude some of the original addressees, you can add or delete names as you wish. ·

> **TIP**
>
> When you choose Reply to All, Notes copies every name except yours from the address information on the first message and puts them in the cc: field on your new message. However, this doesn't guarantee that your reply will go out to everyone who received the first message. The original sender may have used the bcc: field to send blind courtesy copies. The recipients of the blind copies wouldn't have been listed on the copy you got. If you use Reply to All, Notes doesn't know about these recipients and won't include them on your new message.

Replying with History

There are also times when you need to refer to the original message in your reply. Say someone has sent you a message asking several questions that you'd like to answer individually. For these situations, Notes gives you the option to create a Reply with History. Clicking on this button or choosing Create ➤ Reply with History also opens up a new, preaddressed message, but with the contents of the original message copied to the Body field, as in Figure 1.12.

Here, you can annotate and edit the original text as much as you like, adding your responses and comments before sending the message. The section on Permanent Pen in Chapter 6 shows you how to make your comments stand out. If you do use Reply with History, you can help your message's recipients by including just the parts to which your responses refer.

Again, you can use the Reply to All button to have Notes add in the names of all the original addressees.

Forwarding a Message

Sometimes you'll get an e-mail message that you think someone else should know about. You don't need to write a whole new message to explain the first one to your new recipient. Instead you can pass on the message by clicking on the Forward button at the top of the message or by choosing Actions ➤ Forward.

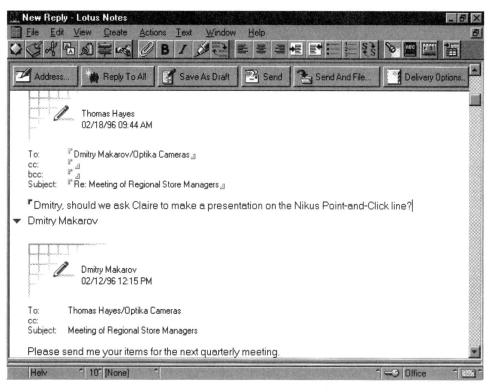

FIGURE 1.12: A Reply with History lets you add your comments to a copy of the original message.

Either method starts a new message that contains a copy of the original one preceded by a line telling the recipient that this is a message you have forwarded. You can address this new memo to whomever you want. You can also edit the text that Notes has copied from the original message. You might want to add a couple of sentences to explain where the original message came from and what it's about. Or you might want to remove parts of it to highlight a particular point.

Keeping Notes Running While You Use Other Software

When you have finished working with Notes for the moment, you *could* close the program entirely. That may seem like the obvious choice, and if your computer is not very fast and you are going to be using particularly demanding software (for example, a desktop publishing or sophisticated image-processing program), it may be a wise idea to close Notes.

But you do have another choice. Windows, OS/2, the Macintosh, and Unix all allow you to run more than one program at the same time. This is called *multitasking,* but it's a lot easier than it sounds.

Why would you want to do that—surely you can only type in one place at a time? Well, that's true. There are quite a few reasons you might want to have Notes running at the same time as your other software, but one reason makes particular sense.

When Notes is still running on your computer, it continues to check every so often to see if you have received any new mail. If you have received any, Notes tells your computer to beep, even if you are currently using a completely different program. Then you can switch to Notes at your convenience and read your new mail. For this reason, most Notes users run Notes whenever they're at their desks.

Here are some easy ways to switch to Notes:

In Windows 95 or NT, click on the Notes button on the Taskbar along the bottom of the screen. If Notes isn't listed, launch it from the Start menu as you normally would.

In Windows 3.1, press Ctrl+Esc to bring up the Task List shown in Figure 1.13. Choose Notes from the Task List and click on OK. If it isn't listed, choose Program Manager (or your Windows shell, such as Norton Desktop) and click on OK. Then launch Notes as you normally would.

In OS/2, press Ctrl+Esc to bring up the Task List. Choose Notes from the Task List. If it isn't listed, choose Main and launch Notes as you normally would.

On the Macintosh, pull down the Application menu and choose Notes. If the program you want isn't listed, choose Finder from the Application menu and launch Notes as you normally would.

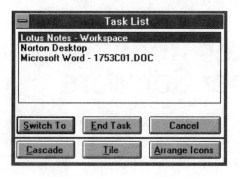

FIGURE 1.13:
The Task List lets Windows 3.1 and OS/2 users switch to other programs.

Leaving Notes

Occasionally, however, you may decide to tear yourself away from your desk (to go home, for instance). When you need to close Notes, any one of the following will do it:

- Choose File ➤ Exit Notes (File ➤ Quit on the Macintosh).
- Press Alt+F4 (⌘ on the Macintosh).
- Double-click on the Application control icon. This is the tiny Notes icon (Windows 95 or NT) or long bar (Windows 3.1) in a square box in the top left-hand corner of the Notes window.
- Choose Close from the Application control menu. This menu appears when you click once on the Application control icon.
- In Windows 95 or NT, click on the main Notes window's Close button (the small box with an × in it at the top right-hand corner of the window).

If you stay away from Notes too long, and start to suffer withdrawal symptoms, you can always restart the program and turn to Chapter 2, where you can learn how to use views and folders to organize your mail.

Chapter 2

ORGANIZING YOUR MAIL

FEATURING

- **The All Documents view**
- **Filing messages in folders**
- **Using drag-and-drop with folders**
- **Customizing views**
- **Previewing messages**
- **Other mailbox views**

So you're only one chapter into this book and you already know how to send and receive electronic messages. Isn't that mainly what Notes does? What's the rest of this book going to be about?

Yes, a big part of Notes is e-mail. But e-mail is a lot more than just sending and receiving messages. This chapter will give you a few more tools to work with so you can manage what shortly may become a flood of e-mail.

The All Documents View of Your Mailbox

In Chapter 1 we briefly saw the All Documents view of the Notes mailbox. You can see this view again in Figure 2.1. A view like this is the first thing you will see each time you open your mailbox.

If Notes is running on your computer but you don't see this view of your mail, here is how to get it:

- If you are reading or writing a message, use one of the several alternatives for closing a window offered in "Closing a Message" in Chapter 1. If other messages appear, keep closing them until you get back to your mailbox view.
- If you are looking at your workspace, find the icon for your Notes mailbox and double-click on it.

You should now have a screen that looks something like Figure 2.1.

The very top of the screen in Figure 2.1 says, "Thomas Hayes - All Documents - Lotus Notes." This area is called the *title bar*, and whatever is displayed here is intended to tell you what you are looking at. In this case, you are looking at the All Documents view of Thomas Hayes' mail in Lotus Notes.

The right-hand part of the screen is called the *View Pane*. Views are a central part of Notes. They're a good way to look at a lot of information at one time. This view, for instance, shows all the messages Thomas Hayes has sent and received along with a few details about each message.

The view tells us the date of each message, who it is to or from, and what the subject is. Incoming messages are listed in the order in which they were received, with drafts and sent messages listed in the order in which they were written.

Messages sent by Thomas Hayes have a small envelope before the name of the recipient. Drafts that Thomas Hayes has created but not sent have a piece of paper and a pencil next to the name. Messages that Thomas Hayes has received from other people usually have this area blank.

The left-hand part of the screen is the *Navigation Pane*. This gives you a quick way to get to the various parts of your Notes mailbox—to different views and folders, for instance. You've already used it in Chapter 1 to get from your Inbox to the All Documents view.

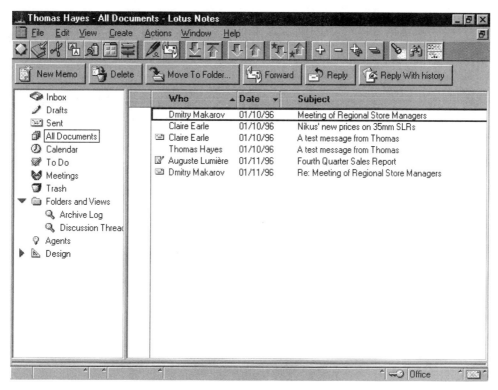

FIGURE 2.1: This Notes view shows all of Thomas Hayes' mail.

Filing Your Mail with Folders

It's great to be able to see all the e-mail you've received in one long list, but often that's not the most helpful way to look at it. After all, few people would keep all their paper mail in one big pile, even if it was in date order.

Fortunately, Notes lets you use folders to organize your mail almost any way you like. You can create as many folders as you need and even put folders inside other folders. This useful feature of Notes allows you to sort information (here, it's e-mail messages) in a way that makes best sense to you. You label the folders and choose what messages should go in each.

Putting a Message into a New Folder

Find a message that you want to file from the All Documents view on your screen. Highlight the message, either by using the ↑ or ↓ cursor keys or by clicking on the message. A thick outline of a rectangle shows which message is highlighted. Then click **Move To Folder...** on the Move To Folder button. Notes will display the dialog box in Figure 2.2. The dialog box shows you all the available folders in which you can put your message. At first you'll just see the choices shown in the figure.

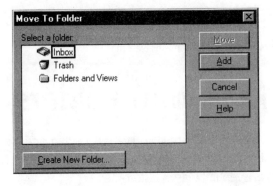

FIGURE 2.2:
Select a folder to
file your message
in, or create a
new one.

The Inbox and Trash are special folders automatically created by Notes. You've already seen the Inbox—it's where Notes puts any new mail it has for you. Trash is where messages go when you delete them. We'll look at deleting messages in Chapter 3.

When you have some folders available to file messages in, Notes lists them under the heading Folders and Views. At the moment, though, you don't have any folders available, so you'll have to create one.

1. Click on Create New Folder to open the dialog box in Figure 2.3.

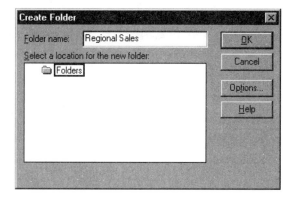

FIGURE 2.3:
Type a name for
your folder and
choose where it
will appear.

2.   In the box at the top, replace Notes' suggestion of Untitled with a more
     appropriate description for your new folder, such as **Regional Sales**.

3.   In the main box, highlight the name of the folder under which you want your
     new folder to appear. For your first folder, you just need to highlight the word
     Folders. Later you can arrange folders within folders, dividing Regional Sales
     into Meetings, Promotions, and Inventory, for example.

4.   Once you have chosen a name and location for your folder, click on OK for
     Notes to record your choices. Notes returns you to the first dialog box, where,
     as Figure 2.4 shows, you now have a new option.

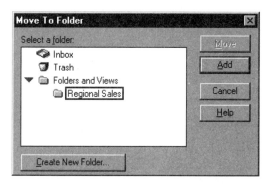

FIGURE 2.4:
Now your new
folder is listed.
Highlight it to tell
Notes where to
file your message.

5.   Highlight the name of your new folder. Click on Move to file your message
     in your new folder, and Notes will return you to your mailbox.

Of course, you don't need a new folder for every message. To file a message in an
existing folder, highlight the message, click on Move to Folder, and then just select the
name of the folder you want.

TIP   You can file received messages as you read them. The Move to Folder button appears at the top of messages you read as well.

TIP   Use the Send and File button at the top of a new memo to choose a folder for it at the same time as you mail it.

Working with Folders

There's no point putting messages in folders unless you can look at them—so how do you do it? All folders apart from the Inbox and Trash are listed under the item Folders and Views in the Navigation Pane on the left-hand side of your screen.

Like many things in Notes, the list of Folders and Views can be expanded or collapsed. If the blue-green triangle in the margin next to the folder icon is pointing to the right, the list is collapsed. If the triangle is pointing down, it's expanded. Click on the triangle to expand or collapse the list.

Expand the list and you'll see several items indented underneath it. The folders are identified by folder icons, and the views are identified by magnifying-glass icons. The difference between folders and views is explained later in this chapter.

Some of the folders themselves may have triangles next to them, indicating that they contain other folders and can be expanded. Figure 2.5 shows the folder hierarchy in a typical mailbox. You can see the contents of any folder simply by highlighting the folder's name. Notes changes the right-hand pane to display the contents of that folder.

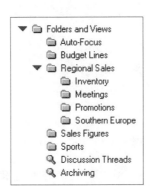

FIGURE 2.5:
A typical Notes user's mailbox will have a number of folders, some "nested" inside others.

> **TIP**
>
> In Notes jargon, the triangles that show whether something is expanded or collapsed are called *twisties*. It's good to know some Notes jargon to impress your Notes administrator, though examples less silly than this one are probably more impressive.

Selecting Messages to File

Now that you know how to file your mail in folders, you may well want to organize all the mail that has accumulated in your mailbox. Storing your mail in folders gives you a much easier way to find old messages than just skimming through a chronological list.

You could select each message in turn, click on Move to Folder, pick an appropriate folder, and click on OK. But if a number of messages have accumulated, that soon gets pretty tedious. There is an easier way: You can select a group of messages and file them all at once. Here's how to do it:

1. Find an unfiled message that is one of several you would like to put in the same folder.
2. Select the message with either of the following methods:

   - Press the spacebar when the message is highlighted.
   - Click on the blank column to the left of the message.

3. As shown in Figure 2.6, a checkmark appears in the left-hand margin, indicating that this message has been selected.
4. Repeat steps 1–3 to select additional messages.
5. When you have selected all the messages you want to categorize, click on Move to Folder to file all the selected messages.

This method of selecting messages is an important one in Notes. Although here we're just using it to file mail more efficiently, you'll later find that the same technique can be used to manipulate groups of messages very simply.

Moving Messages between Folders

When you put a message in a folder, it stays there when you leave Notes. Tomorrow when you arrive at work and open your Notes mailbox, your messages will still be organized in the same folders. But on occasion you might want to put a message in a different folder, put it in more than one folder, or remove it from a folder.

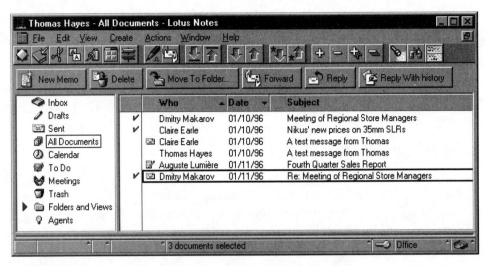

FIGURE 2.6: The messages you select have checkmarks in the left-hand margin.

To move a message from one folder to another:

1. Highlight the message and click on Move to Folder.
2. Select the new folder and click on the Move button.

Clicking on the Add button instead puts your message in *both* the new folder *and* whatever folders it was in originally.

> **TIP** Because your Inbox is a folder, clicking on Move when filing received messages will take the message out of the Inbox and put it into the new folder. It's a good idea to move messages out of your Inbox regularly to make it easier to deal with the new messages you receive.

To remove a message from a folder:

1. Open the folder and highlight the message.
2. Choose Actions ➤ Remove from Folder. You'll notice that another option on the Actions menu, Move to Folder, gives you an alternative way to file messages.

You can use all these techniques with multiple messages. Just checkmark the messages you want to work with first. If you want to create a new empty folder without filing a message, choose Create ➤ Folder.

> **NOTE** You have a couple of other options for organizing your mail, aside from placing messages in folders. Later in this chapter you can see other views of your mailbox that let you look at your messages grouped in different ways. Chapter 17 explains how to keep a To Do list by creating Tasks from messages you receive.

Using Drag-and-Drop with Folders

One really easy way to organize your messages and folders is to *drag and drop* them. Drag-and-drop is a computer buzzphrase, but in practice it means that you can arrange your Notes mailbox using only the mouse. Here are some ways to use drag-and-drop techniques with folders.

Dragging Messages between Folders

To drag a message into a folder:

1. Open the view or folder that contains the message you want to move.
2. Make sure the destination folder is listed in the Navigation Pane, but don't select it.
3. In the View Pane, click on the message you want to put into this folder.
4. Holding down the left mouse button, drag the cursor toward the folder in which you want to file the message. The cursor changes to a page icon like the one shown here.
5. Still holding down the mouse button, move the cursor onto the name of the folder. Notes will highlight the folder's name when you have the cursor in the right position.
6. Release the left mouse button. Notes moves the message to the new folder.

Normally, dragging a message to a new folder indicates to Notes that you want to move it rather than copy it to that folder. If you want to copy the message, hold down Ctrl when you click on the message to begin dragging it. Notes shows an icon with a page and a plus sign to confirm that you are copying the message. Note that if you drag the message from the All Documents view, however, Notes assumes you want to copy it.

You can drag several messages at a time into a folder by selecting them (placing checkmarks next to them) and then dragging one of them to the folder you want. If you are moving the messages, Notes shows an icon of several sheets of paper. You can hold down Ctrl while you drag to copy the messages rather than move them. Notes adds a plus to its icon.

Using Drag-and-Drop to Change the Folder Hierarchy

You can also use the drag-and-drop technique to move folders around. Click on the folder you want to move and drag the cursor (which changes to a sheet of paper again) to its new parent folder. When you release the left mouse button, Notes rearranges your folder hierarchy to put the folder you dragged in its new place.

Any folders that were contained in the folder you dragged move along with it. There are some obvious limits to how you can rearrange folders:

- You can't drag a folder into its parent folder.
- You can't drag a folder into itself.
- You can't drag a folder into any of its children (any folders that are contained in the one you are dragging).

NOTE

Using drag-and-drop to reorder folders can be a little tricky. Although it's supposed to work as I've described, you may find that Notes doesn't want to interpret your mouse movements properly. If you experience problems, try dragging folders with the right mouse button instead of the left button. Alternatively, click on a folder's icon with the right mouse button, choose Move from the menu that appears, and then choose a new location for your folder from the dialog box that Notes provides.

Customizing Views

Looking at your mail listed by the date it was created or received, as the All Documents view shows it, is generally quite useful. Sometimes, however, you'd like Notes to list your messages by the names of the people who wrote them (or to whom *you* wrote).

If a column title in a Notes view has one or two small triangles at its right-hand edge, you can change the way Notes lists the information in this column by clicking on the column heading.

Date ▼ Try clicking on the Date column heading in the All Documents view. Notes changes the view from sorting in ascending order of date (earliest first) to sorting in descending order (latest first). Notice that Notes has changed the little triangle at the top of the column from gray to blue. This tells you Notes has changed the view to sort on this column.

Who ▲ Now try clicking on the Who column heading. Notes re-sorts the view by the name of each message's author or recipient. Now the triangle on the Who column is highlighted in blue. The direction the triangle points tells you how Notes sorts the column when you click on the heading. Upward-pointing triangles mean that Notes will sort in ascending order and downward-pointing ones mean descending. If you click again on a re-sorted column, Notes will return the view to normal.

Sometimes, although not in your mailbox, you'll see a column heading that displays **Price** ⬍ a double triangle. This means that you can click once to sort the column in ascending order and click again to sort it in descending order. Clicking a third time returns the view to its original state.

Supplier ⬈ Finally, you may sometimes see a small arrow with a twist in it at the top of a view column. This indicates that if you click on the column heading, Notes will open a different view, usually one that sorts on the information in the column you clicked. Often, there will be an on-screen explanation, such as "Click here to switch to the Supplier view."

Another way you can alter views to suit your needs is to change column widths. If you run the mouse pointer slowly along the column headings in any view, you'll notice that as the pointer moves over the dividing line between one column and the next it changes shape to a vertical line with two horizontal arrows. If you click and hold the left mouse button when the pointer is like this, Notes lets you drag the column divider to make the column wider or narrower. Fine-tuning column widths can help you in views that contain a lot of information or if you have a small monitor.

Previewing Messages

Skimming through the names, dates, and subjects listed in your mailbox when you're trying to track down a particular message is probably becoming second nature. Sometimes, though, it would be easier to find the message you seek if you had a little more information to work with. Notes will preview messages for you in a separate pane so you can decide which to open. Open the Preview Pane in any view by choosing View ➤ Document Preview. Notes will add an extra pane at the bottom of the window, as in Figure 2.7. As you highlight messages in the View Pane (in the top-right corner of the window), Notes changes the Preview Pane to display each new message.

The preview in Figure 2.7 looks a little different from the regular message. The address information has been collapsed to fit in more of the body of the message. You'll often find that previews are modified a little to ensure that the key information in the document will be visible.

The right-pointing triangle, or "twisty," next to the recipient's name lets you expand the message to show the full address information and the subject if you wish. The other, lower twisty lets you expand or collapse the portion of this Reply with History that was copied from the original message.

The Preview Pane works as a toggle: By choosing View ➤ Document Preview again, you return to the regular Navigation and View Panes. When the Preview Pane is open, Notes places a checkmark next to the Document Preview choice on the View menu.

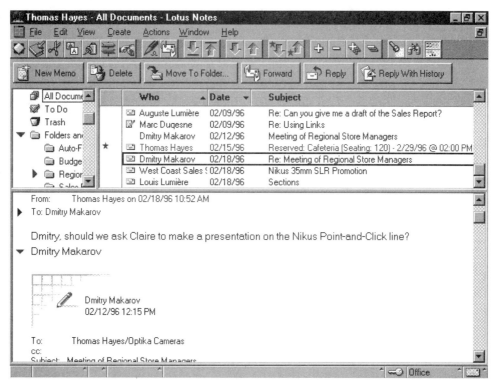

FIGURE 2.7: The Preview Pane lets you try before you buy.

Changing the Size of a Pane

Notes allows you to customize the size of the three panes to suit your needs. To change the size of a pane, place the cursor at its junction with a neighboring pane. Notes will switch the cursor to a vertical or horizontal bar with two small perpendicular arrows. When this bar appears, you can click and hold the left mouse button to drag the edge of the pane to a new position. Placing the cursor at the intersection of the three panes makes Notes display a crosshair-type cursor with which you can resize all three panes at once.

| TIP | If you want to quickly switch the view to show a large Preview Pane and small Navigation and View Panes, choose View ➤ Zoom Preview. Notes expands the Preview Pane to take up the bulk of the screen. This command works as a toggle: Choose View ➤ Zoom Preview again to revert to the earlier view. |

Rearranging Panes

You can also change the relative positions of the three panes. Choosing View ➤ Arrange Preview displays the dialog box in Figure 2.8. Here you can choose between the standard arrangement with the Preview Pane at the bottom of the window and variants with it on the right-hand side of the window or in the bottom-right corner.

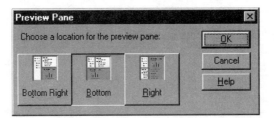

FIGURE 2.8:
You can reshuffle and resize the three-pane window.

Other Views of Your Mailbox

As well as the All Documents view of your mailbox, there are several others you may find useful.

The Sent view and Drafts view are both very straightforward. Click on Sent in the Navigator Pane and Notes will show you only the messages that you have written and mailed to other people. If you get a lot of Notes mail, this can help you find messages you've written among the sea of incoming notifications. The Drafts view shows only messages you have written but not sent. It can help you find things you wrote but then put aside.

The Discussion Threads view is very helpful if you're trying to follow an e-mail conversation that has been going back and forth for a while. The ease with which you can forward and cc: messages in Notes can quickly lead to an issue being debated by half a dozen people copying their messages to each other. The Discussion Threads view may help you in sorting out who's replying to what. You will find this view listed after your private folders under Folders and Views in the Navigation Pane. Click on the icon of a magnifying glass and you'll see something like Figure 2.9.

The key difference between this view and the All Documents view is that here Notes indents replies underneath the message to which they are replying. This helps you keep track of discussions to which several people have contributed, such as the

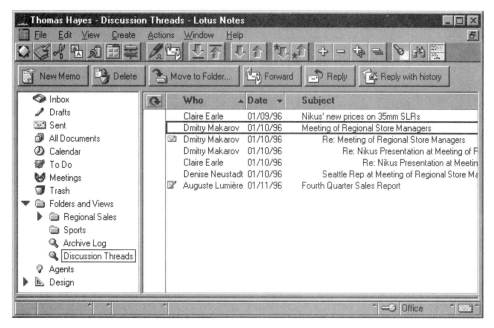

FIGURE 2.9: The Discussion Threads view helps you keep track of complex e-mail exchanges.

one in Figure 2.9 where two people have replied to the highlighted message and one of the replies itself has a chain of replies. Of course, Notes can only include messages and replies in your own mailbox as part of this structure. Replies that weren't copied to you won't show up.

NOTE
There are four other views available in your mailbox, but they work in conjunction with Notes features we haven't discussed yet. The Calendar and Meetings views let you track upcoming events and appointments. You can find out more about them in Chapter 4. The To Do view lets you see items you've assigned to your "task" list. The Archiving view shows details of any messages Notes has moved out of your mailbox to save space. You can find out more about the To Do and Archiving views in Chapters 17 and 18.

The Difference between Views and Folders

You may have noticed that when we looked briefly at the Inbox in Chapter 1, I referred to it as a folder, whereas all the other lists of your mail are called views. When you created your own lists of messages, these were called folders, too. So what's the difference between a folder and a view?

A *view* is a list of the documents in a Notes database (for the moment, you can think of it as a list of the messages in your mailbox). It can list all the documents (like the All Documents and Discussion Threads views) or just those that fulfill certain criteria (mailed documents for the Sent view; unmailed ones for the Drafts view).

A *folder* is also a list of the documents in a Notes database. The difference is that you put documents into folders and take them out. This is most obvious with the personal folders you created to organize your mail: Messages only get into these folders because you put them there, and they only get out because you take them out.

Special folders, like the Inbox and Trash, may also gain and lose documents in other ways. If you open the Trash folder, you can click on Empty Trash to have Notes remove all its documents. When Notes gets new mail for you, it automatically places it in the Inbox folder. However, you can still add messages to these folders and remove them at any time you want. For example, you can (and should) move messages out of your Inbox once you have acted on them. In contrast, the Sent view will always display *all* messages you have mailed and saved.

When you create your own folders, Notes bases their design on that of the database's default view or folder. For your mailbox, this means that your folders will have the same columns as the Inbox.

Often in this book, I'll refer to actions you can perform in a view. To take an example from the next chapter, I might describe how you can delete messages at the view level. Unless I specifically exclude folders, these actions will also work there.

"Refreshing" Mailbox Views

In Chapter 1 you found out that you can bring the current view of your mailbox up to date by choosing View ➤ Refresh. In fact, you have three ways to refresh any view:

- Choose View ➤ Refresh.
- Press F9.
 - Click on the View Refresh box. This is the box toward the top-left corner of the View Pane where the left-hand column meets the row that contains the column headings. A blue arrow pointing in a circle appears there when the view has not been refreshed to take account of a change, such as a new e-mail message.

Now you should be comfortable with sending Notes messages to your close colleagues, and with reading and organizing the messages you receive. You may, however, wonder how you tell Notes that your message is for the Mike Smith in accounting and not the one in sales. Will Notes let you send a message to your whole workgroup without having to type in each of their names? And how do you get rid of messages you no longer need? Read on.

Chapter 3

THE FINE POINTS OF ADDRESSING

FEATURING

- **Addressing messages**
- **The Public Name & Address Book**
- **Sending a message to a group**
- **Read-only and edit modes**
- **Deleting messages**

Chapters 1 and 2 have covered the key features of Notes mail. You know how to read and write messages and organize your mail with folders and views. However, there are a couple more skills you'll need to round out a basic knowledge of Notes mail.

Notes provides several more sophisticated ways to address your messages than just typing and hoping. The first half of this chapter shows you how to use them. Also, you may have wondered if Notes gives you any way to remove messages entirely. There are several techniques, and each is explained in the second half of this chapter.

Message Addressing

So far, the only way you've been shown to address Notes messages is to begin typing a person's name into the To or cc field and hope that Notes will provide the right name. Most of the time this *does* work, but there will be times when you don't quite know how someone's name is spelled or when Notes just doesn't seem to be finding the name you want. Thankfully, your mailbox has some sophisticated features tucked away for solving these and other riddles.

What If Notes Doesn't Know Whom to Send My Message To?

Notes deals with your mail a little differently depending on whether your computer is permanently connected to a network (most desktop computers) or connected only occasionally (most notebook computers).

If you have a permanent network connection, Notes will check all the addresses in your message at the time you send it against a list called the Public Name & Address Book. If you are using Notes remotely, Notes checks the addresses against your Personal Name & Address Book (see Chapters 13 and 18). If Notes finds a name it doesn't recognize among those to whom you have addressed your message, it will bring up a dialog box on the screen. Here, your choices are:

- Choose a name from a list of similar names that Notes provides.
- Skip this name and have Notes carry on sending the message to any other addressees.
- Cancel sending the message entirely.

If Notes finds a problem with one of the addresses in your message, it will send you a Delivery Failure Report. This is a special type of message that explains why Notes couldn't deliver your original message. If you receive a report of this type, you'll need to use the tools described later in this chapter to check the way you addressed your original message.

If Notes complains about a name you've used, or if you're not sure of a name when you're addressing a message, Notes gives you an easy way to look it up.

Looking Up Names in the Public Name & Address Book

As I have mentioned a few times already, Notes uses a list called the Public Name & Address Book to keep track of the names and e-mail addresses of Notes users. In fact, this is just what Lotus calls it. The copy you use will have your company's name on it. It may be called something like "Optika Cameras' Address Book."

Notes uses the Public Name & Address Book to keep track of all the people in your company who use Notes and how to get their mail to them. However, you can use it, too, to look up the names of people to whom you want to send messages. Notes gives you a special way to look up names in the Public Name & Address Book while you're writing a message.

Open your mailbox and click on New Memo. Notes puts the insertion point in the To: field of a blank message. Say you want to send a message to your boss but you can't remember her name (okay, this is just an example). Open up the Public Name & Address Book to check on the name of your boss either by clicking on the Address button or by choosing Actions ➤ Address. Either option opens the Mail Address dialog box, which looks like Figure 3.1.

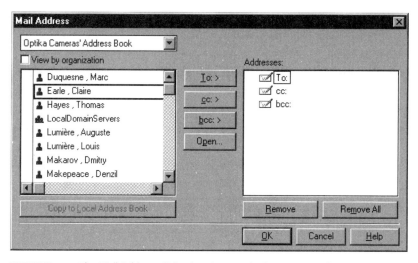

FIGURE 3.1: The Mail Address dialog box lets you look up names of Notes users.

On the left side of this dialog box is a series of rows that mostly list the names of people in your company who have Notes. The names are listed alphabetically by last name. You have three ways to find the name you are looking for:

- Click on the scroll bar to the right of the list to move up and down through the list until you find the name you want.
- Click in the list box and then press the ↑, ↓, PgUp, and PgDn keys to move to the name you want.
- Click in the list box and then type the first few letters of the person's last name. Notes will briefly bring up a Quick Search dialog box. When you press Enter or click on OK, Notes checks to see if the letters you typed match the first few letters of any name in the address book. If there is a match, Notes highlights the name as a suggestion.

Once you find the name of the person to whom you want to send your message, use either of these ways to add it to the list of names on your memo:

- Highlight the name and click on one of the three buttons marked To, cc, or bcc.
- Drag the name to one of the envelopes marked To, cc, or bcc in the Addresses box on the right of the dialog box.

Whichever method you use, Notes will add the new name to any others already listed in the Addresses box. If you find that you added a name in the wrong place, you can drag it to one of the other sections (say, from cc to bcc). If you want to delete a name from the Addresses box, highlight it and click on Remove. Remove All deletes all the names from the Addresses box.

Once you have selected the addresses you require, click on OK to add them to the relevant fields of your memo. Clicking on Cancel leaves your memo as it was.

In the top-left corner of the Mail Address dialog box is a list box that contains the name of your company's Public Name & Address Book. Click on the triangle at its right-hand end to see other address books available to you. Choosing an address book from this list tells Notes to display the names from that address book in the box below.

Most often this list shows your company's Public Name & Address Book and your own Personal Name & Address Book. Chapter 18 explains how to use your Personal Name & Address Book. Large companies may have several Public Name & Address Books. If your company is one of them, you will have extra choices here.

If you work for a company where many people use Notes, you may find it helpful to check the "View by organization" box. This tells Notes to group the names in the address list hierarchically.

Sending a Message to a Group

It probably didn't escape you that some names in the list you scrolled through didn't look much like the names of real people. The address list has two main types of entries: people entries and group entries. Each is identified by its own icon in the left-hand column.

People entries are the names of real people who use Notes and display an icon of a single person. They make up the bulk of the entries in any Public Name & Address Book.

Group entries are a convenience that Notes offers you. By addressing a message to a group, you can avoid the task of typing in the names of many different people. Group entries display an icon of three people.

Before you send a message to a group, though, you will want to find out who is in it. Highlight a group name in the list (look for the icon with three people to the left of the name) and click on the Open button in the center of the dialog box. Notes should display a screen similar to Figure 3.2. The members of the group are listed in the bottom field shown in Figure 3.2. If you address a message to this group name, Notes sends it to all the people in this list.

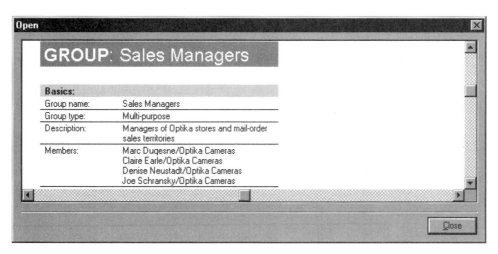

FIGURE 3.2: The Group document lists all members of a Name & Address Book group.

Groups are created by the people in your company who are entrusted with maintaining the Public Name & Address Book. The groups should have been chosen to make sense within your company.

Scroll down below the Members field and open the Administration section by clicking on the "twisty" triangle next to the title. The Owners field lists the names of people who can make changes to the group. If you think the list of members needs to be updated or modified, get in touch with one of these people or contact your Notes administrator.

> **NOTE** If you regularly write to a group of people, you can follow the instructions in Chapter 18 to create a group in your Personal Name & Address Book. If you think other people will want to send messages to this same group, get in touch with your Notes administrator to see if this group should be made available in the Public Name & Address Book.

Switching between Read-Only and Edit Modes

When you create a new message, Notes lets you type information into each field and say to whom to send the message and what it's about. Earlier we saw how you can tell which fields Notes lets you write in by the little L-shaped angle brackets at the top left and bottom right of each field.

When you open a message you've received, Notes doesn't display any angle brackets, and you can't type any new information in any of the fields. The fields are called *read-only*, since you can't write in them.

Notes is clever enough to know most of the time when it should display a message in edit mode and when it should use read-only mode. Sometimes, however, you may need to change from one mode to the other. To toggle between modes, press Ctrl+E or choose Actions ➤ Edit Document.

> **TIP** To switch from read-only to edit mode you can also double-click with the left mouse button anywhere in the message. This technique does *not* work to change back from edit mode to read-only mode.

If you make changes to a message in edit mode and you try to switch back to read-only mode, Notes asks you first if you want to save and/or mail those changes. If you just completed a draft you were working on earlier, you probably want to mail and save the changed message. If you have made some changes but still need to do more work, you might want to save without mailing.

Actions ➤ Edit Document (Ctrl+E) is quite versatile. You can also use this command at the view level to open the highlighted message in edit mode. This saves you the trouble of first opening the message in read-only mode and then switching to edit mode.

> **TIP** You may have noticed that switching from read-only to edit mode and back again changes the look of messages slightly. In particular, the buttons at the top of messages are different. This is because some buttons, such as the Send button, are most useful when you are writing a new message and others, such as the Forward and Reply buttons, make more sense when you are reading a message.

Deleting Messages

Now your messages are filed away in an appropriate array of folders. It's a good idea to keep many of the messages you send and a fair number of the ones you receive. Certainly, if a message contains information you think you might need to refer to later, you ought to keep it. But that leaves a large number of messages that you don't need to keep. You can delete these messages so that they no longer clutter up your mailbox.

WARNING Deleting a message and removing it from a folder are very different things. Taking a message out of a folder just changes the way your mail is filed. Even if you take all your messages out of their folders, they still exist in your mailbox and you can see them in the All Documents view. When you delete a message, Notes puts it in the Trash folder prior to removing it entirely. Once it is gone from the Trash, you can't retrieve it.

Deleting messages works a little differently depending on whether you are looking at a view of your mailbox or at a single message.

Deleting Messages from a View or Folder

At the view level you can delete a single message or many. To delete just one message, highlight it in the view. Then use any of the following methods to move it to the Trash folder:

- Press Delete.
- Choose Edit ➤ Clear.
- Click on the Delete button.
- Drag the message to the Trash folder.

Notes places a small icon of a trashcan in the margin to the left of the message you highlighted. This means that the message has been placed in the Trash folder.

Messages marked with the trashcan icon haven't been deleted yet, so you can still change your mind and restore them. However, when you leave your mailbox or ask Notes to refresh the view, you are asked whether you want to permanently delete any messages you have marked in this way, as in Figure 3.3.

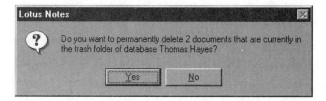

FIGURE 3.3: If you move messages to the Trash folder and then leave your mailbox or ask Notes to refresh the view, you have the option to permanently remove these messages from your mailbox.

If you choose Yes, Notes removes the messages from your mailbox and there is no way you can get them back. If you choose No, Notes leaves the messages in the Trash folder.

> **TIP**
>
> **If you find that you've permanently deleted a very important Notes document, you *do* have a couple of options. If it was something that someone else sent you, your best course of action is to ask him or her to resend it. Failing that, if it was a really unique and important document that would take a long time to reproduce, you might want to ask your Notes administrator if there's a backup anywhere. Bear in mind that even if there is a backup, it may take someone several hours to restore it.**

Of course, if you put a message into the trash and change your mind, you need to know how to "undelete" your message. One way to do this is to move the message out of the Trash folder just like you would with any other folder.

Open the Trash folder by clicking on the Trash icon in the Navigation Pane, and you'll see something like Figure 3.4. Highlight the message you want to undelete, then choose one of the following options:

- Drag it out of the Trash folder and into another folder.
- Click on the Remove from Trash button.
- Choose Actions ➤ Remove from Trash.
- Choose Edit ➤ Undo Delete.
- Press Ctrl+Z.
- Press Delete.

The last three methods leave the message in the Trash folder temporarily, but remove the trashcan icon. If you leave the Trash folder and return, you'll find that the message you undeleted is no longer listed.

The Trash folder also gives you an Empty Trash button to click on if you want to permanently delete everything in the folder.

You don't have to be in the Trash folder to undelete a message. In other views and folders, pressing the Delete key a second time is probably the easiest way to undelete messages.

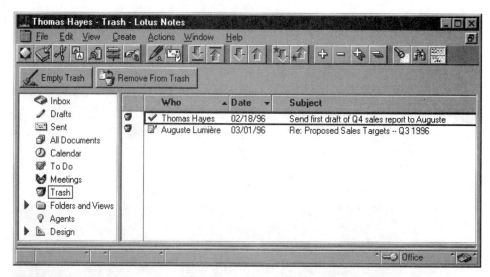

FIGURE 3.4: The Trash folder contains all the messages that Notes will later delete.

Deleting More Than One Message

To delete more than one message at a time, select each message with the technique you used in Chapter 2 to move a group of messages to a folder (see "Selecting Messages to File"). Each message that you are going to delete will have a checkmark next to it. Then press Delete, click on Delete, choose Edit ➤ Clear, or drag the messages to the Trash folder as you would with a single message.

As well as deleting more than one message at a time, you can also undelete several messages. Select each message that you want to undelete and use any of the methods you would use to undelete a single message.

Deleting the Message You Are Reading

You don't need to be looking at a view of your mailbox to delete messages; you can delete the very message you are reading. You just need to be sure you are looking at the message in read-only mode. (If you are in edit mode, then you will probably end up deleting some of the words in the message but not the message itself.) Once you are looking at the message you want to delete in read-only mode, choose Edit ➤ Clear, press Delete, or click on the Delete button.

Notes will move the message to the Trash folder and automatically show you the next message in the view. (If there are no more messages in the view, Notes takes you automatically back to the view level.) If you close the new message and go back to the view, you should see a trashcan icon next to the message you marked for deletion.

Undeleting a message is best done from a mailbox view, where you can use the methods you learned earlier to remove the trashcan icon and restore the message.

If you deleted a message and you're now looking at the next one, you can press the Backspace key and Notes will take you back to the message you deleted. Notice that the title bar at the top of your screen tells you that this message has been deleted, as in Figure 3.5. Unfortunately, there's no direct way to undelete the message from here. To do this, you have to close the message and go back to a mailbox view.

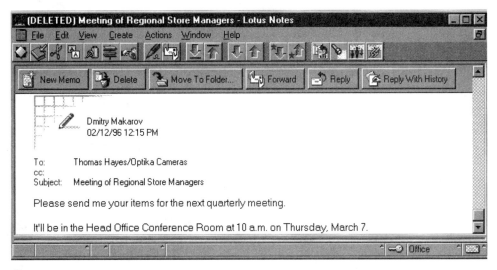

FIGURE 3.5: You can tell by looking at the title bar whether the message you have opened has been placed in the trash folder.

> **NOTE** Chapter 18 deals with managing your mailbox in more detail. It offers suggestions on how to keep your mailbox at a manageable size.

Understanding addressing and knowing how to delete messages completes your core set of mail skills. You know all the basics of sending and receiving messages. Next up: Chapter 4 looks at the key points of using Notes to schedule meetings.

Chapter 4

USING THE CALENDAR

- **Appointments, meetings, and reminders**
- **Events and anniversaries**
- **Using your calendar**
- **Setting alarms**
- **Repeating events**

Now that you are comfortable sending messages back and forth, you may find that you sometimes use Notes memos to propose meetings to your coworkers, who then respond via Notes. In fact, Notes 4.5 has built-in functions that handle booking meetings much better than a memo can. These features also let you record your own appointments and keep track of birthdays, conferences, and anything else that you can fit into a calendar format.

The place for this information is the Calendar view of your mailbox. The Calendar view works like an intelligent datebook or desk diary, showing you the meetings to which you have been invited, along with your own appointments and reminders, and any events or anniversaries you choose to record. You can even combine the calendar with Notes' To Do functions (see Chapter 17) to form a sophisticated personal information manager.

Creating a Calendar Entry

You switch to the Calendar view by clicking on the Calendar item in the Navigation Pane. You will then see something like the view in Figure 4.1, although your screen will probably appear emptier. Of course, you are unlikely to have many items on your calendar if you have not used it before, so this section deals with the most straightforward calendar operations: creating appointments, reminders, events, and anniversaries.

> **NOTE**
>
> **If you don't see entries for the Calendar and Meetings views in the Navigation Pane in your mailbox, it probably means that your Notes mail database has not been updated to the version that comes with Notes 4.5. Ask your Notes administrator whether you are in fact using Notes 4.5 and, if so, whether she or he can update the design of your mailbox.**

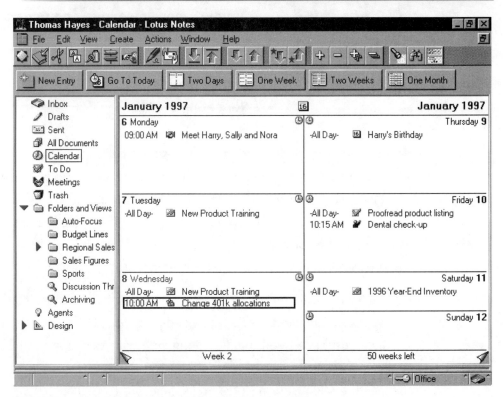

FIGURE 4.1: A typical Calendar view shows a variety of entries.

Notes lets you display a variety of items on the calendar in your mailbox. Some you will use quite regularly, such as appointments; others, more rarely, such as anniversaries. The basic components of each are quite similar, so we'll look at them all together, with two exceptions:

- Recording meetings and inviting people to them involves coordinating your schedule with theirs. Because this is a little more complex, we'll look at it later in the chapter.
- You can also choose to show individual items from your To Do list on your calendar. This is covered in Chapter 17.

This section will look at how to create four types of Calendar Entries: appointments, events (such as a conference or training course), reminders (to jog your memory), and anniversaries (birthdays and other annual celebrations).

Once you are looking at the Calendar view (Figure 4.1), you have several ways to create a new calendar item. You can:

- Click on the New Entry button on the Action Bar (above the Navigation Pane).
- Choose Create ➤ Calendar Entry.
- Double-click on a blank space on any day on the calendar.

Any of these three actions will open a new Calendar Entry document, which will look like the one in Figure 4.2, but with an additional "Invitations" section at the bottom.

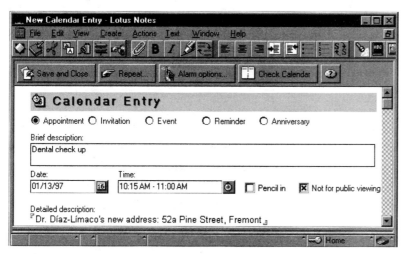

FIGURE 4.2: An appointment is one of the simpler forms of Calendar Entry.

Now you are ready to create your first Calendar Entry:

1. Tell Notes whether you want to record an appointment, event, reminder, or anniversary by selecting the appropriate radio button at the top of the document. Notes then removes the Invitations section, which is only needed for meetings.
2. Now enter a brief description of the item you want to record.
3. Next, change the date and time details, if necessary. You can either type in a new date in standard format, or click on the button marked *16* next to the field to invoke a mini-calendar, like the one in Figure 4.3, from which you can choose the date.

FIGURE 4.3:
Notes lets you use a mini-calendar to choose the date of your appointment.

Within this calendar you can use the ↑, ↓, ←, and → keys to move to the date you want. Use the PgUp and PgDn keys (or, alternatively, click on the small triangles at either side of the month's name) to move backwards or forwards by a month at a time. To move backwards or forwards one year at a time, use Ctrl+PgUp and Ctrl+PgDn.

4. Appointments are recorded with a specific start and finish time. You can simply type in these starting and finishing times for your appointment if you wish, but you can also click on the stopwatch button next to the field to use a special dialog box like the one in Figure 4.4. To change the starting time for the appointment just drag the upper of the two black-on-yellow times to a new position on the "timeline." To change the finishing time, drag the lower one. To move the whole appointment without changing its length, drag the duration indicator. The times move in 15-minute increments and Notes won't let you set an appointment that ends before it starts. Triangular gray icons at the top and bottom of the box let you scroll the timeline to display earlier or later times. When you are satisfied with your settings, click on the small green checkmark, or simply click in a different field on the form.

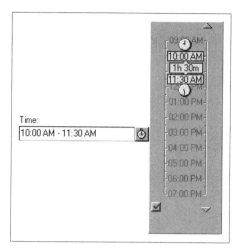

FIGURE 4.4:
A "timeline" lets you choose the starting and finishing times for an appointment.

5. Reminders are recorded with a single time that you can edit similarly. For events, you should enter the event's duration in days.

6. Next, a pair of checkboxes let you tell Notes how much it should tell people about whether you are available at this time. Allowing other Notes users to check your availability is explained in the section "Setting Your Calendar Profile" in Chapter 17, so I'll just describe these options briefly here:

- Check Pencil In if you haven't yet confirmed that the Calendar Entry you are adding will, in fact, take place. Notes will report this time as free when other users check on your availability. When you confirm the item, you should make sure to reopen the Calendar Entry and remove the check next to Pencil In. Because of the nature of reminders, Notes doesn't let you pencil them in. In contrast, Notes checks Pencil In by default for anniversaries, on the assumption that celebrating an anniversary is unlikely to mean you are unavailable for meetings.
- The Not for Public Viewing checkbox is useful for personal appointments and reminders. It tells Notes not to show this item to users who can read your calendar. Letting other users read your calendar is also described in "Setting Your Calendar Profile" in Chapter 17.

7. If your Calendar Entry needs further explanation or annotation, you can provide these in the Detailed Description field.

8. **Save and Close** Clicking on the Save and Close button is a fine way to add this new entry to your calendar. All the usual methods for closing documents will also work, too. When you close the new document, Notes returns you to the Calendar view.

WARNING If you absent-mindedly try to add an appointment to your schedule for a time that has already passed, Notes will warn you of your *faux pas* as you try to close the new Calendar Entry.

Two other buttons on the Action Bar above your Calendar Entry merit some description here (the remaining two you will meet later in the chapter). Clicking on the blue question mark on a yellow background calls up a dialog box with context-sensitive (but rudimentary) guidelines on using Notes' calendaring features. Clicking on the Check Calendar button switches to your Calendar view to let you check on other Calendar Entries. Close the Calendar view and Notes takes you back to your new Calendar Entry.

Viewing Your Calendar

Take another look at the Calendar view on your screen (or at Figure 4.1, if you prefer). When you first open it, it will show your calendar items for the current week, with the current day displayed in red. As well as the one-week view, you can also have Notes show you the calendar two days, two weeks, or one month at a time, using the buttons on the Action Bar. These options are also available from the View ➤ Calendar submenu.

Getting Around in the Calendar View

There are a number of ways to move around in your calendar. You can use the ↑, ↓, ←, and → keys to highlight any item or date in the view. By highlighting an item and pressing Enter (or by double-clicking on it), you can view and edit the relevant Calendar Entry, just as you might with a memo.

NOTE You can change the date or time of a Calendar Entry by opening and editing it. However, you can also reschedule entries by dragging them to a different day or time in the calendar. For more information, see the section "Rescheduling with Drag-and-Drop" at the end of this chapter.

Pressing Enter when a date is highlighted (or double-clicking on a date) tells Notes to switch to a two-day view for this day.

You can click on the small folded-over page corners at the lower left and lower right (or use the PgUp and PgDn keys) to move a Calendar view backwards and forwards in time. The view will change by the same increment as the period you are displaying (one week at a time for the one-week view, and so on).

TIP	Lotus's technical term for the folded-over page corners that let you flip the calendar to view earlier or later dates is "dog-ears." No, really, it is.

To quickly switch to a different date, click on the 16 button at the top of the view to display a mini-calendar like the one available on the Calendar Entry form. Choosing View ➤ Calendar ➤ Go To brings up a dialog box that also allows you to switch to a different date. To get your calendar back to the present, click on the Go to Today button on the Action Bar, or choose View ➤ Calendar ➤ Go to Today.

Item Descriptions and Time Slots

Notes lists items chronologically on your calendar. Anniversaries, events, and items from your To Do list come first on each day, as they are not assigned a specific time. Instead, Notes displays them as occurring all day. Then Notes lists appointments, meetings, and any reminders you have set yourself, in the order they occur. Next to the time, Notes displays one of seven small icons, which are shown in Table 4.1, to indicate the type of entry.

Table 4.1: Calendar Icons

Icon	Calendar Entry
	Appointment
	Invitation (sent)
	Invitation (received)
	Event
	Reminder
	Anniversary
	To Do Item

After the icon, Notes displays a brief description of the item. Often, Notes does not have enough room to display all the calendar items for a particular day. In this case, Notes provides a pair of arrow icons that you can use to scroll up and down the day's calendar. Also, Notes may not have enough room to display a full line of information about some Calendar Entries (in the one-month view, for example). If you move the cursor onto one of these truncated entries, without clicking the mouse button, Notes will pop up a box with a more complete description.

If the times set for two appointments or meetings overlap, Notes displays a red bar to the left of the conflicting entries to alert you. If the calendar contains any entries you have not yet read, these are listed in red.

By default, Notes displays items in the two-day view in one-hour time slots that run from 7:00 A.M. to 7:00 P.M. Notes shows a line for each hour, with your appointments, meetings, and reminders placed chronologically and highlighted in pale blue. You can display or hide time slots for any day in any type of Calendar view by choosing View ➤ Calendar ➤ Show Time Slots. An alternative way to show and hide time slots (except in the one-month view) is to click on the small clock icon for the day.

> **TIP**
>
> You can select items in the Calendar view in much the same way you would select messages in the other views of your mailbox. Pressing the spacebar places a checkmark next to the highlighted message to indicate that you have selected it. You can select (and deselect) further items either with the spacebar or by clicking in the margin to the left of the item. You can then print, copy, or delete multiple calendar items as you would multiple messages.

Simple Meeting Functions

Because meetings involve coordinating your schedule with those of other people, they are a little more complex than other types of Calendar Entry. Notes provides a range of sophisticated functions that let you automate the scheduling of meetings, check availability, send invitations, confirm attendance, and even delegate someone else to attend in your place. Some of these functions are a little complex for Chapter 4, so they are covered separately in Chapter 17.

Depending on the functions of your job, you may never need to schedule a meeting yourself, but you are more than likely to receive occasional meeting invitations from other people. Even if you don't plan to schedule many meetings yourself, you may want to read through this section to understand how meetings are arranged in Notes.

Scheduling a Meeting

You record a meeting in the same way you would any other item on your calendar—by creating a new Calendar Entry. This time you can leave the Invitation radio button selected. Your screen should look something like Figure 4.5.

Fill in the Calendar Entry section as you would for an appointment. Take care that your descriptions are intelligible, as Notes will use them later on to notify your invitees of the meeting.

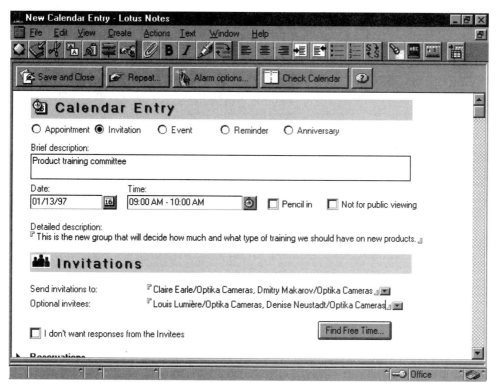

FIGURE 4.5: When you create a meeting invitation, Notes adds a new Invitations section to the standard Calendar Entry form.

Sending Out Invitations

After scheduling your meeting, Notes gives you two fields in which to list the people you want to invite. In the Send Invitations To field, list all the people who should attend your meeting. Use the Optional Invitees field to list people you want to invite to the meeting but whose attendance is not as critical. Later, if you want to find the best time for the meeting, Notes will put a lower priority on scheduling a time when the optional invitees are free. You can list multiple names in these fields, separated by commas, or click on the small button to the right of each field to bring up a standard address dialog box.

These are the only items that you *must* provide to invite people to a meeting. If you want, you can click on Save and Close right now to enter the meeting in your calendar and send out invitations. Notes also offers you several other options and tools to use with your invitation. They are only mentioned briefly in this chapter but you can find full descriptions in Chapter 17.

If you do close this new Calendar Entry now, Notes will ask you, "Do you want to send this to the people/resources you invited?" You may be a little puzzled by this question. "Resources" refers to the in-built functions to reserve rooms and equipment that are contained in the Reservations section and described in Chapter 17. As far as you are concerned at the moment, Notes is just asking whether it should send out invitations to your meeting, so you should click on Yes.

Other Invitation Options

Here's a brief summary of other functions you can use with invitations; you can find more details in Chapter 17. Below the two fields for invitees' names, you can check a box to tell Notes you don't want to request responses from the invitees. You might want to send "broadcast invitations" like this for meetings with many attendees. When you create repeating meetings (described later in this chapter), Notes issues broadcast invitations by default.

If you are having (or anticipate) trouble finding the most convenient time for your meeting, click on the Find Free Time button to open a dialog box that lets you scan the Freetime Schedules of the invitees you have selected.

At the bottom of the invitation is a collapsed section labeled Reservations. You can click on the small triangle to the left of the section to expand it (click again to return it to the collapsed state). The Reservations section offers you three buttons to click to reserve a room or resource for your meeting, *providing that your company has chosen to implement these features*. You can choose between reserving a specific room or reserving whatever room is available at a particular time. You can also choose to reserve a specific resource for your meeting, such as an overhead projector or a large-screen computer monitor.

Responding to Invitations

Probably, you are likely to need to respond to meeting invitations much more frequently than to actually send them yourself. Here's how to do it in Notes.

When you receive meeting invitations, they will show up in your mailbox just like regular messages. The subject will start with the word "Invitation" and then list the meeting's title, date, and time. Open up the invitation and you will see something like Figure 4.6.

Notes tells you who is organizing the meeting, what time it will start and end, where it will take place (if this information is known), and what it is about. You can click to expand the Invitees section to see who has been invited, and read any extra details that the meeting's organizer has provided.

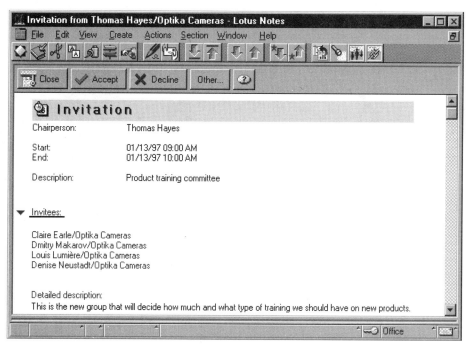

FIGURE 4.6: When you receive an invitation to a meeting, the choices are quite simple.

There are several actions you can take:

Accept You can click on this button on the Action Bar to agree to attend the meeting.

Decline You can click on this button on the Action Bar to choose not to attend the meeting.

Other You can click on this button on the Action Bar to open an Options dialog box that lets you perform a range of other actions. You may find up to five choices here:

- Two options let you Accept or Reject the invitation. These are equivalent to clicking on the Accept and Reject buttons on the Action Bar, but also let you enclose comments for the meeting's chairperson.
- If you are not sure whether you'll be able to attend, you can Pencil In the invitation. This works just like accepting the invitation, except that Notes keeps the time free in your calendar for the moment. If you need to, you can add comments to send to the chairperson.
- If you can't attend the meeting yourself, choose Delegate to have Notes open a dialog box in which you can nominate someone else to attend. Notes then tells the chairperson that you have delegated your attendance, and notifies your chosen stand-in.

WARNING Notes will not let you delegate attendance at a meeting to someone else on the list of invitees. If you name someone who has already been invited, Notes will warn you and ask you to pick again.

- If you want to suggest holding the meeting at a different time or in a different place, choose Propose Alternative Time/Location. Notes displays a new Proposed Change section on the invitation, and you can enter any combination of a new date, a new time, or a new location. Notes gives you space to explain why you would like to make the change. Notes then sends a counterproposal to the meeting's chairperson, and will let you know whether the chairperson accepts or declines your suggestion.

No Buttons If the invitation you have received doesn't have Accept and Decline buttons, that most likely means it is a broadcast invitation. You are being notified of the meeting but there is no need for you to respond. Broadcast meetings are not placed on your calendar automatically, but if you would like to include this meeting, click on the Add to Calendar button. Alternatively, you can click on Other to pencil it in.

Close Click on this button on the Action Bar to leave the invitation without yet accepting or declining it. Remember to give your answer soon.

Check Calendar You may also see this button, which you can click to view your other appointments.

If, later on, you change your mind about attending a meeting, you can open the invitation and make a new choice. Maybe you want to reschedule a meeting for which you initially accepted the invitation, or to attend a meeting that you earlier declined. In some cases, Notes will warn you that your earlier course of action (declining or delegating) may have caused you to miss important notifications about the meeting.

> **NOTE** Notes lets you configure your mailbox to automatically accept meeting invitations (either from certain named people or from everyone). Also, you can have Notes automatically remove meeting invitations from your Inbox once you have responded to them (or have added broadcast meetings to your calendar). To find out more about these options, see Chapter 17.

The Meetings View

Each meeting invitation appears automatically in your Inbox. In addition, once you accept an invitation (or add a broadcast invitation to your calendar) it shows up in the Calendar view.

Sometimes, however, you might like to see your meetings and appointments listed line by line in the conventional Notes view format. Click on Meetings in the Navigation Pane, and Notes will show you the Meetings view of your mailbox. It will look something like the one in Figure 4.7.

This simple view lists all the Calendar Entries you have created for yourself, as well as any meetings to which you have been invited. You can switch the view between showing your most recent appointments last in the list and first in the list by clicking on the Meeting Time header.

If you have created any repeating events (see the section "Setting up a Repeating Event" later in this chapter), Notes groups them together here under the heading "Do Not Delete - Repeat Parent for...."

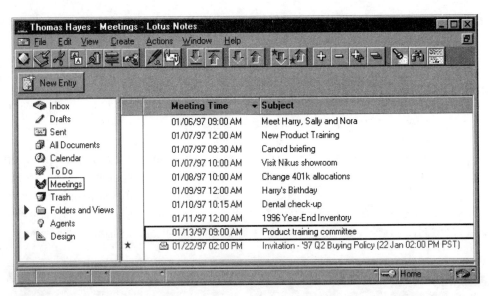

FIGURE 4.7: The Meetings view lets you look at a chronological list of meetings and appointments.

Alarms and Repeating Events

Two buttons on the Action Bar at the top of each Calendar Entry give you access to simple add-on functions that may make the calendar more useful to you. You can have Notes give you an audible and visible warning of certain events, and have particular calendar items repeat on a defined schedule.

Setting an Alarm

Follow these directions to set an alarm:

1. Click on the Alarm Options button on the Action Bar above the Calendar Entry. Notes then opens the Set Alarm dialog box, shown in Figure 4.8.

NOTE Initially, Notes is set to have the alarm system disabled. The first time you want to set an alarm, you will see a dialog box telling you that your Calendar Profile is not yet set up to allow alarms and asking if you want to change this. Click on Yes and Notes will whir away behind the scenes making the necessary changes.

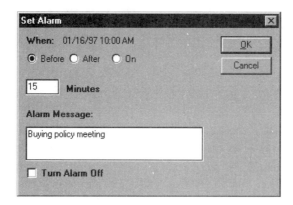

FIGURE 4.8:
The Set Alarm dialog box is quite straightforward.

2. Notes asks you to specify when the alarm should appear. For appointments and meetings, you can have the alarm occur a certain number of minutes before or after the start time you have set for the event, or on some other date and time that you specify. For reminders the default is for the alarm to occur at the date and time you have already set, but you can change this if you like. Alarms for events and anniversaries occur by default at midnight at the start of the date in question, which means that unless you work the night shift, you will see these alarms as soon as you start Notes the next morning.

3. If you like, specify the message that will appear on your alarm (by default, it is the same description that you provided for the event).

4. Click on OK to confirm the alarm or on Cancel to abandon the process. Notes adds a sentence at the top of the document to confirm that you have set an alarm for this Calendar Entry.

5. You can then save and close the Calendar Entry as normal.

When the time you, set comes around, Notes will beep and display a dialog box warning you of the appointment or meeting. You can then either click on Done to turn off the alarm, or click on Snooze to have Notes repeat the alarm a little later. By default, clicking on Snooze suspends the alarm for 10 minutes, but if you want it to repeat later or sooner, you can enter a different length of time.

WARNING In order for an alarm to work, you must be running Notes on your computer. If you are unsure how to keep Notes running while you use other software, see the section on this at the end of Chapter 1.

If the times you set for some alarms passed while the program was not running on your computer, Notes will display a dialog box to let you know about those alarms the next time you start the program. Once you have read the list of alarms that you missed, you can then click on Done to close the box. If you want Notes to repeat some of these alarms later, select them in the list (change the snooze delay if you like) and click on Snooze.

If, after you set an alarm for a calendar item, you decide that you do not need it, open the relevant Calendar Entry and click on the Alarm Options button. Then check the box marked Turn Alarm Off and click on OK. Notes cancels the alarm.

> **NOTE** You can have Notes automatically set alarms for all Calendar Entries of certain types. To find out about this, see Chapter 17.

Setting Up a Repeating Event

Some types of meetings, events, and appointments happen on a regular schedule. Maybe your department has planning meetings every three weeks, or maybe you have to organize the biennial Venice Film Festival. To save you having to create a separate Calendar Entry for each occurrence of the event, Notes lets you tell it the schedule on which these events repeat.

You create a repeating event in the same way that you would create any other calendar item. Use the following directions to set up your event:

1. Once you have entered all the details and made all the selections you need to, click on the Repeat button on the Action Bar. This opens the Repeat Rules dialog box, shown in Figure 4.9.

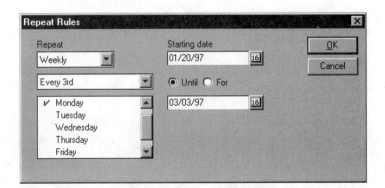

FIGURE 4.9:
Use the Repeat Rules dialog box to tell Notes how often to repeat an event, and for how long.

NOTE You can only create a repeating event from a *new* Calendar Entry. To repeat a Calendar Entry you have already saved and closed, create a new Calendar Entry with the same details and then click on the Repeat button *before* saving and closing the entry.

You need to tell Notes two things in the Repeat Rules dialog box: how often you want the event to occur, and for how long to keep repeating it.

2. The first list box gives you six basic choices of repetition frequency: Daily, Weekly, Monthly by Date, Monthly by Day, Yearly, and Custom. Your choice here just determines the basic unit you want Notes to use to count how often your event will occur. For example, if you want to schedule a meeting every three weeks, you should choose the Weekly option here. Use Monthly by Date if you want a meeting to happen on the 28th day of every month; use Monthly by Day if you want it on the fourth Friday. The Custom option lets you define repeating meetings with erratic schedules.

3. Once you have chosen the basic frequency, you get to refine it:

For Daily events, you can choose to have them occur every day, or every so many days (from 2 to 31).

For Weekly events, you can choose to have them occur every week, or every so many weeks (from 2 to 8). Then select the day of the week on which the event should be scheduled.

For Monthly events, you can choose to have them occur every month, or every so many months (from 2 to 12). If you chose the By Date option, you then select the date of the month on which your event should occur. If you chose the By Day option, you specify meeting dates in the form 1st Monday, 3rd Friday, or last Wednesday of the month.

For Yearly events, you can choose to have them occur every year, or to skip years. If you really need to, Notes lets you schedule an event to repeat only every 10 years.

For Custom events, Notes gives you a list box into which you type the dates of each meeting in order.

4. Next, Notes asks you for the date of the first event. By default this is the same as the date you already provided for the Calendar Entry, so you should not need to change this.

5. You can specify the length of time for which you want the event to repeat in one of two ways. Choose Until, and Notes lets you type in a date after which no more events should be scheduled (or select a date from a pop-up calendar). Choose For, and Notes lets you tell it to repeat the meeting for a certain number of days, weeks, months, or years.

6. Lastly, for all events apart from weekly ones, you can tell Notes what to do if the event falls on a weekend. You can choose not to move the event, to move it to the Friday before or the Monday after, to move it to the nearest weekday, or to delete the event completely.

7. Then, as usual, you click on OK to confirm the repetition schedule you have set up, or click on Cancel to abandon it. When you click on Save and Close, Notes tells you on the status bar at the bottom of the screen that it is creating the repeating appointments you have specified.

> **NOTE** When you create meeting invitations with a repeating schedule, Notes automatically sends broadcast invitations to the invitees. These inform the invitees of the meeting, but do not require them to respond.

Viewing Repeating Events

Notes displays the multiple entries you have created in the Calendar and Meetings views. In the Meetings view, you will see them grouped together under the parent heading "Do Not Delete - Repeat Parent for…." You cannot edit the parent entry here; if you try to delete it, Notes converts each of the repeating events into a separate, non-repeating calendar item.

If you just want to look at the repeat schedule for a series of events, open one of the events and choose Actions ➤ View Repeat Info.

Changing Repeating Events

If you want to change some of the details recorded for a repeating event, open the Calendar Entry you wish to change (*not* the parent entry). You can change all fields on the form with the following exceptions for repeating meetings: You cannot check for free time; you cannot invite more people or remove invitees from the list; and you cannot reserve a new room or resource or cancel a room or resource reservation.

When you click on Save and Close, Notes will ask you to decide if the changes you have made should apply to just this occurrence of the event, all occurrences, or only those before or after the occurrence you have edited.

NOTE   If you change the date or time of a repeating meeting entry, Notes sends out new invitations.

If all you want to do is change the date or time of one or more repeating events, you may find it easier to use the drag-and-drop capabilities of the Calendar view, described in the next section.

Rescheduling with Drag-and-Drop

The Calendar view of your Notes mailbox offers a unique capability to reschedule events by dragging them to a different time or date. You can use this capability with both once-only and repeating events.

To reschedule an event with drag-and-drop:

1. Move the cursor to the event's listing in the Calendar view.
2. Click and hold the left mouse button. The cursor should change from an arrow to a sheet of paper and a small clock face, like the one shown here.
3. You can now move the event to a new time, a new date, or both:
   - To change the date of an event, drag the cursor to the new date. If the date you want is not shown in the current Calendar view, drag the cursor to one of the "dog-ears" at the bottom corners of the view to have Notes scroll the view forward or backward.
   - To change the time of an event, drag the cursor to the new time. If the calendar does not show time slots for the date you want, drag the cursor to the small clock face icon for that date to have Notes display them. Then drag the cursor to the new time for the meeting. You can scroll the list of time slots by dragging the cursor onto one of the scroll arrows.
4. Position the cursor on the new date and/or time and release the left mouse button.
5. If you are rescheduling a repeating event, Notes will ask you whether you want to change just this occurrence, all occurrences, or all those before or after this one.

You now have all the basic skills to use Notes in scheduling your working day and communicating with your colleagues. I have tried to show you practical Notes techniques in the first four chapters, because the only reason to learn new software is so that you can do something useful with it. However, I have avoided too much detailed explanation of the myriad features of the Notes landscape. If the idea of a Notes geography lesson doesn't appeal, think of Chapter 5 more as a package tour: "All the best sights in 20 minutes."

Part 2

Working with Notes Documents

Chapter 5

FINDING YOUR WAY AROUND IN NOTES

FEATURING

- **Understanding the different parts of Notes**
- **Working with Workspace icons and pages**
- **What Notes tells you on the status bar**
- **Clicking SmartIcons to do what you want**
- **Using shortcut menus and the Action Bar**
- **Working with multiple windows**

When you start working with any new software, all you want to do is get some results. But as you get more familiar with using it to do your job, you start to wonder about all the brightly colored buttons and icons and what they might do. After four chapters of looking at the mundane details of e-mail and calendars, this one steps back to show you an array of clever features that make using Notes much easier.

Although for the next few chapters we're still going to be working in your mailbox, the techniques you learn here will also be useful when you start using Notes' information-sharing functions in Part Three: Sharing Information.

Forms, Documents, Messages, and Memos

So far I've been referring to reading and writing *messages* in your Notes mailbox, but Notes has sometimes used the word *document* instead. You also know that your messages are sometimes called *memos*, and you may even have heard the terms *form* and *database*.

So what's the difference? Now might be a good time to define a few terms:

Term	Meaning
Document	The general name for anything you or someone else creates in Notes.
Message	A document that has been (or will be) sent through Notes mail. In your mailbox, *message* and *document* mean the same thing. In other parts of Notes you use documents that you don't generally mail to other people, so they aren't usually called messages.
Memo	The most generic kind of message. Reply and Reply with History are some other kinds of Notes messages.
Form	The "template" for a document. A Notes *form* is different from a Notes document in much the same way that a paper form is different from a paper document. When you save a document, Notes stores just the information in the fields of that document. It doesn't store the labels next to the fields, or any buttons or graphics. That kind of information comes from the form. The next time you open the document, Notes first uses the form to determine where to place each item on the screen, what font and color to use, and so on. Then it gets the actual information–the fields–from the document you saved.
View	A particular way of looking at the information in a Notes database (which is defined below). It is always made up of rows, and each row gives you information about a particular document. A view shows all the docu-ments that match a certain criterion.
Folder	A place you can put Notes documents to organize them in your own way. With some special folders, such as your Inbox, Notes may also add and remove documents itself. Folders look a lot like views but contain only what is put in them. The differences between folders and views are examined at the end of Chapter 2.
Database	A self-contained collection of documents, forms, views, and folders. The documents hold the actual data; the forms, views, and folders tell Notes how to present the data to you. You have already used two databases: your own Notes mailbox (also known as your *mail database*) and your company's Public Name & Address Book.

In a mail database, the documents are all messages that you have sent or received, and the forms are called things like Memo and Reply with History. Each form appears separately on the Create menu. Having different forms lets a Reply with History work a bit differently than a Memo. For example, the Reply with History form automatically copies the subject and body from the original message.

We didn't actually look at a view of the Public Name & Address Book directly. Instead, we saw a special Mail Address dialog box that showed us the names of people and groups to whom you can send Notes messages. But we did look at a Group document in this database (that is, a document created with the Group form). This database also has a form that you can use to provide information about an individual person (the names in the address book come from this form).

A database can be stored on your own computer, in which case it is yours to use and to modify, or on a central computer, in which case it can be made available to all the Notes users in your company, a single person, or any selection of people.

The Notes Workspace Revisited

In Chapter 1, we briefly looked at the Notes workspace, the gray page that Notes displays when you start the program. The workspace contains the icon you use to open your mailbox. By now, you may have guessed that the other icons in the workspace are for opening other Notes databases.

Depending on your company and the work you do in Notes, you will see a different combination of icons here. However, one of the icons in the workspace should bear the name of your company's Public Name & Address Book. You can browse in here when you have a spare moment, to get an idea of the information it contains and how to navigate through Notes. There's more information on Name & Address Books in Chapter 18.

Pages and Tabs

The seven tabbed pages are a fairly prominent part of the Notes workspace. If you have a color monitor, each tab is a different color. Some may already carry a short piece of descriptive text, but most will probably be blank.

NOTE

The rightmost tab is the Replicator and doesn't work like the other tabs. The Replicator lets mobile Notes users exchange mail and Freetime Schedules, and keep any shared Notes databases up to date. Using Notes as a remote user is described in Chapter 13.

The six regular tabbed pages have a simple function: They are a way for you to store and organize icons. At the moment, it may seem as if you have more than enough space on the one displayed page without needing five other pages. However, most Notes users quickly accumulate many database icons, and the tabs can help you maintain some semblance of order. It's a good idea to keep the first workspace page just for your mail and for Name & Address Books. Then you can arrange other icons on the other pages in whatever way makes best sense for your job.

Notes places a light gray border around whichever is the current tab. (If you're using a monochrome screen, a *lot* of things will be gray, but the colors Notes uses translate quite well to most monochrome displays. Telling the difference between various shades of gray soon becomes second-nature.) Click once on one of the six tabs. A new page replaces the old one on your screen.

Along with showing a new page, Notes may also be showing you new icons. More likely, there are no icons at all on this page. To get back to the page we first looked at, click on its tab, probably the farthest to the left.

Changing the Color of Tabs

Now *double-click* on the tab for the page that's currently displayed. Notes shows an InfoBox like that in Figure 5.1. You'll find InfoBoxes to be a very useful way to change settings in Notes. They're described more fully in Chapter 6, but this one is simple enough that we can use it without having to examine it too carefully.

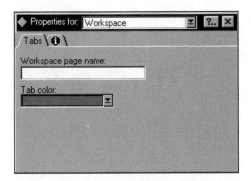

FIGURE 5.1:
Using an InfoBox to assign a name and color to a workspace tab

If the tab you double-clicked on was blank, then the box marked Workspace Page Name will be empty. In that case, type **Mail & Addresses** to tell Notes what you want to display on this tab.

Click on the triangle to the right of the Tab color box to pop up a matrix showing all 240 colors Notes can use for this tab, as in Figure 5.2. One of the squares in the matrix will be highlighted already. To change this tab's color, just click on a different square. If you want Notes to name the various colors for you, drag the cursor to different squares in the matrix and Notes will display the name of each. When you're happy with the name and color for this tab, click on the close box (the box with an × in it at the top-right corner of the InfoBox).

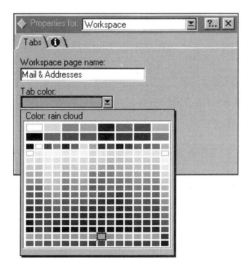

FIGURE 5.2:
Each of the 240 colors available in Notes has its own name.

Repositioning Icons on the Page

To organize your workspace to best suit your needs, you should arrange how Notes displays icons on the six tabbed pages. To move an icon to a different spot on the same page:

1. Place the cursor on the icon you want to move.
2. Click and hold the left mouse button.
3. Drag the icon to its new position.
4. Release the left mouse button.

You can also use this drag-and-drop method to reposition several icons at a time:

1. Click once on the first icon you want to move.
2. Hold down the Shift key on the keyboard.
3. Click once on each additional icon you want to move as a group. As you click on the icons, their appearance changes, and it looks as if you had depressed a series of buttons.
4. Click on the last icon you want to move as part of this group and hold the mouse button down.
5. Drag the icons to their new position.
6. Release the left mouse button.
7. Release the Shift key.

Notes makes the new positions of the icons you have moved conform to the same regular grid that it uses for the others on the page. If you drop one icon on top of another, Notes moves the existing icon (and any below it) further down on the page to make room for the new icon. You can put many icons on each page. If there isn't room to display them all at once, Notes provides scroll bars.

Moving Icons to Different Pages

Moving icons from one page to another is very similar to moving icons to a different position on the same page:

1. Select the icon or icons you want to move as described above.
2. Drag the cursor to the tab for the page to which you want to move the icon(s). When the cursor is positioned properly, the name of the tab is highlighted.
3. Release the left mouse button (and the Shift key if you were moving a group of icons). The icons will disappear from the current page. If you click on the appropriate tab, you can see where Notes has placed them on the new page.

> **TIP** If the icons on a page become too unruly, choose View ➤ Arrange Icons to line them all up in rows from left to right and top to bottom.

Adding and Deleting Workspace Pages

Once you have found out which Notes databases you'll be working with and have added their icons to your workspace, you may decide that six tabbed pages is too few or too many. Notes lets you add or delete as many workspace pages as you like, so long as you keep at least one and no more than thirty-two.

To add a workspace page:

1. Select the tab to the right of where you want the new page to appear.
2. Choose Create ➤ Workspace Page.
3. If this is the first new workspace page you have added, Notes will display the dialog box in Figure 5.3. Versions of Notes prior to Notes 4.0 were limited to six workspace pages. If you are unsure whether you might have to switch back to an earlier version of Notes, check with your Notes administrator before proceeding. Otherwise, you can click on Yes here.

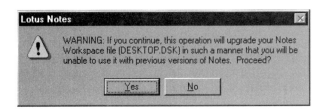

FIGURE 5.3:
If you add work-space pages, you can't use your workspace file with earlier versions of Notes.

4. Notes will place the new tab to the left of the one you selected. You can now choose a name and a color for the new tab in the usual way.

To delete a workspace page:

1. Select the tab you want to remove.
2. Press Delete or choose Edit ➤ Clear.
3. Notes will ask you if you're sure you want to remove the page. Click on Yes.

 **WARNING** If you delete a workspace page with database icons on it, Notes will remove the icons as well. If you want to continue to access these databases, first drag the icons to another page.

The Title and Menu Bars

At the very top of the screen, Notes displays a title bar and a menu bar. You should be familiar with these bars from using other applications that run on your computer.

There's not much special you need to know about them. The *title bar* tells you that you're using Notes and what you're currently doing in the workspace. You use the *menu bar* to choose menu commands and give Notes instructions on many tasks you want to do.

> **NOTE** You can often press shortcut key combinations instead of making menu choices. Common menu choices have SmartIcon equivalents.

SmartIcons

Although you can navigate through Notes by choosing items from the menu bar or by pressing key combinations, often the easiest way to accomplish a task in Notes is to click on a SmartIcon. SmartIcons are the small buttons in a line on the screen, usually below the menu bar.

Most SmartIcons duplicate menu choices. Click and hold down the right mouse button on any SmartIcon (or just let the cursor rest on it for a few seconds) and Notes will tell you what the icon does (on the Macintosh, use Balloon Help). If you have used other Lotus applications before, you may be familiar with some of the SmartIcons already. Other software companies use similar devices that they often call "toolbars."

Changing SmartIcon Settings

To change where Notes displays the SmartIcons on the screen, choose File ➤ Tools ➤ SmartIcons from the menu bar. Notes brings up the SmartIcons dialog box shown in Figure 5.4. The Position item on the right side of the dialog box lets you tell Notes where to display SmartIcons: along one of the four edges of the screen or as a floating palette. A *floating palette* is a set of SmartIcons you can drag anywhere you want on the screen.

On the right side of the dialog box, three checkboxes are under the heading Show:

- The first checkbox, labeled Icon Bar, determines whether Notes displays SmartIcons at all.
- The second checkbox, Context Icons, lets you choose whether to have Notes display additional icons that are appropriate to what you're doing at any moment. Context Icons are usually very useful, offering you text-editing commands in a document and navigation commands in a view, for example; so you'd be wise to leave this option checked.

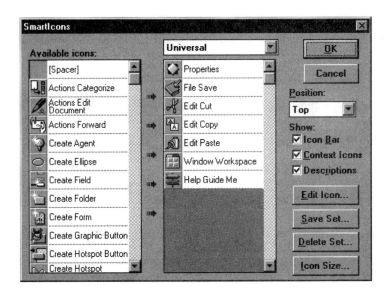

FIGURE 5.4:
One of the things you can do in the SmartIcons dialog box is tell Notes where and what size to display SmartIcons.

- The final checkbox, Descriptions, tells Notes whether to automatically describe SmartIcons when you rest the cursor on them.

In Windows and OS/2 you can choose the size of the SmartIcons that Notes displays. Click on the Icon Size button in the bottom-right corner of the dialog box and Notes lets you choose between small icons (suitable for VGA monitors) and larger icons (suitable for Super VGA monitors).

NOTE Other options in the SmartIcons dialog box let you design your own SmartIcons and choose new sets of SmartIcons. You probably won't need to customize SmartIcons until you become quite an accomplished Notes user. If you do want to make a set of your favorite SmartIcons, you can find instructions in Notes' own online help. The Notes Help database is described in Chapter 9.

Using SmartIcons

There are about 150 SmartIcons available to you. From now on in this book, if a SmartIcon is available for a particular task, it will appear in the text. Table 5.1 offers a quick summary of SmartIcons that you can use instead of menu choices for some of the tasks you have already learned.

TABLE 5.1: SmartIcons for Common Notes Tasks

SmartIcon	Function	SmartIcon	Function	SmartIcon	Function
	Mail Open		File Save		View Refresh
	Create Mail Memo		Actions Edit Document		Edit Clear
	Mail Address		File Exit Notes		Edit Undo
	Mail Send Document		Create Folder Database		File Open
	Actions Forward		View Show/Hide Preview Pane		File Tools SmartIcons

The Status Bar

Along the bottom of the screen, Notes displays the status bar. It is shown in Figure 5.5. If you're using Windows 95, the status bar will probably be shown above the Windows Taskbar. Some items here provide you with information on what Notes is doing. Others let you tell Notes what to do. We'll take a look at them from left to right.

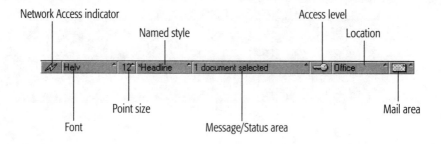

FIGURE 5.5: The status bar tells you a lot about how your copy of Notes is set up.

TIP If the combination of the Windows 95 Taskbar and the Notes status bar seems too cluttered, choose Settings ➤ Taskbar from the Start Menu. Then check the box marked Auto Hide on the Taskbar Options tab. Windows reduces the Taskbar to a thin line that expands into the Taskbar when you move the cursor to the bottom of the screen.

The Network Access indicator is a small box that displays a yellow lightning bolt when Notes is communicating over your network. If you use Notes over a dial-up connection, you'll see a small modem icon (a box with lights) here when Notes is using the modem.

The next three parts of the status bar display the current font, point size, and named style when you are creating or editing a document. Often, however, nothing is shown here because the cursor is not located on text whose font, point size, or style you can alter (if you are reading a document or working in a dialog box, for example). The tiny triangles on each of these parts of the status bar indicate that they also work as pop-up lists. You can change the font, point size, or style of text by clicking on these areas of the status bar and making a new choice.

NOTE See Chapter 6 for more information on formatting text.

The long bar that follows is the Message/Status area. This shows the most recent informational or warning message that Notes has displayed on your computer. Try clicking on the Message/Status area. Notes will pop up a list of the most recent messages it has displayed.

NOTE In previous versions of Notes, the pop-up list showed up to the last nine messages. Notes 4.5 increases the limit to 19 messages.

The Access Level indicator tells you what access rights you have to the current database. It can show one of seven icons, representing the Manager, Designer, Editor, Author, Reader, Depositor, and No Access levels. You can find a quick guide to these icons inside the back cover of this book. If you click on the Access Level indicator, Notes gives you a description of your access level for the current database in the Message/Status area. Chapter 9 covers access levels in detail.

The Location indicator tells mobile Notes users which set of location information Notes is using. Using Notes on the road is covered in Chapter 13.

The rightmost box on the status bar tells you about your mail. Normally it displays an envelope icon, but when you have new mail you'll see an inbox icon here. If you click on this area, Notes pops up a menu with various mail-related commands. Two commands you can use already are Open Mail, to open your Notes mailbox, and Create Memo. You can also use this menu to scan for unread mail (see Chapter 18). Mobile Notes users will find some additional mail commands here.

Field Help

Usually, you can work out what information to enter in which field of a document from the labels next to each field and the general context of the document. Sometimes, however, you'll find yourself working with a strange form in a strange database and you could use a few helpful hints.

In these circumstances, choose View ➤ Show ➤ Field Help to have Notes display a thin ribbon above the status bar. (You'll need to be in edit mode to choose this option.) On this ribbon, Notes displays any help text supplied by the database's designer. Usually, you can expect to find a fuller description of what to enter in the field. You can leave this option on as long as you like; to cancel it, choose View ➤ Show ➤ Field Help again.

Shortcut Menus and the Action Bar

Two other features of the Notes landscape are intended to give you quick access to a range of appropriate actions.

A shortcut menu is a pop-up list of the most common actions for a particular situation. You display the shortcut menu by clicking the right mouse button on the item or area of the screen you want to affect. For example, you'll get a different shortcut menu by clicking on the body field of a memo than you would by clicking on the To field. Clicking on a view or on the workspace will also produce different sets of commands. Macintosh mice have only one button, so Mac users must hold the Option key while clicking on an area of the screen in order to display the shortcut menu.

You've already used the Action Bar quite a bit. It's the row of buttons underneath the SmartIcons in most views, folders, and documents. Again, it's context-sensitive, offering you actions that differ depending on whether you're reading mail in your Inbox or reworking a draft.

Buttons on the Action Bar are often duplicated as choices on the Action menu. Each button has a caption to let you know what it does. If the Action Bar provides a particularly useful option, I will highlight it at the appropriate point in the text.

Working with Windows

When you are done reading a document, you have two choices. One is to close the document, which will automatically take you back to the previous view or document you were looking at. That's the method you learned in Chapter 1. The other option is to leave the document open and go back to your workspace, a view, or another document you were looking at before.

To learn about the second option, open a message in your mailbox. Click on Window on the menu bar and you'll see something like Figure 5.6. At the bottom of the menu that appears, Notes lists the windows that are open, in order.

The list in Figure 5.6 is a typical one, showing us that Thomas Hayes has three windows open, showing the workspace, the All Documents view of his mailbox, and a report he's writing. If Notes can't fit a window's full name in the menu, it truncates it and uses three dots to tell you there's more.

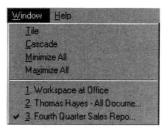

FIGURE 5.6:
The bottom of the Window menu tells you what Notes windows you have open.

Of course, not all of these windows may be visible at the moment. The checkmark next to the name of the report indicates that this is the current window and, in fact, probably only this window is visible on the screen.

 Select the Workspace from the Window menu, or click on the Window Workspace SmartIcon, and Notes shows you the workspace again.

Select the All Documents view and Notes switches back to that view of your mail.

The options at the top of the Window menu should be familiar to you from other programs you have used:

- Choose Window ➤ Tile, or click on the Window Tile SmartIcon, to arrange all open windows so that they take up an equal amount of space on the screen.

- Choose Window ➤ Cascade, or click on the Window Cascade SmartIcon, to arrange all open windows so that they overlap and the title bars of all are visible.
- Window ➤ Minimize All reduces each open window to an icon at the bottom left of the screen.
- The last option, Window ➤ Maximize All, makes all the open windows expand to the size of the full screen. Of course, this means that you can only see one of them, the current window.

> **TIP**
>
> If several windows are open and you want to switch between them without using the mouse, press Ctrl+F6. Each time you press these keys, Notes moves to a different window. In this way you can cycle through them all.

> **NOTE**
>
> When you close a window, Notes will switch to whichever window you used last. If you were looking at the workspace recently, Notes may take you back there even though there are other windows open. If you'd prefer Notes to take you to any other open window in these situations in preference to the workspace (the way it behaved in earlier versions), then you can set it to behave this way. Chapter 14 explains how.

Moving Around in Documents

You can use quite a few shortcuts to move around the screen when you are composing or editing a document. Your basic tools are the four arrow keys to move left, right, up, and down. You can also move the cursor by clicking the mouse. Table 5.2 summarizes the more sophisticated options available to help you move around in documents.

Table 5.2: Moving Around in Documents

Pressing	Moves the Cursor	Pressing	Moves the Cursor
Home	To the beginning of the line	Ctrl+End	To the last field in the document
End	To the end of the line	Tab (in a rich-text field*)	To the next tab stop
Ctrl+→	One word to the right	Tab (elsewhere)	To the next field
Ctrl+←	One word to the left	Shift+Tab (elsewhere)	To the previous field
Ctrl+Home	To the first field in the document	PgUp	Up by one screenful†
		PgDn	Down by one screenful†

* Rich- and plain-text fields and tab stops are explained in Chapter 6.

† A small dash on the left edge of the screen shows where the previous screen was.

So the next time your bosses ask how they can have two Notes documents open alongside each other, or what those funny colored buttons at the top of the screen do, you'll stun them with your firm grasp of the Notes interface. The next chapter shows you how to stun them without them even asking—you'll find out how to format text in all sorts of styles and fonts, how to print out messages and calendar items, and how to check your spelling on that memo asking for a raise.

Chapter 6

BUILDING A BETTER MEMO

FEATURING

- **Printing documents and views**
- **Checking spelling**
- **Changing type fonts, sizes, and styles**
- **Using InfoBoxes**
- **Selecting blocks of text**
- **Editing documents with Permanent Pen**
- **Formatting lists**
- **Setting paragraph alignment**
- **Using Named Paragraph Styles**

Are you feeling a little cramped just sending plain text in your messages? Maybe you'd like to add a little emphasis by putting some words in bold letters, or italics, or by displaying them in bright red. Or maybe you want to create a list where each item is numbered in the left margin.

Most of this chapter is devoted to showing you how to enhance your messages in these and other ways. First of all, though, we're going to deal with two other functions that you're sure to use: printing and the spelling checker.

A Primer on Printing

Remember the paperless office? Computers were going to make paper documents obsolete. Instead, today's word processors and spreadsheets—hooked to high-speed, high-quality laser printers—have made printing so easy that far more paper is being generated than ever before.

Notes does a great deal to reduce the amount of paper you need to use. E-mail, electronic documentation, and "workflow applications" all help to reduce the need to put information on paper to get it from your mind to someone else's. Nevertheless, there are still going to be plenty of times when you want a "hard copy."

Notes provides many of the same options for printing that you are probably familiar with from other software. The two basic types of items that you can print are documents and views.

Printing Documents

Let's start with printing documents. Say company headquarters has sent you a message with an updated version of the evacuation procedure for your building. You are reading the message and decide you need to post the procedure on several bulletin boards around your office. To print the document, you choose one of the following options to open the File Print dialog box shown in Figure 6.1:

- Choose File ➤ Print.
- Press Ctrl+P.
 - Click on the File Print SmartIcon.

NOTE If you are using Notes on a Macintosh computer, you won't see the dialog boxes in Figures 6.1 and 6.2. Instead Notes displays the standard dialog box for the type of printer you are using.

Many of the options in the File Print dialog box will be familiar to you from other software. You can tell Notes whether to print the whole document or just a range of pages. You can also choose how many copies of the document to print.

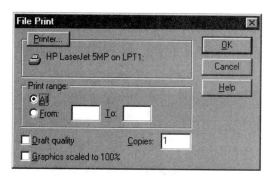

FIGURE 6.1:
The File Print dialog box lets you tell Notes how you want to print the current document.

> **TIP** If you enter a number in the From field and leave the To field blank, Notes prints from the page you specify to the end of the document.

If your printer gives you a draft option to print pages faster at a lower quality, then you can tell Notes to use this mode. You can also force Notes to print any graphics at their full original size (an advanced option you might want to try if you find particular graphics printing badly).

If the printer shown is not the one to which you want to print, you can click on the Printer button to display a dialog box listing all installed printers. You can set attributes specific to the printer you are using, such as paper size, which paper tray to use, and whether to use duplex printing, by clicking on the Setup button in this dialog box.

> **TIP** If you're a Unix user, you'll need to click on the Printer button and select a printer the first time you try to print in Notes.

When you have chosen what to print and how, click on OK. If you decide not to print after all, click on Cancel. Windows and OS/2 users will see a message box, with a Cancel button they can use to interrupt printing. Macintosh users can stop printing by pressing ⌘+. (that is, by pressing the Command and period keys together).

Printing from a View or Folder

As well as printing from within a document, you can also print from a view or folder. As usual in a view, you can highlight a single document to print or use the mouse or spacebar to select a group of documents.

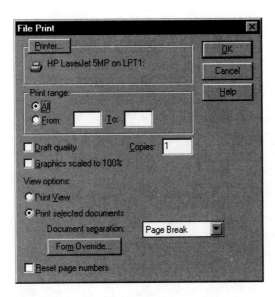 Once you have chosen the documents you are interested in, select File ➤ Print, press Ctrl+P, or click on the File Print SmartIcon. You'll see the File Print dialog box shown in Figure 6.2.

FIGURE 6.2:
The File Print dialog box for a view gives you a few more options.

This File Print dialog box has an upper section that offers the same options you have when printing from a document and a lower section that gives you options that are specific to printing from a view.

The first of your new options is whether to print the view or to print the documents you selected. If you choose to print the view, what comes out of your printer will look a lot like the view you were just looking at: rows and columns. If you checkmarked several rows in the view before you chose to print, Notes prints just those rows. If you choose to print selected documents instead, Notes prints each of the documents you selected (or the highlighted document if you didn't select any).

You have an additional choice if you opt to print selected documents: Document Separation. Your first option is to start a new page for each new document (Page Break), as if you had opened up each one and printed it. Alternatively, you can separate each document from the previous one by just a line across the page (Extra Line) or print each document straight after the previous one (No Separation).

If you choose either Extra Line or No Separation, Notes numbers the pages consecutively until it runs out of stuff to print. But if you choose to have a Page Break between documents, you can also check the Reset Page Numbers box to have Notes restart page numbering at 1 each time Notes starts printing a new document. Otherwise, the page numbering keeps increasing incrementally regardless of what document Notes is printing.

Printing Calendar Entries

Notes gives you several ways to print items from your calendar. Unfortunately, one type of output you might naturally expect—a printed calendar—is not available. Instead you can print full Calendar Entry documents, lists of items grouped by day, and lists in the style of the meetings view.

 To print a Calendar Entry that you have opened for reading or editing, choose File ➤ Print or click on the File Print SmartIcon.

To print multiple Calendar Entries, select them in the Calendar or Meetings view. (In the Calendar view, you must hold down the Shift key as you click to select the first item to force Notes to display selection checkmarks.) Then, when you tell Notes to print, choose the Print Selected Documents option. Calendar Entries are quite compact and you may want to choose a Document Separation setting of No Separation or Extra Line to fit several on a page.

From the Calendar view, you can also print calendar listings, showing some or all of the events for one or more days. To print listings for several entries, select them in the view and use the Print View option in the Print dialog box. If you choose this option with no items selected in the view, Notes prints your entire calendar.

To print all the Calendar Entries for one or more days, use the Print Selected Days option instead (you don't need to select entries in the view first of all). Enter in the boxes provided the first and last dates for which you want to print listings.

To print a chronological view with slightly more details about each item, switch to the Meetings view and choose the Print View option. Again, you can select just certain items if you prefer.

Other Print Options

Beyond what we've looked at here, a number of other options are available when you want to print. You can find out more about all the following options in Notes' own online help, which is described in Chapter 9.

Form Override is available from a button in the File Print dialog box. You use this option to tell Notes on what form you want documents to print.

Choosing File ➤ Page Setup lets you tell Notes information about margins and cropping (on the Macintosh, choose File ➤ Print and then click on Margins).

On the Printer tabs in the Document Properties and Database Properties InfoBoxes, you can set header and footer information for either the whole database or an individual document.

Checking Your Spelling

Notes has a pretty reasonable spell-checker, so if you want to have an excuse for sending memos with misspelled words, you had better not read this section.

You need to be in Edit mode to check spelling. You have the option to just check spelling in a portion of text that you select, or to check spelling in the entire document. Start the spelling checker by choosing Edit ➤ Check Spelling or clicking on the Edit Check Spelling SmartIcon. If you select some text before giving this command, Notes confines its spelling check to that text. Otherwise, Notes checks the whole document.

If Notes finds what it thinks is a misspelling, you will see the Spell Check dialog box shown in Figure 6.3. This dialog box gives you several choices as to how to handle the word.

FIGURE 6.3:
The Spell Check dialog box lets you decide how to deal with words Notes thinks are misspelled.

Skip This tells Notes that you want to disregard this occurrence of the word but still be warned if it comes up again.

Skip All This tells Notes that you want to regard this and any other occurrence of this word in the document as correct.

Define This tells Notes that the word is spelled right and you never want Notes to complain about it again.

Guess Select one of Notes' suggestions from the Guess box if this is the word you meant.

Edit   Type a correction in the Replace box if Notes hasn't come up with an appropriate suggestion.

Replace   Click on Replace to substitute the contents of the Replace box for the word in the document.

Done   This stops the spelling check.

If Notes thinks every word in the document (or the text you selected) is spelled right, it displays a message box that says "No misspellings found." If Notes does find misspellings but you correct them all, the spell-checker bids you adieu with a message box that says "Spelling Complete."

> **NOTE**   When you use **Define** to tell Notes that a word is spelled correctly, Notes puts these words on a list that it always refers to when it checks spelling in documents. If you add a word to the list by mistake, you may want to edit the list to remove the misspelled word. Chapter 14 tells you how to do this. Chapter 14 is also the place to look if you would like to change the language that Notes uses to check spelling. Variant forms of English and medical dictionaries are also available.

Formatting Your Documents

If you are familiar with word processing software, you may already have tried to get Notes to format your documents with more sophistication. Maybe you've already discovered how to change the font or the color of text. Most of the rest of this chapter deals with two ways to make your documents better convey what you want to say: by formatting text and by adding nontext elements.

How Notes Handles Text

Each Notes field handles text in one of two ways:

- *Plain-text* fields store only the letters and words you type, not the font, size, or color they happen to be written in. The field displays your words in a font, size, and color chosen by the person who designed the form you're using.

- *Rich-text* fields store the text you type along with information about what color, size, and font to display it in. Rich-text fields can also include all sorts of other items, such as tables, buttons, and links to other Notes documents. Although the person who designed the form can determine what font, size, and color you start typing in, you can change these formats at any time.

So, in looking at how to format text, we're mainly going to be dealing with rich-text fields. Rich-text and plain-text fields look the same when they're empty. If you want to check whether you can format the text in the field you are using, look on the Text menu. If you are not in a rich-text field, the Text Properties option is dimmed.

The field's purpose may also give you a clue. Database designers tend to use rich-text fields where they expect people to want to be able to enter free-form information. On the memo form, for instance, the Body field is the only rich-text field available to you. The form's designers made the (perhaps warranted) assumption that you wouldn't need to put a table or bright-red, 24-point Symbol text in the cc field.

A Look at InfoBoxes

When you edit and format text, you're going to be using InfoBoxes a lot. The first InfoBox you saw was a pretty simple one in Chapter 5 that allows you to change the name and color of a workspace tab.

You have a lot more choices to make in formatting text, so the InfoBoxes you see will be more complex, but the principle is still the same. Many of the options you need in order to format text can be set from the Text Properties InfoBox, shown in Figure 6.4.

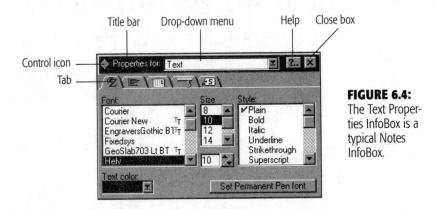

FIGURE 6.4:
The Text Properties InfoBox is a typical Notes InfoBox.

Once you're in edit mode in a rich-text field, you can open this InfoBox in any of the following ways:

- Choose Edit ➤ Properties.
- Choose Text Properties from the shortcut menu that appears when you right-click in the field.
 - Click on the Properties SmartIcon.
- Choose Text ➤ Text Properties.
- Press Ctrl+K.

The first three options will also work to open any type of InfoBox.

So what's so special about InfoBoxes? Their key feature is that they let you change a wide range of options for an item and *see* those changes reflected as you make them.

Once you've opened an InfoBox, it "floats" on top of the active Notes window until you decide to close it. As you make changes in the InfoBox, Notes applies them to the item you are working with. If you want, you can select a new item in the main Notes window and then use the InfoBox to change *its* attributes.

In Notes parlance, InfoBoxes let you view and alter the *properties* of items. Each InfoBox has between one and eight tabs you can select, and each tab usually groups a number of related properties. In the Text Properties InfoBox, the tabs set the Font, Alignment, Page, Hide, and Named Style properties of text.

We'll return to these tabs in the next section, but first we should quickly look at how you can work with InfoBoxes.

Manipulating InfoBoxes

I already mentioned that you can leave an InfoBox on the screen while you switch to a different piece of text, but you could also switch to a different field and open or close documents, folders, or views while the InfoBox is displayed. All the while, Notes will adjust the InfoBox to display the properties of whatever item is active or highlighted.

Often there will be several items whose properties you might want to edit. For example, if you are typing in the body field of a new mail memo, you might want to format text or edit some property of the document as a whole, or even make some adjustment to the settings for your entire mail database. Initially, Notes displays the InfoBox you're most likely to want, but you can switch to any other appropriate InfoBox by choosing a different item in the list box on the title bar.

You may have to move the InfoBox out of the way to see what effect your changes are having. You can move an InfoBox around the screen by dragging its title bar with the mouse. Double-clicking on the title bar reduces the InfoBox to just the title bar and tabs. This works as a toggle—a second double-click restores the InfoBox.

The box marked ?.. takes you to a section of Notes' "Guide Me" online help specific to the properties you're trying to adjust. Notes Help is described in more detail in Chapter 9.

When you have finished, you can close the InfoBox by clicking once on its close box or twice on the lozenge-like control box in the top-left corner.

Formatting Text at the Insertion Point

When you start typing in a rich-text field, Notes displays the font, size, and color chosen by the person who designed the form you are using. Many forms use Regular, Black, 10-point Helv as the standard font. It shows up well on most monitors. (Helv, by the way, is short for Helvetica, a long-standing favorite with typographers.)

Say that after you have typed two paragraphs, you want to start typing the next in Bold, Dark Blue, 14-point Tms Rmn instead. One way to do this is to open the Text Properties InfoBox shown in Figure 6.4. If the Font page is not already selected, click on its tab. You can modify any combination of text attributes on this tab to get the effect you want.

The Font and Size boxes let you choose the typeface and type height to display. In our example, you would select Tms Rmn from the list of font names and 14 from the list of possible sizes. If the size you want isn't listed, you can type it in the box below the size list.

> **NOTE** Point size is a traditional method for measuring type height. One point is $1/72$", so there are six lines of 12-point text per inch.

Next you can choose whether you want Plain, **Bold**, *Italic*, Underlined, ~~Strikethrough~~, Superscript, or Subscript text. You can apply one or more of these formats in any combination, with two obvious exceptions: Text can't be both superscript and subscript at the same time, and normal text can't have any other formatting. In our example, we would check Bold in the Style box.

You can also choose three special styles for displaying text: Shadow (where the text appears to be casting a shadow on the page), Embossed (text appears to be stamped into the page) and Extruded (text appears to be raised up out of the page). These special styles can't be used in combination with any other.

Last, you can choose a color for your text from the box of 16 colors that appears when you click on the triangle next to Text Color. In our example, we would choose Dark Blue, the fifth box in the bottom row. We'll return to the button marked Set Permanent Pen Font later.

> **TIP**
> **Choose text colors carefully. Most Notes forms are white or light-colored, and white or light-colored text does not show up on these forms very well, if at all.**

When you have made the changes you want, click on the Close box in the top-right corner of the InfoBox. Notes returns you to your document, and any text you type at the insertion point reflects your new choices. You can type your next paragraph in Bold, Dark Blue, 14-point Tms Rmn and then switch to something different if you want.

However, the critical words here are "text you type at the insertion point." If you move the insertion point somewhere else in the document, the text you type will reflect whatever font, size, and color have been set for that particular point. If you move to a part of your document that uses 8-point, Bright Green, Italic Arial, that is what Notes will use for new text you type there. To use a different font, you would need to choose it from the Text Properties InfoBox again.

Formatting Selected Text

As well as telling Notes what font to use when you type new text, you can also change the attributes of existing text. To do this, you need to select the text that you want Notes to alter. This principle is a common one, and you should be familiar with it from other software that runs on your computer. You can use the mouse or the keyboard to select text. Notes shows selected text in *reverse video*. This means that if the regular text is black on a white background, selected text is white on a black background.

Shortcuts for Selecting Text

There are many shortcuts to select text in edit mode using the mouse, keyboard, and menus. Table 6.1 summarizes them. You can use any selection methods in combination to highlight exactly what you want.

Table 6.1: Techniques for Selecting Text

Press/Choose	To Select
Shift+→	One character to right of insertion point
Shift+←	One character to left of insertion point
Ctrl+Shift+→	One word to right of insertion point
Ctrl+Shift+←	One word to left of insertion point
Shift+Home	To beginning of line
Shift+End	To end of line
Shift+↑	To the same point on the line above
Shift+↓	To the same point on the line below
Ctrl+Shift+Home	To beginning of current field
Ctrl+Shift+End	To end of current field
Double-click	The word you click on
Shift+click	From the insertion point to the point at which the left mouse button is clicked
Edit ➤ Select All	All the text in the current field
Ctrl+A	All the text in the current field
Edit ➤ Deselect All	Removes any selection highlighting you may have applied, or you can simply click the cursor elsewhere in the document.

If you need to select a slew of text, there are a couple of tried and tested techniques.

- Place the insertion point at the beginning of the text you want to select. Use the window's scroll bars to move to the end of the text you want to select. Hold down the Shift key and click the mouse at the appropriate point.
- Alternatively, place the insertion point at the beginning of the text you want to select. Shift-click somewhere lower down the page and continue to hold the left mouse button and Shift key down as you move the mouse pointer toward the bottom edge of the window. Notes will obligingly scroll the window so you select more and more of the document. When you get to the end of the passage you wish to select, release the left mouse button. This option can scroll somewhat wildly and is generally less predictable.

Working with Selected Text

Our digression into the niceties of selecting text in Notes did have a purpose to it: You need to know how to select text in order to change the formatting of words you have already written.

Now that you know how to select text and how to set font attributes for the text at the insertion point, learning how to set the font for selected text is just a matter of putting the two skills together.

If you open the Text Properties InfoBox (by choosing Edit ➤ Properties or by clicking on the Properties SmartIcon) when you already have text selected, then the changes you make apply to the selected text rather than to the attributes Notes uses at the insertion point. Choose the text format you want, as you did before. But now, as you move to each new property in the InfoBox, Notes implements any changes you have made to the text you selected in the main window.

TIP

If you change your mind about text formatting you have applied, you can try using Edit ➤ Undo (Ctrl+Z) to reverse the change. Unfortunately, Notes will not always allow you to undo your action. If the Undo option is displayed in gray, it is unusable. You may wonder how you know in advance whether your action can be undone—the answer is a little esoteric. If you make a text formatting change while the "focus" is on the main Notes window (that is, while the InfoBox is displayed with a gray title bar) then that formatting change is reversible. If, however, the InfoBox has the "focus" (and the main Notes window has a gray title bar) then you can't reverse your formatting. Tricky, isn't it?

Other Ways to Change the Font

As you may remember from Chapter 5, two items on the status bar tell you the font and point size of the current selection (or of the text at the insertion point if no text is selected).

Each item also functions as a pop-up menu. Click once on the font name and you can choose a new font from the list. Click once on the font size and you can choose a new point size.

Four items from Text InfoBox's Font tab and a couple of new but related items are also available in the form of SmartIcons, menu options, and shortcut keys. Table 6.2 summarizes your many options for changing fonts and point size.

Table 6.2: Options for Changing Fonts and Point Size

SmartIcon	Menu Choice	Keyboard	Action
N	Text ➤ Normal Text	Ctrl+T	Makes selection plain text
B	Text ➤ Bold	Ctrl+B	Makes selection bold
I	Text ➤ Italic	Ctrl+I	Italicizes selection
U	Text ➤ Underline	Ctrl+U	Underlines selection
A'A	Text ➤ Enlarge Size	F2	Increases the point size to the next higher value
A'A	Text ➤ Reduce Size	Shift+F2	Decreases the point size to the next lower value
	Text ➤ Color ➤ <name>		Changes the color of the selected text to one of nine popular options

Using Permanent Pen for Editing

You may find that you want to add comments to someone else's message or document, and you'd like these comments to stand out from the rest of the text in a different font or color. You could use the Text Properties InfoBox to choose a new format, and then type your comments in, say, bold red type. But you'll find that when you move somewhere else in the document, any other comments you type will take on the attributes of the text at the insertion point. If you use this approach, you have to change the font every time you want to make a comment.

Notes gives you an easy solution. You can select something called Permanent Pen to put all your comments in the same format, regardless of the format of the rest of the document. You can turn on Permanent Pen by either choosing Text ➤ Permanent Pen or by clicking on the Text Permanent Pen SmartIcon. The same actions turn off Permanent Pen.

Initially, Permanent Pen is set to be bold red text. If you want to choose a different format, open the Text Properties InfoBox, select the combination of font, size, style, and color you want, and click on Set Permanent Pen Font to set the new format. Notes will then use this format any time you select Permanent Pen.

> **TIP**
>
> **If you regularly review and exchange documents with the same group of Notes users, you may each want to choose a distinctive Permanent Pen format. Then you'll be able to tell at a glance whose comments are whose.**

Paragraph Formatting

As well as changing the font and color of text, you can also apply a number of types of paragraph formatting. Paragraph formats apply to one or more paragraphs. A *paragraph* is defined as being all the text between one press of the Enter key and the next.

Paragraph formatting works quite like the text formatting you've already learned. You need to be in edit mode to change formatting. You can select a number of paragraphs to format. If no text is selected, Notes formats the current paragraph—that is, the paragraph where the insertion point is located.

As with text formatting, the Text Properties InfoBox and SmartIcons let you set paragraph formatting, but Notes also provides a couple of quick methods to format lists and something called the ruler to let you set certain paragraph attributes. Each method is detailed in the pages that follow.

Making a Numbered or Bulleted List

Notes gives you a quick way to create numbered or bulleted lists. To create either kind of list, you need to be in edit mode. Then, to create a numbered list:

1. Select the paragraphs you wish to make into a list, or, if you haven't yet typed the list, place the insertion point where you want the list to start.
2. Choose Text ➤ Numbers, or click on the Text Numbers SmartIcon.
3. Notes numbers the current or selected paragraphs sequentially in the margin.

To create a bulleted list, choose Text ➤ Bullets or click on the Text Bullets SmartIcon at step 2.

As you type each new paragraph, Notes will place the appropriate number (or a bullet) in the margin. If you insert a paragraph in a numbered list, Notes rearranges the numbering to compensate. When you come to the end of the list, choose Text ➤ Numbers or Text ➤ Bullets again to end the list formatting.

You can use these formats to create "nested" lists, too. Choose Text ➤ Indent, or press F8, to indent the current or selected paragraphs ¼". If the paragraph is formatted as a numbered list, Notes will restart the numbering for the new level of the list. Text ➤ Outdent (Shift+F8) reverses this action.

One effective technique is to use the numbered and bulleted list formats for different levels of a list. Indenting paragraphs is covered in more detail in the next sections of this chapter.

Formatting Paragraphs with the Ruler

If you are in edit mode in a document, you can display a formatting ruler along the top of the Notes window. The ruler is shown in Figure 6.5. To display the ruler:

- Select View ➤ Ruler.
- Press Ctrl+R.
 - Click on the View Ruler SmartIcon.

Notes changes the markings on the ruler to match the paragraph settings at the insertion point. You can drag markers on the ruler to change the left margin, the distance that the first line of a paragraph is indented, and the tab settings for the current paragraph or for selected paragraphs.

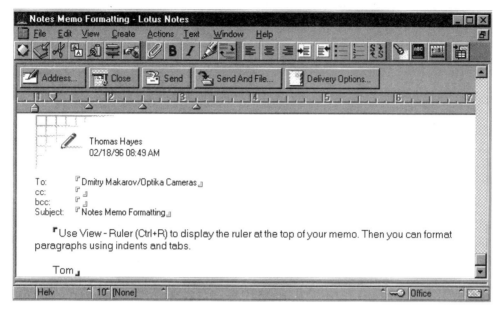

FIGURE 6.5: When you choose View ➤ Ruler, Notes displays your margin and tab settings on a ruler above your document.

Setting Left Margins and Indents

You'll see two "pentagon pointers" toward the left end of the ruler. Here's what they do:

- The *left margin marker* is the lower pentagon pointer. It shows the distance the paragraph is indented from the left edge of the page.
- The *first line margin marker* is the upper pentagon pointer. It shows the distance the first line of the paragraph is indented from the left edge of the page.

You can use the two left margin markers to set up the style of indentation you want to use for one or more paragraphs. For example, you might want to set off quoted material from the rest of a memo. You can have Notes indent the quote more than the rest of the memo, as in Figure 6.6.

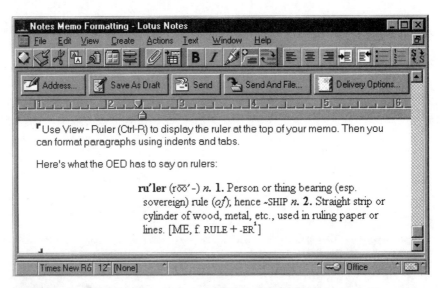

FIGURE 6.6: You can use the ruler to set indents for quoted material.

To change the left margin for the first line of the paragraph, place the insertion point in the paragraph and drag the upper pointer to a new position. To change the left margin for the subsequent lines of text, drag the triangular part of the lower pointer to a new position.

To move both markers together while retaining their relative positions, drag the square part of the lower pointer. To make the first line indent the same as the left margin, double-click on either pentagon pointer. Notes moves the other pointer level with the one you double-clicked.

Setting Tab Stops

Tab markers are upward pointing arrows that show where tab stops are in the current paragraph. They work just like the tab stops on a typewriter or a word processor: Pressing the Tab key moves the insertion point to the next tab stop to the right.

You might use tabs in Notes when you want to draw up a table quickly or when you need more flexibility in an outline than Notes' built-in list functions offer. Notes provides four kinds of tab markers:

 • *Left tabs* align text along its left edge, as you might do with text in a table. You can create a left tab for the current or selected paragraphs by clicking on the ruler where you want the tab to appear.

• *Right tabs* align text along its right edge and work well for most columns of numbers. Create a right tab by right-clicking on the ruler where you want the tab. On the Macintosh use Option+click.

 • *Decimal tabs* align numbers so that the decimal point is at the tab stop. You can make a decimal tab by Shift+clicking on the ruler.

 • *Center tabs* center text about the tab point. You can make a center tab by Shift+right-clicking on the ruler. On the Macintosh use Shift+Option+click.

You can use the mouse to drag tabs to new positions. To delete a tab, click on it with the left mouse button. Windows, OS/2, and Unix users can also right-click on a tab marker to bring up a shortcut menu to change the tab to another type or delete it. If you want to move a tab that's hidden by the left margin marker, hold down the Shift key while you click.

By default, Notes places tab stops every ½". These default tab stops are not marked on the ruler. If you add tab stops manually, Notes only applies these default tab stops to the right of whatever manual stops you have created. If a paragraph has a *hanging indent* (where the first line margin is to the left of the margin for the rest of the paragraph), Notes also interprets the left margin marker as a tab stop.

TIP
Notes doesn't really let you specify the right margin for the page. You can set a right margin for printing, but for viewing Notes just makes sure all the text fits on the screen. There are cases when Notes displays the right margin and other information on the ruler. For more information, see "The Pagination Tab" later in this chapter and "Adding Tables to Documents" in Chapter 8.

Formatting Paragraphs with an InfoBox

The other principal way to change paragraph formatting is to use the Text Properties InfoBox. Here you can define the same settings as you can with the ruler, and you can perform other formatting functions, too. To display the Text Properties InfoBox, use any of the five methods listed under "A Look at InfoBoxes" earlier in this chapter.

Again, the effect of the paragraph formatting changes you make in this InfoBox depends on whether any text is selected. Changes apply to all paragraphs in which text is selected. If no text is selected, your changes only apply to the paragraph where the insertion point is located.

The Alignment Tab

Of the two tabs that deal with paragraph formatting, the Alignment tab, shown in Figure 6.7, lets you set margins, paragraph justification, line spacing, and list format. A quick way to open the Text Properties InfoBox directly to the Alignment tab is to press Ctrl+J or click on the Paragraph Properties SmartIcon. You have the following options on this tab:

Alignment Lets you tell Notes how to line up the text in the selected or current paragraph. Notes uses symbols to display the five different types of alignment you can use—they are left, center, right, full, and no wrap. The icons for the first four give you a good idea how they work; paragraphs formatted with no wrap alignment trail off the right edge of the screen until Notes reaches a "hard return" (where you pressed the Enter key).

First Line Lets you choose where the selected paragraphs' first lines begin, relative to the left margin that applies for the rest of the paragraph. Your choices are to have both margins the same or to indent or outdent the first line. With the last two options, you can specify the amount of indent or outdent. This option is equivalent to moving the first line marker on the ruler.

List Lets you choose Notes' numbered or bulleted list formats for selected paragraphs. It's equivalent to Text ➤ Numbers or Text ➤ Bullets.

Left Margin Changing this setting is equivalent to moving the left margin marker on the ruler.

Spacing Tells Notes how much space to put between one line and the next and between one paragraph and the next. The Spacing options are:

- *Interline* tells Notes how much space to leave between each line in the current or selected paragraph. You can choose single spacing (the standard setting), or 1½, or double spacing.
- *Above* determines how much space to put between this paragraph and the previous one.
- *Below* determines how much space to put between this paragraph and the next.

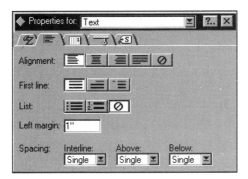

FIGURE 6.7:
The Alignment
tab of the Text
Properties InfoBox

The Pagination Tab

The Pagination tab also lets you format paragraphs. Shown in Figure 6.8, this tab tells Notes how to determine page breaks, where to put tab stops, and where to put the right margin.

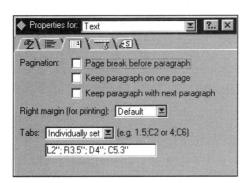

FIGURE 6.8:
The Pagination
tab of the Text
Properties InfoBox

The first section, Pagination, tells Notes how to print the current or selected paragraph if it is close to a page break. You can use the three settings here in any combination:

Page Break before Paragraph Tells Notes to always begin this paragraph on a new page.

Keep Paragraph on One Page Tells Notes to make sure the whole paragraph prints on the same page (providing that the paragraph itself is not longer than a page). This prevents what typesetters call *widows* and *orphans*, which are paragraphs that are split onto two pages, with just a couple of lines on each page.

Keep Paragraph with Next Paragraph Tells Notes to make sure this paragraph and the next both print on the same page.

There's more about page breaks in the next section, "Other Ways to Apply Paragraph Formatting."

You're unlikely to need to set a right margin for an individual paragraph, especially as Notes only uses right margins when you print a document, but if you need to, Notes lets you override its default setting. The right margin is measured from the left edge of the paper, so a setting of 7.5" would produce a 1"-wide right margin on 8.5"-wide paper.

> **NOTE** You can use File ➤ Page Setup (on the Macintosh, choose File ➤ Print and then click on Margins) to set printing margins for the document as a whole. For more information on setting a right margin and displaying it on the ruler, see "Text and Paragraph Formatting in Tables" in Chapter 8.

The Tabs section at the bottom of the InfoBox lets you choose between individually set tabs, like the ones you set with the ruler, and evenly spaced tabs, at whatever frequency you desire.

You can type the locations of new tab stops into the box at the bottom. If you just type a number, Notes interprets it as a left tab at that number of inches or centimeters (depending on the default measurement unit). You can prefix the number with **R** (for right), **C** (for center), or **D** (for decimal) to specify a particular type of tab, or even with **L** to be doubly sure of a left tab.

For multiple tabs, separate each from the next with a semicolon. Any tabs you set earlier with the ruler should be listed in the box already. You can also remove a tab stop by deleting its entry here.

Other Ways to Apply Paragraph Formatting

You can use SmartIcons and menu choices to set some types of paragraph formatting, as well as using the ruler and the Text Properties InfoBox. Table 6.3 lists techniques for formatting paragraphs.

Table 6.3: Paragraph Formatting Options

SmartIcon	Menu Choice	Keyboard	Action
	Text ➤ Align Paragraph ➤ Left		Left-aligns selected paragraphs
	Text ➤ Align Paragraph ➤ Right		Right-aligns selected paragraphs
	Text ➤ Align Paragraph ➤ Center		Centers selected paragraphs
	Text ➤ Align Paragraph ➤ Full		Aligns selected paragraphs flush to both margins
	Text ➤ Align Paragraph ➤ No Wrap		Removes alignment from selected paragraphs
	Text ➤ Spacing		Opens menu to set spacing below paragraph
			Cycles through three paragraph spacing choices
	Create ➤ Page Break	Ctrl+L	Makes Notes begin paragraph on a new page
	Text ➤ Indent	F8	Indents this paragraph ¼" more
		F7	Indents first line of paragraph ¼" more
	Text ➤ Outdent	Shift+F8	Indents this paragraph ¼" less
		Shift+F7	Indents first line of paragraph ¼" less

If you create "manual," or "hard," page breaks via the dialog box, keyboard, SmartIcon, or menu choice, Notes shows them on the screen as a thin line running from one side of the window across to the other. You can also have Notes show you where it will place "automatic" or "soft" page breaks if you print the document. To do this, choose View ➤ Show ➤ Page Breaks.

If you want to see exactly where hard returns, spaces, tabs, and other "nonprinting" characters appear in your document, choose View ➤ Show ➤ Hidden Characters. Notes displays a centered dot for each space, a paragraph character for each hard return, and so on. You may be familiar with this type of display from word processing software you have used.

Notes lets you know exactly which items (page breaks, hidden characters, etc.) it is set to display by placing checkmarks next to their entries on the View ➤ Show menu.

Using Named Paragraph Styles

Once you start to use paragraph formatting in your Notes documents, you may become tired of frequently having to select paragraphs and define a number of different attributes for them.

Notes offers you a shortcut to help you always present particular types of information in the same way. Notes paragraph styles are a way to store a certain combination of paragraph and font formatting choices so that you can apply them to other paragraphs later. You give each style a name, say "Heading" or "Note," so that you can retrieve it later.

NOTE	Paragraph styles have changed vastly in recent versions of Notes, with the ability to include text formatting information and use styles throughout a database. If you have recently upgraded from Notes 3.x and previously ignored the very limited paragraph styles, you should try the much more flexible named styles now available.

Styles can include any combination of parameters you want from the first four tabs in the Text Properties InfoBox. If you often write a particular kind of memo in Notes, you may want to create one or more styles in your mail database to make the task easier.

Some of the most common uses for named styles are to easily apply consistent formats for headings and subheadings, lists, outlines, and reports.

Creating a Named Style

To create a named style, you must first be in edit mode with the insertion point in a paragraph that has the attributes you want to assign to your new style. Then do the following:

1. Open the Text Properties InfoBox and click on the Named Styles tab, shown in Figure 6.9.

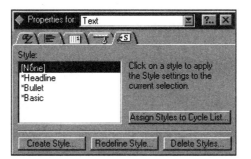

FIGURE 6.9:
The Named Styles tab helps you manage paragraph styles.

2. Click on the Create Style button to open the Create Named Style dialog box, shown in Figure 6.10.

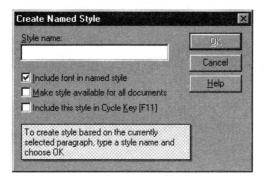

FIGURE 6.10:
Name your new style and tell Notes where and how you want to use it.

3. Type a name for your style.

4. If you want, you can also:

- Choose whether to include font attributes in the style (the default is to include them).
- Allow other documents to use the same style (usually a good idea).

- Make this style available via the Style Cycle Key (F11), which is described later in this chapter.

5. Once you have chosen a name for your new style and selected any options, click on OK.

Applying Named Styles

Once you've defined a paragraph style, you can apply it to other paragraphs in the same document. If you chose to make the style available throughout the database, then you can use it in other documents, too.

To apply a style, select the paragraphs to which you want to apply it. Then choose the style from one of these lists:

- The pop-up list on the status bar
- The list under Text ➤ Named Styles
- The list on the Named Styles tab in the Text Properties InfoBox

If you use several styles a lot, you can make choosing among them even easier by assigning them to the Style Cycle Key. Then you can cycle through these selected styles by pressing F11 or by clicking on the Text Style Cycle Key SmartIcon. Notes applies each style in turn to the selection or current paragraph.

To choose which styles Notes uses for the Style Cycle Key, click on the Assign Styles to Cycle List button on the Named Styles tab (Figure 6.9). Notes displays a list of all available styles. Place checkmarks next to those you want to be available through F11.

Changing, Copying, and Deleting Named Styles

To change the attributes of an existing style:

1. Select a paragraph with the new attributes.
2. Open the Text Properties InfoBox and click on the Named Styles tab.
3. Click on Redefine Style.
4. Select the style you wish to alter.
5. Click on OK.

Notes changes the definition to match the paragraph you selected. Any paragraphs already formatted with this named style will be reformatted to match your changed definition.

As well as defining brand new named styles, you can also copy existing ones. To create a new style based on an existing one:

1. Format one or more paragraphs in the existing style.
2. Choose the style [None] for these paragraphs. Notes will leave the paragraphs formatted as before, but they are no longer marked with the existing style name.
3. Make whatever formatting changes you want for the new style (for example, to change the text color or first line indent). These changes do not affect the existing style.
4. Open the Text Properties InfoBox, switch to the Named Styles tab, and click on Create Style.
5. Name your new style as you would normally.

If you decide that you don't need one of the styles you have created, you can delete it by clicking on the Delete Style button on the Named Styles tab, selecting the style name, and clicking on OK. Any paragraphs already formatted with the style are assigned the style [None].

You now know how to use fonts and paragraph formatting to make your text much more presentable. As you concoct ever more sophisticated memos, you will want to bring in work you have created in other software. You might incorporate the text of a letter you wrote in Microsoft Word or some sales figures from a Lotus 1-2-3 worksheet. Read Chapter 7 to find out all about getting Notes to work with your other software.

Chapter 7

MOVING YOUR INFORMATION AROUND

- **Cutting and pasting via the Clipboard**
- **Importing and exporting files from other programs**
- **Attaching files to Notes documents**
- **Linking and embedding objects**
- **Subscribing to Macintosh data**

You'll find Notes useful on its own for its ability to help you communicate and share information with your colleagues, but Notes can also add value to the other computer programs you use. Notes gives you a variety of ways to incorporate information from other programs into your documents. Some ways let you bring parts of other documents straight into Notes format. Others emphasize keeping information in its original form so that the recipient can work with it just as you do.

Cutting, Copying, and Pasting

Before we get into adding all sorts of fancy stuff to your documents, we ought to brush up on three basic (and related) techniques. By cutting, copying, and pasting, you can move all sorts of items between one document and another. Often, you can also use these techniques to move information between Notes and other programs. You have probably used these techniques in other software that runs on your computer.

To cut or copy an item from a document, you must select that item. To paste an item into a document, you must be in edit mode. All of these techniques depend on something called the *Clipboard*, which is just the place your computer puts stuff while you move it from one document to another. You don't usually see the Clipboard (it's just there in the background), but your computer can display what's on the Clipboard if you need to see it.

You can cut, copy, and paste all sorts of items in Notes, such as plain text, formatted text, tables, buttons, graphics, links to other Notes documents or databases, whole Notes documents, and multiple Notes documents.

Cutting

In Notes, any of the following actions cuts a selected item from a document. Cutting removes what you have selected from the document and places it on the Clipboard:

- Choose Edit ➤ Cut.
- Press Ctrl+X.
- Right-click on your selection and choose Cut from the floating menu.

 - Click on the Edit Cut SmartIcon.

Copying

Similarly, any of the following actions copies a selected item from a document. Copying leaves the selected item in the document and places a copy of it on the Clipboard.

- Choose Edit ➤ Copy.
- Press Ctrl+C.
- Right-click on your selection and choose Copy from the floating menu.

 - Click on the Edit Copy SmartIcon.

Pasting

When you have cut or copied something to the Clipboard, it stays there until you cut or copy something else to take its place, you close your operating system, or you shut down your computer.

You can paste the item from the Clipboard into the same or another document by placing the insertion point where you want the item to appear and doing one of the following:

- Choose Edit ➤ Paste.
- Press Ctrl+V.
- Right-click at the insertion point and choose Paste from the floating menu.

- Click on the Edit Paste SmartIcon.

If text or another portion of your document is selected at the time you choose Paste, the contents of the Clipboard will *replace* your selection.

When you paste an item into a document, a copy of it remains on the Clipboard as well. That means you can paste extra copies of it elsewhere (in the same document or another one) as many times as you want.

When you cut or copy information from one context and paste it somewhere different, your computer and Notes do their best to interpret the information properly. If you copy formatted text from a word processing document into the body of a Notes memo, it should look fairly similar to the original. However, on some occasions a square peg doesn't go into a round hole: If you paste formatted text into a plain-text field, Notes removes the formatting. If you paste other rich-text items there, Notes politely ignores you.

To find out more about using cut, copy, and paste, consult Notes' Help database (described in Chapter 9) and the documentation for your operating system.

Copying Information from Other Programs to Notes

These three techniques—cut, copy, and paste—are the basis for many operations in Notes. They also provide the easiest way to get information from other programs into a Notes document. You can quite simply copy data into Notes from other programs. Here's a general description of the procedure:

1. Switch to the program that you used to create the data.
2. Open the file that contains the data.
3. Select the portion you want to copy.

4. Copy or cut the data to the Clipboard using whatever commands the program uses (Edit ➤ Cut and Edit ➤ Copy are fairly standard).
5. Switch to Notes.
6. In edit mode, open the document into which you want to paste the data.
7. Place the insertion point where you want the data to appear.
8. Choose Edit ➤ Paste.

If you are unsatisfied with the results, you can try to import the data directly from a file (see "Importing Files" below).

Copying Notes Information to Other Programs

You can use a similar procedure to copy information from a Notes document into another application. If you choose to copy while you are in edit mode, the maximum you can select and copy is the contents of a single field. If you select and copy in read-only mode, you can copy as much as the whole document, including field labels and other nonfield text on the form.

Either way, the basic procedure for copying Notes information to other programs is:

1. Switch to Notes.
2. Open the document that contains the data you want to copy.
3. Select what you want to copy.
4. Copy or cut the data to the Clipboard with Edit ➤ Cut or Edit ➤ Copy.
5. Switch to the program to which you want to copy the data.
6. Open the document into which you want to paste the data.
7. Place the insertion point where you want the data to appear.
8. Use the application's paste command (usually Edit ➤ Paste).

Importing Files

Notes comes equipped with *filters* that allow it to read the files used by a variety of popular word processing, spreadsheet, database, and graphics packages. Filters give you a way to incorporate information from other software without needing to launch the appropriate package and cut and paste via the Clipboard.

File Types You Can Import into Notes

Table 7.1 shows the various types of files that you can import into a Notes document.

Table 7.1: File Types You Can Import into Notes

Plain Text Files
> ASCII text
> Binary files incorporating text

Word Processing Files
> Corel WordPerfect 5.x, 6.0, and 6.1
> Frame Technologies FrameMaker 3.0/4.0 (.MIF) (Unix only)
> Interleaf ASCII Version 5 or later (Unix only)
> Lotus Ami Pro (.SAM)
> MacWrite II (via Claris XTND)
> Microsoft Word Rich Text Format (.RTF) (including embedded bitmaps)
> Microsoft Word 6.0 (.DOC) (Windows only)

Picture Files
> ANSI Metafile (.CGM, .GMF)
> Bitmap (.BMP) (not Unix)
> CompuServe Graphics Interchange Format (.GIF)
> JPEG Image (.JPG)
> Lotus 1-2-3 and Symphony graphics (.PIC) (not Unix)
> MacPaint (via Claris XTND)
> PC Paintbrush (.PCX)
> TIFF 5.0 image (.TIF) (uncompressed only)
> Windows and OS/2 Clipboard
> Macintosh Clipboard

Worksheet and Database Files
> Lotus 1-2-3 and Symphony
> Microsoft Excel 4.0/5.0 (Windows only)
> Tabular Text
> Structured Text

Files labeled *not Unix* cannot be imported into the Unix versions of Notes. Files labeled *Windows only* or *Unix only* can only be imported into the version of Notes for that operating system.

You can only import whole files, so if you don't need all the information in a file, you have the choice of either importing the whole file and then deleting the parts you don't need, or saving a copy of the file that only includes the parts you want to import.

Selecting a File to Import

To import a file into a document, place the insertion point where you wish the imported data to appear and then open the Import dialog box. This dialog box looks like Figure 7.1 in Windows, OS/2, and Unix. Because the Macintosh uses a different file system, Mac users will see a slightly different box. You can open the Import dialog box in either of the following ways:

- Choose File ➤ Import.

 - Click on the File Import SmartIcon.

The Import dialog box works in the same way most file selection dialog boxes do. For Windows, OS/2, and Unix:

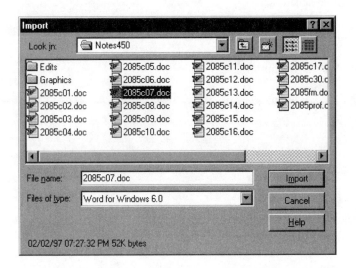

FIGURE 7.1:
The Import dialog box lets you tell Notes what file to import and in what format to expect data.

1. Under Files of Type, select the category of file you want to import.
2. Use either of these techniques to choose the file you want to import:

   - Select the file's drive and directory and then select the file.
   - Enter the path and name of the file in the File Name box.

3. Click on Import.

For the Macintosh:

1. Under Show, select the category of file you want to import.
2. Choose the file's drive and folder.
3. Select the file.
4. Click on Open.

The Files of Type or Show box lets you specify a file type. This tells Notes that it should only display files of this type for you to choose from and also how to treat the file you eventually select.

If You Have Trouble Importing a File

Once you have imported the file, take a look at how Notes has formatted the new information. If you are unhappy with the results or if Notes told you that it could not import the file, you have several options:

- You can open the file in the program that created it and copy it to Notes via the Clipboard.
- You can open the file in the program that created it and save a copy in a format used by a different version of the same software, then try importing this new copy of the file. In general, the filters available in Notes support the most current versions of software available at the time Notes 4.5 was originally released. So if you are using software released very recently, you may need to save your document in an earlier file format for Notes to successfully import it. The Files of Type box in the Import dialog box tells you precisely what file versions Notes can import.
- If the type of file you are using isn't supported by Notes or if importing this way isn't giving good results, see if the software that created the file can save it in another format that Notes can import. For example, if you want to import a Quattro Pro spreadsheet, try saving the file in Lotus 1-2-3 format and then importing it into Notes.

Exporting Files

As well as bringing information from other packages into Notes, you can also, as you might expect, take information from Notes documents and export it in a format that can be read by another program.

Export Formats That Notes Supports

You can export documents in the formats used by the software packages listed in Table 7.2.

Table 7.2: Export Formats That Notes Supports

Plain Text Files
  ASCII text
Word Processing Files
  Corel WordPerfect 5.1, 6.0, and 6.1
  Frame Technologies FrameMaker 3.0/4.0 (.MIF) (Unix only)
  Lotus Ami Pro (.SAM)
  Microsoft Word Rich Text Format (.RTF) (including embedded bitmaps)
  Microsoft Word 6.0 (.DOC) (Windows only)
Picture Files
  ANSI Metafile (.CGM)
  TIFF 5.0 image (.TIF) (uncompressed only)
  Windows and OS/2 Clipboard
  Macintosh Clipboard

Files labeled *Windows only* or *Unix only* can only be exported from the version of Notes for that operating system.

You can export a whole document or just a part of it. If you want to export a picture file, however, you can only export one graphic at a time.

To export text or a graphic, you must first open the document (in either read-only mode or edit mode). If you want to export only a portion of the text, select that portion. If you want to export a graphic, select it (if you don't select a graphic, Notes just exports the first graphic in the document).

Once you've opened the document and made the necessary selections, open the Export dialog box, shown in Figure 7.2, in either of these ways:

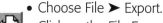

- Choose File ➤ Export.
- Click on the File Export SmartIcon.

Again, Macintosh users will find that their Export dialog box looks slightly different.

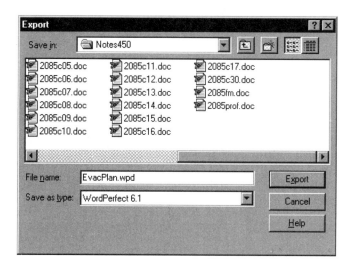

FIGURE 7.2:
The Export dialog box lets you tell Notes in what format you want to save the document or graphic and what filename to give it.

The Export dialog box works the same way as the Import dialog box (see Figure 7.1), except that this time you are specifying a disk drive, directory, filename, and file format for Notes to use in creating this new file.

If you choose the name of a file that already exists, Notes asks whether you want to replace the file (erasing whatever information it currently holds) or cancel exporting. In some cases, you may also get the option to append your export to the existing contents of the file.

> **NOTE**
>
> If you choose to export your file as ASCII text, Notes lets you choose a line length at which Notes will wrap words. Word processors (and Notes) wrap text to fit document margins, but applications that use ASCII text usually have a fixed line length and use hard returns (the Enter key) to end each line. Notes uses the number you enter here to determine where to place hard returns in the Notes document you are converting.

If You Have Trouble Exporting a File

As with importing, if the results of your first exporting attempt are less than satisfactory, you can experiment with different export formats. Look at the documentation for the application into which you want to bring the Notes document. See what types of files *it* can import and compare them to the types of files Notes can export. Try whatever formats Notes and the other application have in common until you find a good match.

Attaching Files to Notes Documents

So far, this chapter has looked at how to incorporate information from one program into another program so that it becomes a part of a new document. There are other ways to connect information to a Notes document, however, that retain more of its original identity.

One easy way to put information from another application in a Notes document is to *attach* a file to the document. With this process, you can take any file and link it to a document. If you mail the document to someone else or if someone else reads the document in a shared database, he or she sees an icon like the one shown here. This icon represents the file you attached.

Q4 Sales.doc

Recipients can *detach* the file (copy it to a hard disk or a diskette), or *launch* it, providing they have a copy of the software that created the file. Additionally, Windows users of Notes can *view* and *print* some files, even if they don't have their own copy of the software that created them.

There are two main reasons why you might want to attach a file rather than import or copy the information into a document:

- You can attach *any* type of file to a document. You don't need to know what application created the file. You don't even need to know what type of file it is. And you don't need to make sure that Notes can import that type of file.
- Other Notes users who receive your message or read the document you created can detach the file and use it just as you did. Importing information works well for word processing documents, but if you want to distribute a slide show from a presentation graphics package or a printer driver, the recipient needs to have the actual file.

Attaching a File

To attach a file to a document:

1. Open the document in edit mode and place the insertion point in a rich-text field at the point where you want the icon for the file to appear.
2. Use either of the following actions to open the Create Attachment(s) dialog box, shown in Figure 7.3.

- Choose File ➤ Attach.
- Click on the File Attach SmartIcon.

The Macintosh Create Attachment(s) dialog box is a little different from the dialog box used in other versions of Notes, but the procedure for attaching a file is similar.

3. Choose the drive and directory (or folder) where the file you want to attach is stored.
4. Scroll through the list of files until the correct name is displayed.
5. Click on the file to select it.

You can attach more than one file to a document at the same time as long as they are all stored in the same directory or folder. To select multiple files, you have two options. You can hold down the Ctrl key and click on each file to attach. Alternatively, to select several files in a row, you can click on the first file of the series and then hold down the Shift key and click on the last file. All the filenames from the first one you clicked to the last will be selected.

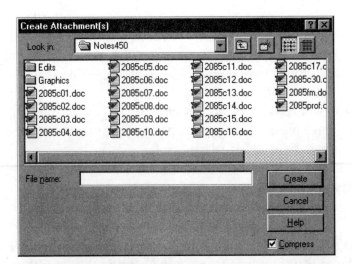

FIGURE 7.3: Choose which files to enclose with your document in the Create Attachment(s) dialog box.

TIP

If you attach several files at the same time, Notes places their icons one after the other in the document. If you want files' icons to be displayed with the text that relates to them, you need to insert them one at a time, moving the insertion point as appropriate.

6. Before you attach the files you have selected, there is one last choice to make. A small checkbox on the right side of the dialog box lets you choose whether to have Notes compress the attached files. Compressed files take up less disk space and can be transmitted more quickly. Unless you know that the files you are attaching are already compressed, I recommend leaving this box checked.

7. As you might expect, clicking on Create (Open on the Macintosh) attaches the file to your document and places an icon for it at the insertion point.

Once you have attached a file to your document, it might look something like Figure 7.4.

FIGURE 7.4: When you attach a file to a document, it shows up as an icon embedded in the text.

TIP

If you are using the Windows version of Notes, you have an additional way to attach individual files to Notes documents. Select a file in File Manager (Windows 3.1), Explorer (Windows 95), or another Windows file utility. Then drag the file to the place where you want it in your Notes document (which has to be in edit mode). Release the mouse button, and Notes will attach the files to whichever rich-text field is nearest the cursor. By some quirk of programming, files attached in this way have their names listed in all uppercase letters.

Once you have attached a file or files to a document, make sure to write a few words that explain what the files are and how someone reading or receiving the document should deal with them. Think how bemused you might be to receive these files with no instructions!

Attached Files in Views

Documents with attached files are often shown differently in views and folders. Figure 7.5 shows how the message in Figure 7.4 is displayed in a folder. The small paperclip icon indicates that this message has an attached file. Sometimes you see the >> symbol instead to indicate an attachment.

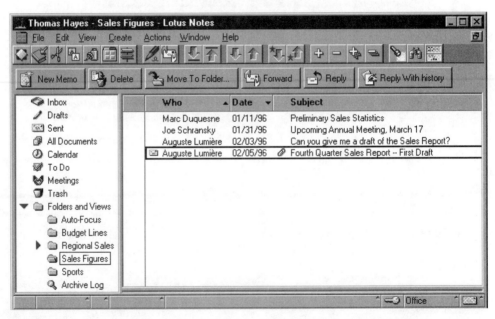

FIGURE 7.5: The paperclip symbol to the left of the Subject field indicates that the message has an attached file.

NOTE Notes may also display a paperclip icon for documents that contain linked or embedded objects, which are described later in this chapter under "Linking, Embedding, and Subscribing."

A Few Words on How Attached Files Work

It is useful to have a clear picture of what Notes is doing when you attach and detach files. When you attach a file to a document, Notes actually makes a copy and leaves the original file untouched. From this point on, the original file and the attached copy lead separate lives.

If you attached the file to a mail message that you then sent to your boss and three coworkers, Notes made more copies. Each copy of the message (five, including the one that's in your own mail database) has its own copy of the file attached.

Say the attached file is a word processing document that your boss wants to look at on her word processor. She detaches the file and stores it on the hard drive of her computer, making another copy (the copy she received in your memo is still there, separate from the copy she placed on her hard drive). If she makes some changes to the document, attaches it to a Notes memo, and mails it back to you, that makes yet another separate copy of the file.

There are two things to bear in mind about all this copying:

- Each copy of a file takes space to store. If it's just a short word processing document, that's not too bad. But if you attached a copy of the page-layout files for your company's annual report to a memo and you mailed the memo to every Notes user in your company, it would take a lot of hard disk space to store all those copies. When you detach a file that you received in a Notes message, you may want to delete the attachment to save space.

NOTE For more on how to remove attachments from documents, see the section "Deleting and Cutting Attached Files" later in this chapter. For general advice on keeping your Notes mailbox to a manageable size, see Chapter 18.

- It can be very time consuming to reconcile different versions of a single file. Say you produce a marketing brochure in Microsoft Word and you attach it to a memo to 10 colleagues, asking them to review it and make amendments where necessary. Even if only half of them send you back edited versions, that's still a lot of files from which to juggle competing advice.

> **NOTE** Some of the Notes database templates examined in Chapter 10 offer more sophisticated approaches to reviewing and revising documents.

Receiving Attached Files

It's quite likely that before you attach any files to a document yourself, you'll receive one in a mail message from someone else. You'll know that you've received an attachment by the paperclip icon in your mailbox view, or the >> symbol before the message subject on the title bar.

What do you do with an attached file? Your choices are any or all of the following:

- Detach the file.
- Launch it.
- View it or print it (if you're a Windows user).
- Delete it.

Come to think of it, I guess you could also ignore the attached file.

You can find out a little more from the Attachment Properties InfoBox, shown in Figure 7.6. The easiest way to open this InfoBox is to double-click on the attachment icon in your document. Alternatively, you can select the icon and either use any of the regular means of opening an InfoBox or choose Attachment ➤ Attachment Properties.

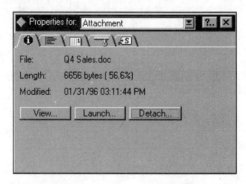

FIGURE 7.6:
The Attachment Properties InfoBox tells you a little more about an attached file and lets you detach it or launch it (and view it or print it, too, if you're a Windows user).

The Attachment Properties InfoBox tells you the name of the file, its size (or length) in bytes, and when it was last modified. If the file has been compressed, the size refers to its original size and the percentage figure next to it indicates how much the file was reduced. Larger percentages equal greater compression.

The buttons at the bottom of the InfoBox let you detach the file or launch it. Windows users also get a button allowing them to view the file (and also print it if they choose).

Detaching Files

You can detach a single file by clicking on the Detach button in the Attachment InfoBox (see Figure 7.6) or by selecting the file's icon in your document and choosing Attachment ➤ Detach. Either action opens the Save Attachment dialog box shown in Figure 7.7. From this dialog box, you can choose a drive and directory in which to store the attached file. If you want to, you can also specify a new name for Notes to use when storing the file. As usual, the dialog box on the Macintosh looks a little different but works in much the same way.

If you want to detach more than one file from a document to the same directory, you can select several files (click on the first, hold down Shift, and click on the last) and then detach them all at the same time by choosing Attachments ➤ Detach All Selected. You will see a somewhat simpler dialog box that lets you choose a drive and directory in which to store the attached files. This dialog box is shown in Figure 7.8. You can also detach all the files attached to a document by selecting one of them and choosing Attachment ➤ Detach All.

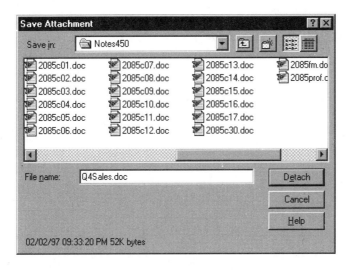

FIGURE 7.7:
If you detach a single file, you can choose a new name for it if you want, as well as a drive and directory (or folder) in which to place the file.

FIGURE 7.8:
If you choose to detach files *en masse*, your only choices are the drive and directory in which to put them.

Once you have stored the file or files on a disk, you can open them in the program that created them or in any other program that reads the type of file you detached.

Launching Attached Files

If you have your own copy of the software that created the attached file, you can bypass the step of detaching the file to a hard disk or diskette and open it straight from the Notes document. You can launch the file by clicking on the Launch button in the Attachment Properties InfoBox (see Figure 7.6) or by selecting the file's icon and then choosing Attachment ➤ Launch. Notes will attempt to start the appropriate program to work with the attached file. Notes uses your operating system's file type registry to determine what software package to use.

WARNING

Launching programs relying on the operating system's registry isn't foolproof. Your computer may launch an application that can't read the file, or it may be unable to choose an application suitable for the file. If you regularly receive files of a particular type that you can't launch properly, read in your operating system's documentation about how to associate a type of file with a particular application. One thing Windows and OS/2 users should watch out for is when the sender has renamed a file with a different three-letter extension. Windows will probably then launch the file in the wrong application or not at all. To view the file, detach it to your hard disk and then open it in the right application. If you want to attach the file to a Notes document later on, rename it with the correct extension so other people can launch the file directly from Notes.

TIP	When Windows launches an attached file, it stores it temporarily with a nonsense name in a temporary directory on your hard disk. On most computers, files in this directory are erased every so often (perhaps each time you start your computer). This works fine if you are just launching the attachment to read it. However, if you want to make changes and keep them for later use, you ought to detach the file instead.

Viewing and Printing Attached Files

If you are using Notes on a Windows computer, you have two other options for working with attached files: You can view and print most types of files even if you don't have your own copy of the software that created them. Notes 4.5 for Windows includes special software filters that let it display and print many common types of attached files.

To view an attached file, either click on View in the Attachment InfoBox or highlight the file's icon and choose Attachment ➤ View. Notes will try to determine the file's type and display it appropriately. If you have received a particularly esoteric type of file, you may get a message telling you that the Notes viewer can't display the file.

If Notes can work with the file, you'll usually see a fair approximation of how the document, image, or spreadsheet would look in the application that created it. With some files, such as program files, the Notes viewer will show you information about the file rather than the full contents of the file itself.

You can change how the file is displayed by setting options available on an extra menu that Notes provides for this purpose. This menu may be labeled Document, Spreadsheet, or Bitmap, for example, depending on the type of file you are viewing.

To print an attached file directly from Notes:

1. Open the file in the Notes viewer.
2. If you want to print only part of the file, select the part you want to print.
3. Choose File ➤ Print. The new menu that Notes has added for the file you are viewing also has a print option.

4. If you don't want to print the entire file, you have the following options:

   - To print just the highlighted portion, choose Selection.
   - To print only certain pages, choose Pages and type the numbers of the first and last pages you want to print.

5. If you want to print more than one copy, enter a number of copies. You can sort multiple copies by selecting Collate Copies.

6. You can change a broad range of more advanced settings by clicking on the Properties button.

7. When you are ready to print, click on OK.

Deleting and Cutting Attached Files

Once a file has been attached to a rich-text field, it behaves a lot like any other item in the field. You can select it on its own or as part of a larger block. You can cut, copy, paste, and delete it.

The main difference in how an attached file behaves is that if you cut or delete it, you can't use Edit ➤ Undo to reverse your action. This means that if you select and delete an attached file, it's gone permanently—your only option is to insert the attachment again, providing you have the original file. To make sure you don't delete attached files by accident, Notes displays a warning before it lets you cut or delete an attachment or paste something in place of an attachment you have selected.

Working with Objects

So far, we've looked at three methods for incorporating information from other programs into Notes documents. Two of them—copying via the Clipboard and importing—sever the link to the original program, making the new data indistinguishable from the other contents of a Notes document. The third method—attaching a file—keeps the data in its original form, but only displays it as an icon in the document.

Notes does, however, offer options that allow you to display data from another program in your Notes document in the format in which it was created. You can choose to allow the data to be edited in the program that created it or within Notes. Data copied like this is often referred to as an *object*, and it can be text, graphics, a spreadsheet, or just about anything else.

You are not likely to use these techniques in your own Notes documents until you become quite a proficient Notes user. However, you may well find that you have to work with a shared Notes database that uses objects to link Notes documents to information created in another application. For example, your company might have a contract library database that provides a Notes "front-end" to a collection of standardized legal contracts written in a word processing package. You would use the Notes database to find the appropriate contract and then open the linked word processing file to copy, edit, and print it.

This section does not attempt to cover the full complexity of working with objects. Rather, it attempts to give you enough information to work with them when you must.

> **NOTE** For more advanced users, several documents in the Notes Help database cover in greater detail the processes of creating, editing, updating, and deleting subscriptions, links, and embedded objects. The Notes Help database is introduced in Chapter 9.

Linking, Embedding, and Subscribing

There are three main ways that objects can be displayed in Notes:

- *Linking* displays the object in your Notes document, but the actual information remains stored in the original file. Changes you make to the original file are reflected in the Notes document. You can double-click on the object to edit it, and Notes will open the object in the software that created it.
- *Embedding* both displays and stores the object in your Notes document. Changes you make to the original file won't affect the object in your Notes document. You can double-click on the object to edit it, but this time Notes will open a small editing window in the Notes document. Although you remain in Notes, you gain the menus, toolbars, and functions of the software that created the object. Embedding is not available to OS/2 users.
- *Subscribing* lets Macintosh System 7 users of Notes link Macintosh data published by other programs to a Notes document. The data can then be made available to any Notes user. You can incorporate data published by another program on your Macintosh or by another Macintosh on the same network. Macintosh users can edit subscribed data.

You may come across subscriptions and linked objects in complex Notes applications. These techniques give users access to files they can edit, review, or update in the original application. Figure 7.9 shows a linked object used in a documentation database.

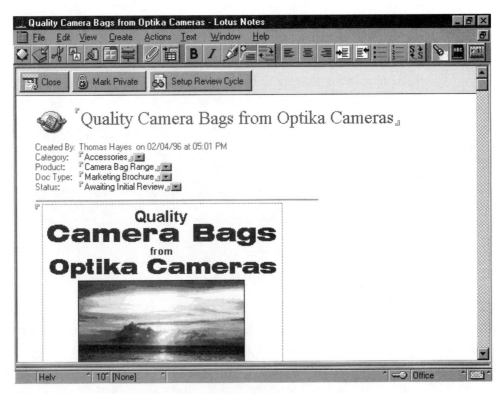

FIGURE 7.9: This linked Microsoft Word document lets all the members of a workgroup review the same copy of proposed product documentation.

You are more likely to see embedded objects in *ad hoc* memos and documents, used mainly as a means of providing information that is editable in the context it was created but not linked to a specific file. Figure 7.10 shows a report with an embedded spreadsheet.

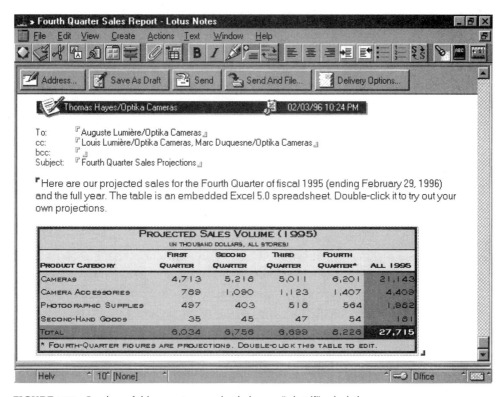

FIGURE 7.10: Readers of this report can make their own "what-if" calculations.

> **NOTE** There are two caveats to using any of these techniques. First, both the person creating the object and anyone who needs to edit it later must have access to the software that created the data. Second, the software has to adhere to certain conventions (with names such as OLE, DDE, and LEL) that provide the mechanics for linking, embedding, and subscribing.

Editing Objects

In general, you can recognize an object incorporated into a Notes document by the dotted border Notes places around it in edit mode, as in Figures 7.9 and 7.10.

Both linking and embedding allow the object's creator a choice of how to display the object in the Notes document. Usually, an object will appear similar to the way it does in the application that created it. Sometimes, however, the object may be represented by an icon or by a rich-text equivalent of the same information. The dotted border is your clue that you are working with an object from another program.

To edit a linked or embedded object, just double-click on the object. You need to have at least Reader-level access to a document and access to the original file to edit a linked object. To edit an embedded object, you need at least Editor-level access to the document. Database access levels are explained in Chapter 9.

To edit a Macintosh subscription, select the subscribed data and choose Edit ➤ Subscriber Options and then Open Publisher.

Now that you have seen how to incorporate information from other software packages into your Notes documents, you will be keen to learn how to make one Notes document link to another. Not only can you link Notes documents together, you can provide links to Notes views, whole Notes databases, and pages on the World Wide Web. These are just some of the rich array of document features explained in Chapter 8.

Chapter 8

COMPOUND DOCUMENTS: GOING BEYOND TEXT

- **Creating and formatting tables**
- **Adding and deleting rows and columns**
- **Merging and splitting cells**
- **Document, view, and database links**
- **Hotspots, pop-ups, URL links, and buttons**
- **Collapsible sections**

Now that you have seen some of the wide variety of things you can put in any Notes document, you may be keen to find out what other bells and whistles you can use in your messages. This chapter looks at four features that you will find in documents. In the "mundane-but-useful" category are tables similar to those found in any word-processing package, and collapsible sections that let you organize and focus documents. In the "not-in-your-word-processor" category are links that take you to electronic references, and hotspots and buttons that pop up information boxes or perform actions.

Adding Tables to Documents

Notes has a built-in facility that lets you create tables as you might in a word processor. Often, creating tables in this way is a lot easier than using tabs to line up columns of text or figures. You can begin a table at any point while you are in edit mode in a rich-text field. Either select Create ➤ Table or click on the Create Table SmartIcon. Notes will ask you to enter the number of rows and columns you want your table to have. Then click on OK and your new table will appear in your document.

You may think your new table looks less than impressive—a grid of thin black lines running across the page, every column the same width and every row the same height. Don't worry, we'll soon examine the settings you can adjust to mold your table to your needs. First, though, we'll look at how to work with data in a table.

Each of the component squares of the table is called a *cell* in Notes terminology and holds one piece of data. You can click in any cell of the table to place the insertion point there so you can begin entering information.

If you type more than will fit across the width of a column, Notes automatically wraps your text onto the next line and increases the height of the current row to compensate. You can also press the Enter key to force Notes to begin a new line within the same cell.

Moving around in a Table

Moving around in a table is quite similar to moving around in text. The main differences are:

- Pressing Tab moves you to the beginning of the next cell in the table.
- If you are in the last cell of the table, pressing Tab adds a blank row of cells to the bottom of the table.
- Pressing Shift+Tab moves you to the end of the previous cell in the table.
- The arrow keys work as usual except when you reach the beginning or end of a cell. If you are at the beginning of a cell, for instance, pressing ← takes you to the end of the previous cell. If you are on the bottom line of the cell, pressing ↓ takes you to the top line of the cell below.

Selecting Parts of a Table

Selecting text in a table is also similar to selecting text in the rest of a document, with just a few subtle differences.

- You can select any portion of text within a single cell.
- If you use the cursor keys or the mouse to extend the selection into an adjacent cell, Notes will select the *whole* of the text in both cells.
- You can further extend your selected text to other adjacent cells, but your selected cells must form a rectangular block.

Text and Paragraph Formatting in Tables

Once you have entered the information into your table, it may look something like Figure 8.1, functional but a little austere.

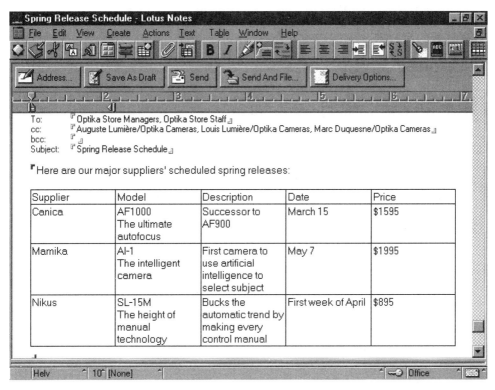

FIGURE 8.1: This table tells it straight, but it could be easier on the eye.

Don't worry that using Notes is going to cast you into an aesthetic wasteland. You have a range of formatting options to help you stamp your style on the tables you create.

To start with, you can use most of the same types of text and paragraph formatting that you learned in Chapter 6. You can change the font, size, and color of text, and set alignment and indents.

Notes doesn't allow you to set the left margin for a cell in the Paragraph Properties InfoBox, but you can use the ruler and table formatting to get a similar effect. First, let's look at two new symbols that appear on the ruler when you're in a table:

- The *column border markers* are two small upright rectangles that show where Notes puts the left and right borders for the current column. You can drag the right-hand marker for any column to adjust the column width.

- The *right margin marker* is a left-pointing triangle that shows the farthest point to the right that Notes can display text in the current cell. If you chose to fully justify text, its right edge would be at this mark. You can drag this marker to adjust the right margin for the current paragraph or, if you select text first, for multiple paragraphs.

There are also left-margin and first-line indent markers that you can drag to format one or more paragraphs in the same way as you did with paragraphs of regular text in Chapter 6.

Changing the Format of Tables

As well as altering the format of text and paragraphs in a table, you can change several attributes of the table itself. These include column widths, the space between rows and between columns, and the style of line that Notes uses for cell borders. You can also merge two or more cells in a table into a single one (and split them again later, if you change your plans), and you can change the background color Notes uses for each cell in the table.

You can change table properties in the Table InfoBox; the Borders tab is shown in Figure 8.2. Move to the cell whose format you want to change and summon the InfoBox either by choosing Table ➤ Properties or by clicking on the Table Properties SmartIcon. You can also use any of the regular methods for opening an InfoBox. If at first you don't see the Borders tab, choose Table from the Properties For drop-down menu on the title bar.

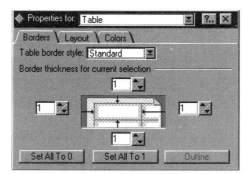

FIGURE 8.2:
The Borders tab in the Table Properties InfoBox lets you specify cell borders.

Your first choice on the Borders tab is whether to display your table with Standard ruled borders, Extruded borders (which make the table seem to be raised from the page), or Embossed borders (where the table appears to be stamped into the page).

Next, you can change the style of lines around whatever cells you have selected. You can choose any thickness of line, from zero (no line at all) and one (a standard, thin line) to 10 (about the width of a marker pen). You have several ways to change the border settings:

- Change the border thickness setting along one edge of the cell diagram in the InfoBox, and Notes changes the style of line used for that edge of every cell you've selected. If you drag the InfoBox by its title bar so that it doesn't obscure the table, you can see the effects of your changes as you make them.
- To quickly change the style of each border around every cell you have selected, use the Set All to 0 and Set All to 1 buttons.
- To place a border around all the selected cells and remove all borders in between them, click on the Outline button. Then your subsequent border choices apply only to the outline around your entire selection.

To change the table's left margin, column widths, and row and column spacing, use the Table InfoBox's Layout tab, shown in Figure 8.3.

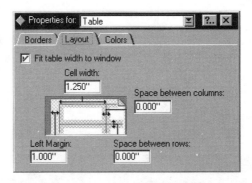

FIGURE 8.3:
The Layout tab lets you alter spacing and layout.

When you check the Fit Table Width to Window checkbox, Notes automatically makes the table fit between the left margin and the right edge of the window. If you change a column's width with Fit Table Width to Window selected, Notes will then adjust the widths of all the columns in the table to make the table fit. Because the amount of information that can be viewed on the screen varies greatly from one computer to the next, you may want to use this option to ensure that your table won't run off the right-hand side of other people's screens.

The Left Margin setting applies to the table as a whole, and it specifies the distance between the left border of the table and the edge of the paper. You can get the same effect by dragging the left-column border marker on the ruler.

The settings for Space between Rows and Space between Columns both apply to the table as a whole. Notes uses these settings to know how far from a cell's contents to draw the cell's borders. If you alter the space between columns, Notes adjusts each cell's margins accordingly. Any space you tell Notes to place between rows in the table is in addition to space that Notes may display because of paragraph formatting.

You can use the Cell Width box to fine-tune the size of columns or as an alternative to dragging the column border markers. Notes ensures that all cells in a column are kept the same width.

The Colors tab lets you set background colors for individual cells or the table as a whole. Use the Background Color field to choose your favorite background hue from the 240 options available. Notes will apply this to whichever cells you have selected. If you want to extend the shading to all of the table, click on Apply to Entire Table. If you want to change the selected cells back so that they have the same background color as the rest of the form, click on the Make Transparent button.

Inserting and Deleting Rows and Columns

Often, tables turn out to have too few or too many rows or columns. Here's how to change the number or rows and columns in a table.

Adding a Single Row or Column

By default, Notes adds new rows above the current row and new columns to the left of the current column. So, place the insertion point in the row below or column to the right of where you want to add a new row or column. Then choose Table ➤ Insert Row or Table ➤ Insert Column. If you are inserting a row, you can also use the Table Insert Row SmartIcon.

If you want to add a row to the bottom of a table or a column to the right-hand edge, place the insertion point anywhere in the table and choose Table ➤ Append Row or Table ➤ Append Column. You can also append a row by pressing the Tab key when you are in the bottom-right cell of a table.

Adding Multiple Rows or Columns

To add more than one row or column to a table, place the insertion point below where you want to add the new rows, or to the right of the new columns. To *append* rows or columns, the insertion point can be anywhere in the table. Then choose Table ➤ Insert Special or click on the Table Insert Special SmartIcon.

Notes displays a simple dialog box. Choose whether to add rows or columns and the number to add. Then click on Insert or Append.

Removing the Selected Row(s) or Column(s)

To remove a single row or column, place the insertion point in that row or column. To remove multiple rows or columns, select at least one cell from each row or column you want to delete. Then choose Table ➤ Delete Selected Row(s) or Table ➤ Delete Selected Column(s). For rows, you can also use the Table Delete Selected Row(s) SmartIcon.

Notes asks you to confirm that you really want to do this, because you can't use Edit ➤ Undo to reverse a deletion later.

> **TIP**   You can use the normal Notes text-editing commands to delete the contents of one or more cells without deleting the cells themselves.

Removing Multiple Rows or Columns

Notes also offers you a way to delete rows or columns without selecting them. Place the insertion point in the top row or left-most column you want to delete and choose Table ➤ Delete Special or click on the Table Delete Special SmartIcon. Notes opens a dialog box in which you can choose whether to delete rows or columns and the number to remove. Click on OK and confirm that you want to delete.

Unless you have dozens of rows or columns to delete, it's probably safer to stick to selecting rows or columns for removal. That way, you can see exactly what will be removed.

Deleting an Entire Table

You can delete the entire table by placing the insertion point in the first row (or column) and deleting all the rows (or columns). You can also delete a whole table by selecting from the end of the last line *before* the table starts until the beginning of the first line *after* the table ends (which highlights the whole table) and then delete it as you would delete any text. The second approach gives you the flexibility of undoing the deletion if you make a mistake.

Merging and Splitting Cells

Sometimes you may want to combine several cells in a table to make a category heading run above several columns, or to group several rows.

Notes 4.5 lets you merge not just cells within a single row or column, but any rectangular block of cells. Simply select the cells you want to merge and choose Table ➤ Merge Cells. Notes takes the information from the selected cells and places it all in a list in the single merged cell.

Merged cells operate much the same as regular cells, their borders and margins displaying on the ruler and in the Table Properties InfoBox. Notes won't allow you to set column widths or margins for horizontally merged cells. Instead, you should alter the widths of unmerged cells in the same columns. There are no such restrictions for vertically merged cells.

If you want to restore a merged cell to its unmerged state, select the cell and choose Table ➤ Split Cell. Notes places all the contents of the merged cell in the top-left cell of those formed by the split.

Table Formatting in Action

Remember the dowdy table of product release information in Figure 8.1? Figure 8.4 shows one way that table might be improved. Here are the changes that I made to transform Figure 8.1 into Figure 8.4:

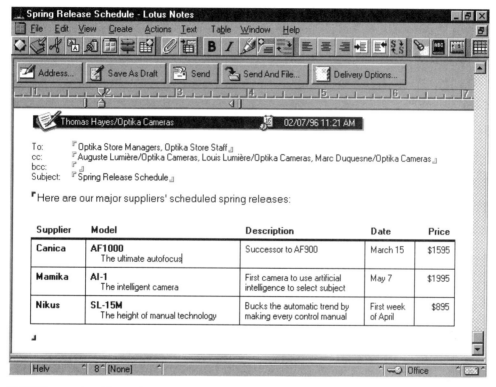

FIGURE 8.4: Good formatting can turn an ugly table into a communicative one. Compare this table with the one in Figure 8.1.

- I selected the whole table and changed the point size from 10-point to 8-point Helv. The smaller type lets me fit more in the table and leads to slightly longer lines, which make the text more readable.
- I also changed the space between rows and space between columns to 0.05" for the entire table. This makes the table feel less cramped than the default zero spacing.
- I made the text bold (by selecting it and pressing Ctrl+B) in three places: the first row headings, and the suppliers' and models' names.

- I also changed the color of the headings in the first row to dark red to help them stand out on color screens.
- I selected the second paragraph in each cell in the second column and used the ruler to indent it by ⅛" to set off the "tag line" for each model.
- I selected the cells in the last column and used Text ➤ Align Paragraph ➤ Right to make the product prices line up properly.
- I selected all the cells in the top row (the column headings) and opened the Cell Borders tab in the Table InfoBox. Then I checked the Outline box, and I specified no borders along the top, left, and right edges, and a double border along the bottom.
- I used the ruler to adjust the column widths to make the best use of the available space.

> **TIP**
>
> This table uses the option Fit Table Width to Window, but I turned this option off while I was adjusting column widths. The reason is that if you alter a column width and make the table wider or narrower than the window, Notes immediately adjusts all the column widths to fit the table on the screen. For example, if you make one column narrower, Notes detects that the table is now narrower than the window and makes *every* column (including the one you just altered) a fraction wider to compensate. It makes for less frustrating editing if you only turn on Fit Table Width to Window when you have established your column widths.

Using Links

As well as features that you might expect to find in a printed document, such as tables and paragraph formatting, Notes can also incorporate elements that no printed document could reproduce. In the remainder of this chapter, you'll find out about hotspots, buttons, collapsible sections, and, first of all, links.

Notes 4.5 provides three types of links that let you quickly jump from one document to another document, view, or new database. These links can appear anywhere in a rich-text field. Often they are used in the same way as you might use a cross-reference in a book.

 • A *DocLink* is a little icon like the one shown here that appears in the text of one Notes document and provides a link to another Notes document. You'll often find DocLinks in documentation databases. The Notes mail database automatically includes a DocLink to the original message each time you make a reply.

 • This is a *View Link*. Click on it and Notes will open a particular view.

 • This is a *Database Link*. Clicking on this icon opens a different database.

You can use a link in either edit mode or read-only mode. In read-only mode, the cursor changes to a pointing finger when you move it onto a link, and Notes displays a summary on the status bar of the document, view, or database to which the link leads.

To follow a link and open the document, view, or database to which it refers, just click on the icon. If you are working without a mouse, press the ← and → keys until the icon has a box around it, like the one shown here. Then press the spacebar to open the linked item. When you are finished reading the linked document, close it and Notes will return you to your place in the original document.

> **TIP**
>
> You can preview a DocLink's destination by choosing View ➤ Document Link Preview. Use the ← and → keys to highlight the correct DocLink in the document. The same menu choice closes the Preview Pane.

Tips for Adding Links

You can make a DocLink to any document you can read, a View Link to any view to which you have access, and a Database Link to any database on your desktop. However, to use links, other Notes users must themselves have the right to read the linked document, view, or database.

This means, for example, that you shouldn't send other people DocLinks to documents in your own mail database. The DocLink will work fine when you test it, because Notes knows to let you read any document in your mail database. But when you mail the message that contains the DocLink to someone else, the DocLink will fail to work. Notes knows that other people aren't supposed to look at your mail database, and therefore it won't open the linked document.

Here are a few good uses for DocLinks:

- To point users to information available in other Notes databases or elsewhere in the same database.
- To link overview documents to more detailed information, and vice versa. This allows readers to see as much or as little detail as they want.
- To link together documents that are being prepared by different authors. This lets several people work independently on sections of a larger presentation.
- To link documents that are frequently updated. If a document that is the target of a link is updated, the DocLink lets that change be reflected elsewhere. If the information had been pasted into another document, the copy would have to be updated each time the original changes.

View and Database Links are principally useful for drawing the attention of other Notes users to a database or view they haven't used before.

Adding Links to Your Documents

Once you have assured yourself that potential users of your link have access to the item to which it refers, you can create the link. Here's how:

1. First, you need to go to your "target" document, view, or database and copy a link to the Clipboard. The target is the item that you want users of your link to end up at when they double-click on the link icon. Specifically:

    - For a DocLink, open the target document or highlight it in a view. Then choose Edit ➤ Copy As Link ➤ Document Link. For DocLinks, you can also use the Edit Copy As Link SmartIcon.
    - For a View Link, open the target view or folder. Then choose Edit ➤ Copy As Link ➤ View Link.
    - For a Database Link, highlight the target database's icon in the workspace. Then choose Edit ➤ Copy As Link ➤ Database Link.

    The status bar will read, "DocLink (or View Link or Database Link) copied to Clipboard. Use Paste to insert it into a document."

2. Open (in edit mode) the document in which you want the link icon to appear.

3. Place the insertion point in a rich-text field where you want to insert the icon.

4. Choose Edit ➤ Paste.

> **NOTE** To find out how to make a link that works by clicking on a piece of text or a graphic, rather than an icon, read the next section.

Using Hotspots and Buttons

Hotspots are areas of a document you can click on while in read-only mode to perform an action, display an annotation, or switch to another document, Web page, view, or database.

A hotspot is usually a piece of text or a graphic that is specially marked so that you know it's clickable. By default, hotspot text has a green rectangle around it to attract your attention. Particular databases may have their own conventions, however; Notes' own Help database uses green underlined text to indicate hotspots that link you to related topics. Hotspot graphics may also have an outline. More commonly, the graphic itself will make it obvious that there's a hotspot, or a caption will tell you.

When you move the cursor to a link hotspot or URL link, Notes displays a pointing hand in place of the usual arrow pointer and tells you on the status bar where the hotspot will take you. Click on the hotspot to follow the link. When you move the cursor to other hotspots, it remains as the standard arrow pointer. To find out what one of these hotspots does, click and hold the left mouse button on it.

- If clicking and holding down the mouse button on the hotspot displays a pop-up annotation or definition, read the text.
- If clicking and holding down the mouse button on the hotspot brings no response, you have an action hotspot. Click on the hotspot to execute the action.

A button is a variant form of an action hotspot. Buttons work in basically the same way, with two minor differences. They always look somewhat similar to the graphic shown here, and buttons work in both read-only and edit modes.

Figure 8.5 shows a memo with some typical hotspots, including one displaying a pop-up annotation.

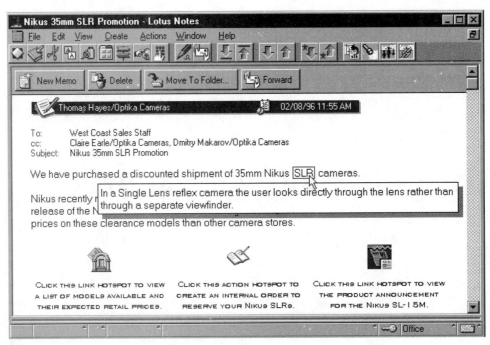

FIGURE 8.5: If you received this memo, you could click on hotspots to find out more about SLR cameras, see a product announcement, view a list of cameras on clearance, or place an internal order.

Creating a Hotspot or Button

At first, you're more likely to be clicking on hotspots than creating them, but if you *do* want to create your own hotspots, here's how. You'll need to decide what type of hotspot you want to add:

- A text pop-up shows a message when you click on highlighted text or a graphic. Pop-ups are particularly useful for providing definitions or explanations to readers who might need extra clarification.
- A link hotspot takes the user to a different document, a view, or another database. Links work well to guide people to related items.
- A URL link takes the user to a Web page in the Web Navigator database. You can find out more about the Web in Chapters 11 and 12.
- An action hotspot can perform one or more of a wide range of actions, such as opening a new document in another database.
- A button does anything an action hotspot can do but is restricted to using text on a gray button as its trigger.

- A formula pop-up uses Notes' formula language to determine the text that displays when you click on the hotspot.

Remember that you need to be in edit mode in a document to create your hotspot or button, and that (with the exception of buttons) you need to be in read-only mode to test it.

TIP   You can set up Notes to create hotspots for Internet URLs automatically. Read the section "Changing Your User Preferences" in Chapter 14.

Creating a Text Pop-Up

1. Select the text or graphic you want to be the hotspot—in other words, the item that Notes highlights to indicate that a hotspot is available.
2. Take one of the following actions to create the hotspot:

    - Choose Create ➤ Hotspot ➤ Text Pop-up.
    - Click on the Create Hotspot Text Pop-up SmartIcon.

    Notes places a rectangle around the text or graphic you selected and opens the Hotspot InfoBox, shown in Figure 8.6.

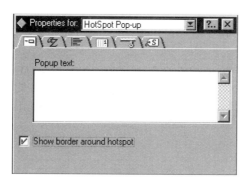

FIGURE 8.6: Type the text of your pop-up annotation into the Hotspot InfoBox.

3. Enter the text you want to pop up when someone clicks on the hotspot.
4. Choose whether or not to display a border around the hotspot.

Creating a Link Hotspot

Follow step 1 in the "Adding Links to Your Documents" section, earlier in this chapter, to copy the link to the Clipboard. Then select the hotspot text or graphic and choose Create ➤ Hotspot ➤ Link Hotspot.

Notes doesn't automatically open the Hotspot InfoBox, but if you want to change the pop-up description of your link or remove the border, you can use Hotspot ➤ Hotspot Properties.

Creating a URL Link

Select the hotspot text or graphic and choose Create ➤ Hotspot ➤ URL Link. Notes opens the URL Link Object InfoBox, where you enter the text of the destination URL and choose whether to display a border. For more information about URLs, check out Chapters 11 and 12.

Creating an Action Hotspot

Select the hotspot text or graphic and choose Create ➤ Hotspot ➤ Action Hotspot. Notes opens both the Hotspot InfoBox and the Programmer's Pane.

Apart from the usual text formatting options, your only choice in the InfoBox is whether or not to display a border. In the Programmer's Pane you choose a simple action to perform or enter a more complicated Notes formula or LotusScript. Actions are examined in the discussion of Agents in Chapter 16. Formulas and LotusScript are beyond the scope of this book; full details are available through Notes' own Help database. When you've chosen an action, click in the document to close the Programmer's Pane.

Creating a Button

Place the insertion point where you want the button. Don't select any text—you'll type that later. Choose Create ➤ Hotspot ➤ Button or click on the Create Hotspot Button SmartIcon. Notes opens both the Button InfoBox and the Programmer's Pane.

Your choices in the Programmer's Pane are the same as for an action hotspot. In the InfoBox you can enter a label for the button and choose whether or not this label should wrap (creating a button of more than one line). If it does wrap, you also need to enter a button width. You can use the Font tab to select a type style for your button.

Creating a Formula Pop-Up

Create ➤ Hotspot ➤ Formula Pop-Up adds a formula-based text pop-up in the same way as you would add a regular text pop-up. Use the Programmer's Pane to supply a Notes formula that produces the text you want to display.

Editing and Deleting Hotspots

You can edit a hotspot at any time by putting the document in edit mode, selecting the hotspot, and choosing Hotspot ➤ Hotspot Properties. This redisplays the Hotspot InfoBox.

For action hotspots, buttons, and formula pop-ups, you can reopen the Programmer's Pane to change the formula you entered by choosing Hotspot ➤ Edit Hotspot (or Button ➤ Edit Button).

To delete a hotspot, select it and choose Hotspot ➤ Remove Hotspot. To delete a button, select it and then press the Delete key or choose Edit ➤ Cut. You can use cut, copy, and paste to reposition a hotspot or button.

Using Collapsible Sections

Sections let you collapse several paragraphs of a document to just a heading and, conversely, expand the heading into several paragraphs. Figure 8.7 shows a document with three sections, the first of which is expanded. Sections are another document feature that, as a beginning Notes user, you are much more likely to be using than creating.

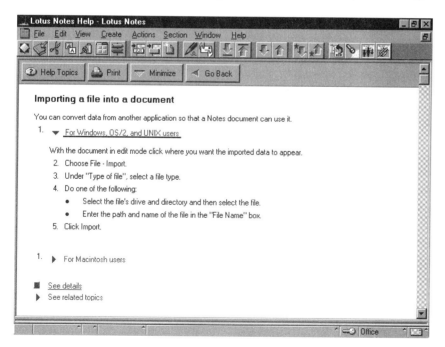

FIGURE 8.7: There are three collapsible sections in this document from Notes' own Help database. The first of them is expanded.

You can detect a section by the twisty triangle to its left. If the triangle is pointing right, the section is collapsed; if it is pointing down, the section is expanded. Click on the twisty or the section title to expand a collapsed section and to collapse an expanded one. If you are working without a mouse, use the ← and → keys to highlight the section title. You can then expand and collapse the section with the spacebar or with Section ➤ Expand and Section ➤ Collapse.

The document's author can choose whether a section should be initially expanded or collapsed. Often a document will have different sections collapsed when you preview it than it will when you view it normally. The author can also specify that particular sections can only be expanded by certain users. These sections can be used to control access to portions of a document.

Sections make it easier to find what you want in a large document. Often a database designer will group the fields on a form into sections to make the form easier to use.

Adding a Section to a Document

To create a section in a document you are writing:

1. Select the title and text that you want to make into the section. By default, Notes makes the first line of your selection into the title, which will show even when the section is collapsed.
2. Choose Create ➤ Section.

If you expand your new section, you'll see that Notes duplicates its title as the first line of the section's text. That's probably not how you'd like the section to appear, so delete the duplicated title.

Editing a Section

Once you have created your new section, you may want to change how it is displayed. To edit a section, place the insertion point on the title line and choose Section ➤ Section Properties to open the Section InfoBox. This InfoBox has four tabs:

- On the Title tab, you can change the section's title text or enter a formula that provides it. You can also choose a border style and color for the title line.

- On the Expand/Collapse tab, you can choose whether your section should be automatically expanded, collapsed, or unaltered in each of four cases: when the document is printed, previewed, being read, and being edited. You can also choose to have the title disappear when the section is expanded, and to have the section only visible in the Preview Pane.
- The Font tab lets you choose a type style for the section title.
- The Hide tab offers paragraph hiding options for advanced users.

To delete a section without removing its contents, place the insertion point on the title line and choose Section ➤ Remove Section. Notes asks you for confirmation (because you can't use Edit ➤ Undo to reverse your action) and then removes the section and the title, but leaves the text.

You now know how to use virtually all the special features you may find in Notes documents, and how to create them too. Reading about hotspots, buttons, collapsible sections, and the like, you may have wondered why you should want to embellish your e-mail with such complex features. In fact, these items are more intended for use in other Notes databases—you might follow a DocLink to see related information in a documentation database, or click on a button to pass a customer on to the next stage in a workflow database.

Chapters 9 and 10 look at the structure of Notes and the types of databases available. Chapters 11 and 12 focus on one of these databases: the Web Navigator.

Part 3

Sharing Information

Chapter

9

GOING BEYOND MAIL

- **Shared databases and what they can do**
- **Notes' network structure**
- **Database access levels**
- **Finding databases and adding them to your workspace**
- **The "About" and "Using" documents**
- **The Notes Help database**

You've seen how Notes does e-mail, and you've found out that it's a pretty effective tool to help you do your job. But many other programs can do about as good a job at e-mail for a much lower price (cc:Mail for example). So why did people at your company pay more to get Notes? The answer lies in shared databases. Notes gives everyone with a computer at your company access to the same information. What kind of information? Everything from news and reference manuals to the status of orders and customer complaints. Turn the page to find out more.

Shared Databases in Notes

Here are some examples of the kinds of databases that might be available to all Notes users, including Notes Mail users:

- Reference documentation for a production process: "Where and how do I get graphics produced for a sales promotion on camera lenses?"
- Human resources procedures: "What do I need to do to get time off for family leave?"
- An electronic discussion about a planned business venture: "The board wants to open three new stores. Who has suggestions about what market we should be aiming for and where?"
- News from a variety of sources, such as major newspapers and wire services, about events in the industry in which you work: "Japan Business News: Nikus SL-15M rollout put on hold."
- A resource reservations log so you can arrange a meeting, reserve an overhead projector, and invite your colleagues without leaving your desk.
- An up-to-date online address and phone book for your whole company.

Here are some examples of databases that might be available to all users except Notes Mail users:

- A specially developed database that handles a key process in the business, such as order-taking or investigating sales leads: "Okay, Atlanta needs two more zoom lenses for the Canica AF900. I can add that to the Cincinnati order I'm placing with the Canica supplier."
- A central customer service database where customer calls can be followed through to their resolution and product improvements can be developed from customer comments: "Armando handled a call from these people last month. Let me see what the problem was."
- A purchasing and requisition database that automates the process of approval and ordering: "Purchase Requisition: Adrian Pagan's request for a notebook computer is attached for your approval."
- A task- and meeting-tracking database that helps ensure progress is made on projects and action taken: "New location search group meeting 11/1/97, four action items outstanding, eight complete."
- Contact directories: "Canica Corp.'s New York rep is Harumi Adachi."

- A range of smaller databases that replace many of the paper forms you have to use now, perhaps letting you order business cards, apply for time off, get a phone installed, and file an expense report electronically.

Those are just a sample of the vast number of possible uses for shared databases. In general, Notes databases can help out with all manner of communication in your company. Notes comes with a number of database templates that your company can use to help it quickly set up databases to perform common business functions.

If you are a Notes Mail user, you can only use databases that are based on nine templates: Mail, Discussion, Document Library (including the special versions of this template for Microsoft Office and Lotus SmartSuite 96), Personal and Public Name & Address Books, Personal and Server Web Navigators, Resource Reservations, and Personal Journal. These nine templates encompass many of Notes' most important features. There is no limit on the number of databases of each type that you can use, so Notes Mail could give you access to a whole suite of reference databases that provide most of the information you need to do your job.

Notes' Network Structure: Servers and Workstations

Before we delve into databases, it's time to look very briefly at how Notes does what it does.

This section is *not* a technical description of Notes' structure. If you need a precise description of how Notes functions, read *Lotus Notes 4.5 Administrator's Guide*, published by Sybex. Here, I'm going to oversimplify shamelessly and gloss over all sorts of details that aren't important to your building a mental picture of what Notes does. In case my skills at drawing mental pictures still need practice, there's a paper-and-ink picture in Figure 9.1.

Notes divides computers into two types, workstations and servers. You use Notes on a Notes workstation. A *Notes workstation* is a regular computer that sits on your desk (or maybe on your lap, if it's a notebook). By contrast, a *Domino server (formerly called a Notes server)* sits in a locked room and is tended by people who have a lot of acronyms in their job titles. If only a few people are using Notes, it's possible for the server to sit on someone's desk (perhaps nobody wanted to pay money to put a computer in a closet), but that isn't usually the case.

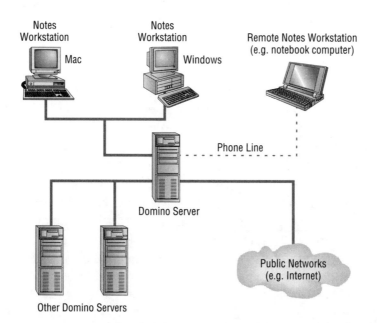

FIGURE 9.1:
Your Notes network, or one that's quite similar

So we have workstations and servers—why? Well, the server does all the stuff that happens behind the scenes. It gets Notes mail from the sender to the recipient, stores all the information in shared databases, and connects to whatever parts of the digital outside world your company has deemed useful. The function of the workstation, of course, is to let you work.

Workstations connect to servers in two main ways. If your Notes workstation is on your desk at work, a bit of cable probably comes out of the back of your computer and plugs into a socket that eventually connects through all sorts of other machines in the locked room to the Domino server. If your Notes workstation is on your desk at home or it's a notebook computer, the wire probably connects instead to a phone line, and each time you want to connect to the server, Notes makes a phone call.

Each server can only handle a certain number of Notes workstations. There isn't a hard and fast limit, but each extra workstation means extra work for the server. Extra workstations make the server accomplish tasks more and more slowly. So, if more than a few people use Notes in your company, your company will have more than one Domino server. Each server is linked to one or more other servers through yet more cables and more machines in locked rooms. The important thing is that everything links together somewhere.

Each workstation usually connects to the same server. One exception is if you are traveling and using Notes on a notebook computer. In this case, you might connect to different servers, depending on where you are working. Even if you connect to the server Alexandria, for example, you can send mail to people who use the server Sogdiana. Also, you can work with shared databases that are stored on Sogdiana as long as the person who manages that database has decided that it's okay for you to have access.

Your company can make all sorts of "external connections" for its Domino servers so they can be hooked up to sources of information or avenues of communication. Outside services don't have to be connected to the same Domino server to which you connect in order for you to use them. If a service is connected to a Domino server somewhere else in your company, then it's a fair bet that you can use it, too, as long as you know how.

Enough theorizing. For now, the important point is that databases you use can be on your own computer, your workgroup's Domino server, or another Domino server in your company or beyond.

Just What Is Domino?

It has been hyped as the biggest innovation since the World Wide Web. It monopolized the ads during the Superbowl. But what exactly *is* Domino?

Domino initially grew out of speculation that the phenomenal rise of Notes as the premier workgroup software would be cut short by the even bigger boom in the use of the World Wide Web. "Who needs Notes," some pundits asked, "when people can use a low-cost browser to view and share information on Web pages?"

Lotus took a long, hard look, and reasoned that Notes and the Web should be complementary and not competitive. There is good justification for this view: Notes offers the robust security and organized information that the Web sorely lacks. But Lotus realized that Notes needed to address the Web's existence in order to remain useful.

In 1995, Lotus offered the first version of the *InterNotes Web Navigator* to let Notes users view Web pages. Lotus also produced the *InterNotes Web Publisher* to let companies produce Web pages from Notes. However, there were some big drawbacks: Web users still could not interact with Notes databases, and pages produced with the Web Publisher were not updated automatically to reflect changes in the underlying Notes database.

In mid-1996, Lotus released *Domino*, a product with three vital capabilities: It simplifies the process of turning Notes databases into Web sites; it works dynamically to keep the same information available on the Web site as in the Notes database; and it applies Notes' strict access control to the whole process.

Domino was viewed favorably by the computer industry, and Lotus realized that it had created a new role for Notes: an easy and secure way to put corporate information onto the Web. Interesting as the first draft of corporate history perhaps, but nothing the average Notes user need worry about. After all, this is a book for Notes users, not systems managers or database designers, and you won't need to build a Domino Web site yourself. However, it's not quite that simple.

Late in 1996, Lotus was ready to release the newest version of Notes. To emphasize its commitment to the Web, Lotus decided to make Domino available with every copy of Notes, and to call the *Notes server* software the *Domino server* instead. Along with this has come a massive marketing campaign, to persuade confused purchasers of business software that Domino is the cure for all Web ills.

Ultimately, you won't see the effects of Domino yourself unless you become a quite advanced Notes user. But you do need to know that what was once the Notes server is now the Domino server.

Database Access Levels

One difference you will notice between shared databases (stored on a Domino server) and most local databases (stored on a Notes workstation or a file server) is that Notes places greater restrictions on who has access to shared databases. When you click on the icon for a shared database, Notes always checks to see who you are and what level of access you are supposed to be allowed.

So what are these access levels and how do you know what level of access you have to a database? At any time, you can check what level of access to the current database you are allowed by looking at the Access Level Indicator (third from the right on the status bar). Table 9.1 summarizes the different Notes access levels, their icons, and what they allow you to do. A simpler version of this table is available as a quick reference guide inside the back cover of this book.

Table 9.1: Notes Access Levels

Icon	Access Level	Rights
	No Access	If you are accorded no access, you can't do a thing with the database. You can't compose or read documents. You can't even add the database's icon to your desktop.
	Depositor or unknown access level	Depositors can add new documents but can't see *any* documents in the database. This access level might be used for a database designed to let people vote on an issue. Notes also displays the Depositor icon when you select a database in the workspace but have not yet opened it. If you click on this icon, Notes opens a dialog box that tells you what access rights you have in this database.
	Reader	Readers can see views and documents but can't compose documents themselves. This is a common access level for people who need to be informed about a process but don't have an active part in it.
	Author	Authors can compose documents, see views, and see other people's documents, but they can only edit documents they composed themselves. This is probably the most common access level, especially for contributory databases, such as discussions.
	Editor	Editors can read, compose, and edit all documents in the database, but they can't modify the database's forms, views, or agents. This is a common access level to use for databases where you expect documents to be modified a number of times by a variety of people.
	Designer	Designers have almost free reign in a database. In addition to everything editors can do, designers can create, modify, and delete forms, views, agents, and the database icon. However, they can't change the database's Access Control List, delete the entire database, or set a number of parameters that control how the database is replicated and presented to users.
	Manager	Managers can do everything that designers can do and everything that they can't do. Managers of shared databases are often members of a company's information systems staff.

Adding Databases to Your Workspace

A number of databases may have been added to your workspace when Notes was set up for you. Or maybe you were sent a memo that let you add a particular database to your workspace just by clicking on a link. If this wasn't the case, however, or if you just want to see what other databases might be available, you'll need to add them yourself.

Adding Special Databases

If your Notes administrator is particularly helpful, he or she may have set up your copy of Notes to give you an easy way to add certain key databases to your workspace. To check whether any of these are available, choose File ➤ Database ➤ Open Special. You'll see a dialog box like that in Figure 9.2.

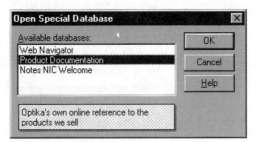

FIGURE 9.2:
The Open Special Database dialog box gives you access to a select few databases.

If you're lucky, you'll see the names of several databases here. You can open one and add its icon to your workspace by selecting its name and clicking on OK. However, it's quite possible that you'll just see a message telling you that there are no special databases defined for your workstation. Don't worry, there are plenty of other places to find databases.

Adding Databases from a Database Library

The next easiest way to find out about new databases and add them to your workspace is to use a database library. This is a special database that describes other databases specifically so that you (and your Notes-using colleagues) can see what's available.

Optika Database Library

Your company may have one or more database libraries, or none at all. If you don't already have an icon for a database library in your workspace (it will probably look like the one next to this paragraph), ask your Notes administrator. If there's no library available, you'll need to use the techniques described in the following sections. If your company does have a database library, the Notes administrator can help you add it to your workspace.

Assuming you have at least one database library available, double-click on its icon to open the library. You'll see a view like that in Figure 9.3.

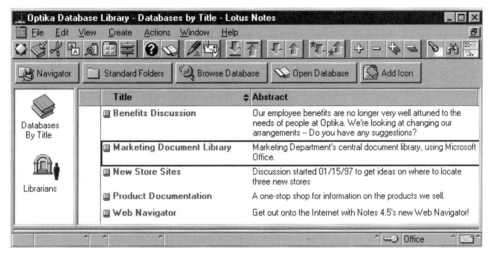

FIGURE 9.3: Libraries let you find interesting and useful Notes databases that are available at your company.

For each database, the library shows its title and an abstract that briefly explains what it does. If you'd like more information about a database, double-click on a row to open the database's description. Here you can also see a more detailed description of the database.

If a database interests you, you have three options on the Action Bar:

- Click on Open Database to add the database's icon to your workspace and open the database itself. Notes will open the database's "About Document," which is described later in this chapter.
- Click on Add Icon to merely place the database's icon in your workspace. This option does not open the database immediately. This lets you add several databases from the library without yet opening them.

- Click on Browse Database to open the database without adding its icon. If you're curious about a particular database, you can take a quick peek first.

If you've added a new database and want to get on with looking at what it contains, skip the next two sections and go to the "About Document" section.

Database libraries contain only what their librarians put into them. There may be many databases on your company's Domino servers that aren't listed in the library. If you can't find a particular database in the library, the next sections cover two other ways to look for databases.

Adding Databases from a Dialog Box

If your company doesn't have a database library, or if the database you're looking for isn't listed in it, you can try to find it yourself by using the Open Database dialog box. This lets you look at the databases available on one or more servers.

You can open the Open Database dialog box, shown in Figure 9.4, in one of these ways:

- Choose File ➤ Database ➤ Open.
- Press Ctrl+O.
- Right-click on the workspace and choose Open Database from the shortcut menu that appears.
- Click on the File Open Database SmartIcon.

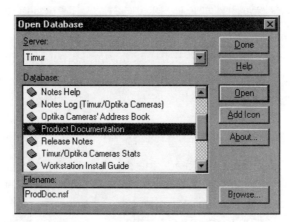

FIGURE 9.4:
The Open Database dialog box lets you browse through the Notes databases that are available to you and add databases to your workspace.

Your first choice to make is where to look for databases. The Server box at the top of the dialog box contains the names of any server for which you already have at least one database in your workspace. It also lists the option Local, which lets you look at databases that are stored on your workstation. If you are just browsing, the best place to start is probably on your own server. To look at what databases a server offers, click on its name.

NOTE

Technically, the Local option lets you open a database on any computer to which you have a regular network connection, as opposed to a Domino server. Depending on what type of network operating system your company uses, you might have access to databases stored on a network file server (which is *not* the same as a Domino server) or on a colleague's workstation. Most of the time, however, you can ignore everything in this paragraph because you'll be looking for databases on a Domino server or in your own local Notes data directory.

TIP

If you've been told that a particular database is available on a particular server and you don't see the server's name in the list on your screen, select the option Other in the Server box to view a list of servers that share the same Public Name & Address Book. If the server isn't listed there, try typing the server's name (exactly) into the Server box and pressing Enter. If you do find a database on a server whose name isn't listed, be aware that using that database may be quite slow, because the information may have to cross some fairly poky communications links.

Once you select a server, Notes displays the databases available in that server's main data folder or directory, as in Figure 9.4. If you are using Notes Mail, you will only see databases that are based on the nine templates you can use.

Notes lists the databases in alphabetical order, followed by any folders (or subdirectories) below the main data directory. Folders may contain other databases. To switch to one, either double-click on its name or click on the name and then click on ⬆.. Open. To return to the parent folder again, double-click on the strange arrow that appears last in the list (and next to this paragraph). Notes lists the selected database's filename at the bottom of the dialog box.

TIP

If you want a more familiar way to navigate through drives and folders to the database file you seek, click on Browse to have Notes open a regular file dialog box. From there, you can choose to display Notes Database Files, Notes Template Files, or All Files. Once you've found the file you want to open, click on Select to have Notes take you back to the Open Database dialog box and place the file's name in the Filename box.

When you see a database that piques your curiosity, you can find out more about it by clicking on the About button. This opens the database's About document (see Figure 9.5 and the section "The About Document" later in this chapter). What Notes displays is a description of the database, written by the person who designed it. This document is also available when you open the database.

If you are lucky, the About document will give you some idea as to the function of the database and help you decide whether it's something that is useful for you. If you're unlucky, you may find that:

- The About document just says general stuff about a certain type of database but doesn't help you work out whether this database is useful. This often happens when databases are based on templates. Rushed or lazy database designers don't always take the time to edit the About document to make it more descriptive.
- You get a message saying that there is no About document available for this database.
- You get a message saying that you are not allowed access to the particular database. If this is the case and you feel you should have access, contact your Notes administrator or use the Database Catalog (described in the next section) to find the name of the database's manager.

When you find a database you like (or hope you're going to like), your options are similar to those in the database library:

Open Notes opens the database right away *and* adds the database icon to your workspace.

Add Icon Notes places the database's icon in your workspace. If you choose this option, Notes does not open the database or close the dialog box, so you can continue looking at the available databases and add more icons if you wish.

Adding Databases from the Database Catalog

There's one other place to look to find databases to add to your workspace. Most servers have a Database Catalog that automatically lists all the databases on that server and on connected servers. This database is less "user-friendly" than the database library, but it can help you track down a database that isn't listed in a library.

First you have to find a copy of the catalog and add it to your workspace. Look for Database Catalog in your server's main data directory. Once you open the catalog, you'll find a number of categorized views that list databases by their titles, managers, servers, and subjects. By opening documents from these views you can find out more about the listed databases.

NOTE Using categorized views is described in more detail in Chapter 14.

Buttons let you open or browse a database or add its icon to your desktop. You will find that many of the databases listed here are inaccessible to you because, although they are "shared databases" stored on a server, they are only intended for limited use. Nevertheless, if you're trying to track down a particular database, the catalog can be very useful.

The About Document

When you open a database for the first time, Notes opens the About document for the database. It's called the About document because its title consists of the word "About" and then the name of the database. You may have seen an About document when you browsed through databases in the Open Database dialog box.

The About document looks a lot like a regular Notes document. Figure 9.5 shows the About document for the standard Notes discussion database.

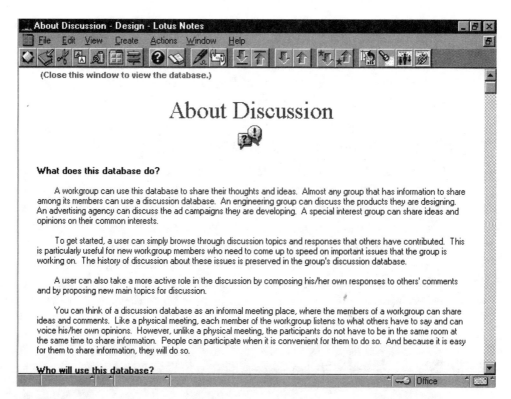

FIGURE 9.5: The About Discussion document gives you general information about how you might use this type of Notes database.

How much information is in an About document depends a lot on how conscientious the person who set up the database was. At best there are some brief, clear guidelines on what the database is supposed to do and how to use it. For a discussion database, a good About document would tell you which people the database was intended for and what things they are invited to discuss.

Often, however, the About document will be little different from the one provided with the database template. It gives some useful information about discussion databases in general, but it doesn't help you find out who's discussing what in the specific database.

Refer to the About document as much or as little as it merits. Once you have read enough of it to brace you for your first plunge into the new database, you can close the document and get the database's main view. If you want to look at the About document again, you can find it on the Help menu at any time, which is also where you'll find the Using document for the database, described next.

The Using Document

The Using document is intended to give you straightforward instructions on how to accomplish specific tasks in the database—with none of the About document's airy speculation on the database's purpose and audience.

A good Using document tells you what each of the database's principal forms does and how to use it. It should also run down which views are available and perhaps lay out any special features the database might have, such as special navigators, links to other databases, and the ability to route documents from person to person.

The Using document isn't as easily compromised by a forgetful database designer. Even if it hasn't been updated, the document's forms and view probably work pretty much the same way. So the Using document is usually a good place to turn for hints on how to use a database.

Notes Database Resources

You'll soon notice that the design of databases varies a great deal. If you need to find out about a particular database, consider the following resources:

- The About and Using documents described previously.
- Any electronic documentation that is provided within the database or perhaps in a separate reference documentation database. For example, Web Navigator users can find useful information in the Lotus Notes and the Internet database.
- Any printed documentation for the database, such as a cheat sheet or a user guide. For example, Lotus Notes and the Internet is sometimes also supplied as a printed booklet.
- If it's a particularly sophisticated database, there may be a demo program that you can run on your computer.
- Any colleagues who you know already use the database.

- The manager of the database. The manager's name may be listed in the About or Using documents. If there's a Memo to Manager form, you can use that (see Chapter 18). The Manager's name will also be listed in the Database Catalog.
- Posting a question in a Q&A or technical support database, if there is one at your company.
- Your Notes administrator.
- As a last resort, consider looking in the database views for someone who has obviously already worked out how to use the database, and then mail your question to him or her.

If you are looking for general help on how to perform a particular operation in Notes, your resources include:

- This book and its index. Although I can't cover everything, I hope to provide answers to the most common questions about Notes.
- The Notes Help and Help Lite databases, explained in the section that follows.
- Notes' context-sensitive Guide Me help (press F1 or click on the Help Guide Me SmartIcon) takes you straight to the appropriate topic in the Help database.
- The Notes documentation databases, which are located in the main Notes data directory on your Domino server. These databases are mostly intended for Notes administrators, but you may find useful items in such databases as the Install Guide for Workstations, the Notes Migration Guide, and the Lotus Notes 4.5 Release Notes.
- The printed Notes documentation, much of which duplicates the documentation databases.
- Your Notes administrator.

Getting Help from the Notes Help Database

The Notes Help database is an online reference to almost every Notes feature that you could want to know about as a Notes user. You can use the Notes Help database in two ways: by browsing through the documents and searching for advice on a particular subject, or by using the context-sensitive Guide Me feature to quickly find your way to the Help documents most appropriate to what you are currently doing.

Help Lite is a smaller version of Help that is intended particularly for people using Notes on a notebook computer. Help Lite contains all the topics you'll need for regular use of Notes, but none of the topics on programming, developing, and managing Notes databases or administering a Notes network.

Taking a Guide

Notes is a very flexible piece of software with a great number of adaptable, but inter-meshed, components. What you need to do with Notes may occasionally take you to parts of the program that aren't covered in detail in this book. But if you run into diffi-culty, or merely become confused, you can almost always use Notes' context-sensitive Guide Me feature to get help.

Figure 9.6 shows a typical Guide Me screen. You can get guidance in any of these ways:

- Press F1.
- Choose Help ➤ Guide Me.
- Click on the Help Guide Me SmartIcon.
- Click on a dialog box's Help button.
- Click on the question mark on the title bar of an InfoBox.
- On the Macintosh, press ⌘+? or Help.

FIGURE 9.6:
Guide Me screens, like this one for opening a data-base, offer a list of choices appro-priate to your situation.

Because there are a number of possible questions a user could have in any situation, Guide Me presents "cascading" lists of choices so you can quickly get the information you need. Lotus says Notes won't present more than eight choices on a Guide Me screen, and it won't require you to step through more than three lists before finding help.

In each list, the green underlined choices are links that you can click on to switch to a more detailed list or to a document in the Notes Help database. Buttons at the top let you print the list, go back to the last screen you were viewing, and tell Notes that you're done and want to close the Help window.

Once you reach a Help database document, you'll also see many other features that you'll be familiar with from other Notes documents. Some useful features that you may see in Help documents are:

- A section at the end marked "See related topics." Click on this title to see a list of links to documents on related subjects.
- A line above the related topics titled "See examples" or "See details" and marked with a green square button. This provides a link to suggestions on how you might use a particular technique.
- Sections that contain information specific to particular operating systems, marked in the form "Click here for Windows NT information."

> **TIP**
> If you try to use Guide Me and receive a message saying, "There is no Help available for that topic," don't give up. Even though you can't get any context-sensitive help, you can still use the methods in the next section to find the information you need.

Striking Out on Your Own

If the Notes advice you crave isn't confined to the context of a certain screen or dialog box, you'll need to do your own searching in the Help database. You can either open the Help database from your workspace by clicking on its icon, shown here, or you can:

- Choose Help ➤ Help Topics.
- Click on the Help Topics SmartIcon.

The Index View

Each time you open the Help database, the first thing you'll see is the Index view, as in Figure 9.7. This view groups the Help documents (marked in the View Pane with icons of a sheet of paper) alphabetically into categories (marked with a twisty triangle).

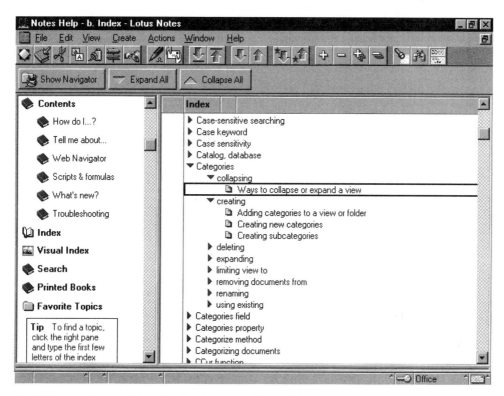

FIGURE 9.7: Notes Help's Index view lets you quickly find documents on any facet of Notes.

You can expand and collapse any category in the view by clicking on the twisty or double-clicking on the category title. Sometimes, as in Figure 9.7, one category will have others indented underneath it. Chapter 14 covers categorized views in more detail.

Click on the View Pane and begin typing the first few letters of the subject you want to look up. Notes opens a dialog box titled Quick Search. Once you've typed enough letters to identify your subject, press Enter or click on OK. If Notes can find a category beginning with those letters, it will scroll the view to the position you indicated.

NOTE As well as searching in Help's Index view, you may be able to make full-text searches of Notes Help. Clicking on the Search hotspot in the Navigation Pane opens a view optimized for full-text searching and provides search instructions. Searching for text in documents and views is described in Chapter 14, while full-text searching is described in Chapter 15.

The Contents Views

Notes also offers six contents views to help you find certain types of information. You can switch to one of these views by clicking on its icon in the Navigation Pane.

- The How Do I...? view works like the table of contents in a book, with categories and subcategories that group documents on each aspect of using Notes. If you want to browse through information on a particular area of Notes, this is a good place to go. If you're using Notes on a note-book computer, you can use the Mobile Help hotspot in Help Lite's Navigation Pane to take you straight to the Mobile Notes topics in How Do I...?
- The Tell Me About... view singles out all the Help database's overview documents, letting you quickly read a summary of, say, printing in Notes.
- The Web Navigator view groups together all the information on using the Personal and Server Web Navigators.
- Scripts & Formulas contains reference information for programming in Notes.
- What's New? includes information for people upgrading from an earlier version of Notes. If you've used Notes before, look here for a quick summary of new features.
- Troubleshooting is the place to go if Notes isn't working as you expected. There are solutions for many common problems, an alphabetical list of error messages, information on Lotus Web sites, and last-minute changes to the program and its documentation.

TIP To find the Notes 4.5 equivalent of a Notes 3.x menu choice, use Help ➤ Release 3 Menu Finder. This opens a special window in which you can pull down Notes 3.x menus and Notes will tell you the corresponding action in Notes 4.5.

The Visual Index

If you have a question about something displayed on the screen in Notes, try using the Visual Index. First, click on the Visual Index hotspot in Help's Navigation Pane. Then choose a subject from the choices Notes displays; workspace management, document contents, view management, and mobile management are likely choices. Then Notes will show you a screen like the one in Figure 9.8, the Visual Index to document features. Click on any of the yellow balloon icons to jump to a Help topic describing that feature.

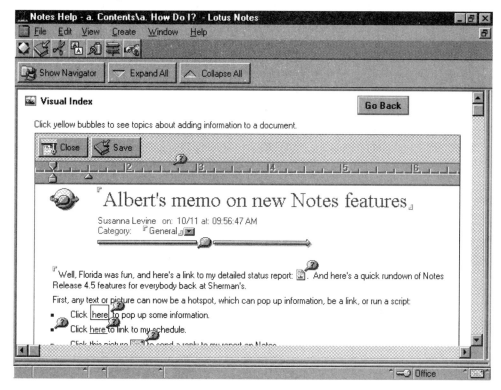

FIGURE 9.8: Click on a yellow balloon in Notes Help's Visual Index to quickly find an explanation of an item in your Notes window.

NOTE The Visual Index is not available in Help Lite.

Printed Books and the User's Guide

The Printed Books view duplicates the content of some of the user manuals supplied with Notes. Until you become a Notes programmer or administrator, you are likely only to be interested in the User's Guide (and this is the only Printed Book included in Help Lite). You may find the methodical and exhaustive approach to each topic in the User's Guide useful.

You may also wish to print out some key sections from the User's Guide if you do not already have your own copy. If you choose to do this, there are two steps you can take to make the resulting pages appear most like a regular booklet: Print no more than one section at a time (select in the view all the documents in the section, or a subset of them); and choose No Separation between documents in the Print dialog box.

Once you have added a few databases to your workspace using the techniques covered in this chapter, you will want to find out how to use them. Chapter 10 takes a detailed look at the main database templates provided with Notes 4.5.

Chapter 10

STANDARD NOTES DATABASES

- **Discussion databases**
- **Document libraries**
- **Special libraries for Microsoft Office and Lotus SmartSuite 96**
- **Personal journals**
- **Resource reservations databases**
- **Other common databases**

You've already taken an extensive look at one of the six standard databases available to Notes Mail users (and all other Notes users): your mail database. We'll spend this chapter taking a tour through four other types: discussion databases, document libraries (including special versions for Microsoft Office and Lotus SmartSuite), personal journals, and resource reservation databases. Chapters 11 and 12 look at Web Navigator databases.

Available Database Templates

Even though the databases covered in this chapter are based on templates that come with Notes, the versions you use at your company may look a little different. Database designers can add or modify views and fields in these databases to suit their particular companies.

Users of Notes Mail shouldn't assume that the selected types of databases that they can use are somehow less useful than those that are available to a regular Notes user. The four databases discussed in this chapter were chosen for Notes Mail because they've proven to be popular and useful at companies that use Notes.

The range of templates that come with Notes changed substantially in Notes 4. Notes 4 introduced several completely new templates, such as the Web Navigator and Personal Journal. Some templates that came with Notes 3, such as News, were not supplied with Notes 4 and most existing templates were substantially upgraded; for example, Notes 3's simple Document Library template gained approval functions and automatic links to two software suites in Notes 4. Notes 4.5 builds on the new range of templates established for Notes 4.

This chapter does not describe the templates and example databases that came with earlier versions of Notes. However, you should experience little difficulty navigating through databases based on these earlier templates and examples. If you need help at any point, seek out the Notes Database Resources suggested in Chapter 9.

Discussion Databases

At many companies that use Notes, discussion databases have revolutionized the way that people make decisions, seek and receive advice, and obtain feedback. But even if you just use them as an easy way to talk over ideas with coworkers, you'll be surprised at how useful discussion databases can be.

Discussion databases can be used in many different ways. In a formal discussion database, you might post a question about a Human Resources policy (perhaps anonymously) and get an authoritative reply. In a very informal discussion database, you and your five closest colleagues might toss up ideas for each other to comment on. In between these extremes are issue-related discussions in which you would get information on a particular subject (a Software Answers forum, for example) and project-related discussions in which you would help plan a new venture.

Discussion databases offer particular advantages over actual meetings and e-mail and phone conversations:

- The database can be made available to as many or few Notes users as you want.
- Newcomers to the discussion can read the existing postings to bring themselves up to speed on an issue or project.
- In a question-and-answer database, users may be able to answer their questions with the help of existing postings.
- People can contribute to the discussion when their schedules permit. Unlike a traditional meeting, not everyone has to be in the same place at the same time.
- There's a built-in record of what was discussed. You can quickly see what has been decided and by whom.
- Users can set up an interest profile to have Notes send them summaries of postings that might interest them.
- In some databases, users can make anonymous comments and responses, letting people convey suggestions and concerns that they might otherwise keep to themselves.
- People who are intimidated by the idea of voicing their ideas in a meeting may find it easier to post comments in a discussion database. Of course, this isn't always true, and sometimes discussion databases make people less forthcoming.

As you may have noticed, documents in discussion databases are often referred to as *postings* (a term from the online world), or as *main topics* and *responses* (the terms Notes uses). The style of writing in a discussion database is determined largely by the subject and the participants. Often postings look a lot like e-mail messages, but you should remember that even if you are replying to one person's comments, your words are probably available to many other Notes users as well.

Main Topic, Response, and Response to Response Documents

One popular use for discussion databases is to let Notes users exchange ideas on new products, markets, and services, and on how to improve existing offerings. A broader range of people can contribute to a database like this than can voice their opinions in a standard meeting. Figure 10.1 shows the main view in a database in which Optika Cameras' employees are helping the company work out where to open three new stores.

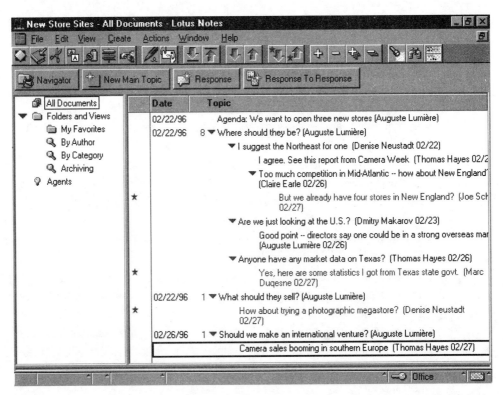

FIGURE 10.1:   This main view of a discussion database shows how people have responded to the original main topics.

Three different types of documents are shown in the view in Figure 10.1:

- *Main Topic* documents have dates to the left of them. They are the starting point for a discussion in some area. Here, they're all written by the chairman, Auguste Lumière. The first one sets the scene for the discussion. Two more— "Where should they be?" and "What should they sell?"—ask specific questions. Another—"Should we make an international venture?"—was written to start a new "thread" of discussion in a particular area.

- *Response* documents are indented one level below the Main Topics to which they refer. "I suggest the Northeast for one" and "How about trying a photographic megastore" are both Responses.

- *Response to Response* documents are indented one level *below* whatever document they refer to. "Too much competition in Mid-Atlantic…" and "But we already have four stores in New England" are both Responses to Responses.

When you are reading a posting like the Response in Figure 10.2 and you decide you want to add your own comments, it's important to know whether you want a simple Response or a Response to Response.

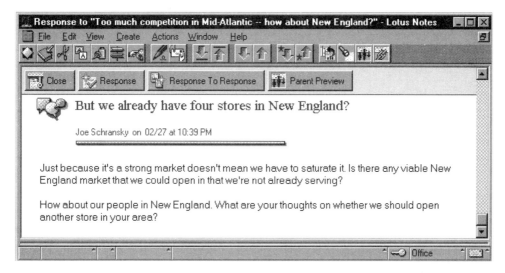

FIGURE 10.2:   If you had comments to add that referred to Joe's opinions, you would choose Response to Response; if you wanted to address the original subject, a plain Response would do.

If you chose to compose a *Response* in Figure 10.2, it would be indented one level under "Where should they be?" in the view and sorted by the date it was composed. That would place it just above "What should they sell?" If instead you chose to compose a *Response to Response,* it would be indented one more level under "But we already have four stores in New England?" So, choose a Response document when your comment refers back to the original point, and a Response to Response document when you are strictly commenting on the substance of the message you're reading.

Some database designers find this setup a little too confusing (I can't imagine why) and pare the structure down to just Main Topic and Response forms. In this situation, the Response is indented under whatever document was open or highlighted when it was composed.

As you've seen, views like the one in Figure 10.1 are set up hierarchically with responses indented below the documents to which they are responding. In these views, you can collapse and expand the response hierarchy just as you might in a categorized view. Discussion databases usually display a twisty triangle in the first column to indicate that a topic is expandable. You may also see older discussion databases that use a plus (+) sign. Expandable hierarchies can occur in categorized views as well, in which case both documents and categories are expandable. Chapter 14 discusses categorized and hierarchical views in more detail.

Other Discussion Database Views and Forms

Discussion databases usually offer three other views: By Category, By Author, and Archiving.

- The *By Category* view is particularly useful in databases that have been around a while. In a technical Q&A database, for example, there may be many main topics, each with a couple of responses. Topics are all listed in order by date in the Main view, which makes it difficult to find a previous query on a subject. But if people have been conscientious about categorizing their questions, the By Category view may help you find what you want.
- The *By Author* view can help you see who's writing what, which can be useful—if only to figure out how your colleagues are spending their free time.
- The *Archiving* functions are similar to those used in your mail database (see Chapter 18) and are used mainly by a database's manager.

When you first contribute to a discussion database, especially one with an audience wider that just your own workgroup, it is polite to complete a Contributor Profile (Create ➤ Contributor Profile) to let other database users know who you are.

Some discussion databases will offer anonymous forms that let you write Responses and Responses to Responses that don't identify the author. If you don't see these forms listed on the Create menu, try using Create ➤ Other. Documents composed with these forms don't contain any record of the author's name, so you can ask difficult questions without fear of repercussion.

Creating an Interest Profile

Notes 4.*x* discussion databases let you set up a personal interest profile. This lets you tell Notes to send you a "newsletter summary" whenever the database receives new documents that:

- Contain your name
- Are written by certain authors
- Are in particular categories
- Contain certain words or phrases

You can specify any combination of these criteria for Notes to look for in new documents. By default, Notes scans for new documents that match your profile every day at 1 a.m. To compose your profile, use Actions ➤ Edit Interest Profile; to have Notes inform you of activity on a particular subject, use Actions ➤ Add Selected Topic to Interest Profile.

Document Libraries

Even more than discussion databases, document libraries differ widely from one company to the next. They can be used to document procedures that relate to particular departments or tasks or to provide an electronic reference for companywide policies. For example, Human Resources and Purchasing guidelines can be kept in document libraries. They can also be used in a more informal way to provide a central repository for a small workgroup.

Notes also provides two variants of the Document Library template that are specifically designed for use with Microsoft Office and Lotus SmartSuite. Most parts of these templates are the same as the basic Document Library template, but their specific features are described at the end of this section.

Figure 10.3 shows an example of a document library that Optika Cameras has set up for salespeople and anyone else who needs to find out about what the company sells. The database contains three kinds of documents:

- Marketing brochures for Optika's own-brand products
- General descriptions of the types of products that Optika sells
- Specific product documentation that Optika receives from vendors

The main document library form is very basic, with fields for a title and category names, and a rich-text field for the document body. This allows you to include a wide variety of types of documents, all of which can be categorized to suit your needs. You may find document libraries that have been tailored to particular uses by the addition of other fields.

The library in Figure 10.3 displays more than one level of categorization by using the backslash technique described in "Using Categorized and Hierarchical Views" in Chapter 14.

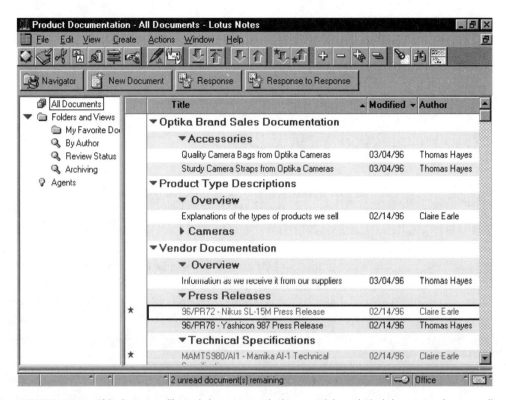

FIGURE 10.3:   This document library is home to marketing materials, technical documents from suppliers, and home-grown descriptions that can help with training.

The employees at Optika Cameras who composed the documents for this database could have used e-mailed product specifications as their starting point. Or the documents could contain scanned copies of printed material received from the manufacturer.

As well as the hierarchical view shown in Figure 10.3, the document library also offers three other views. The By Author and Archiving views work like those in many other Notes databases. The Review Status view is described below.

Using the Document Review Cycle

The Document Library templates have a sophisticated built-in mechanism that lets a workgroup keep track of the process of reviewing documents. Reviews are initiated by the author of the document; the author gets to control who reviews it and how the review process is handled.

Before we examine the full review process, I should also note that a document author can also exert a limited measure of control over a document by clicking on the Mark Private button that appears at the top of a document in edit mode. This hides the document from other database users (apart from any designated reviewers). Private documents are marked with a padlock icon in views. They display a Mark Public button in edit mode that the author can use to make them accessible again.

To start the review process for a document you have written:

1. Click on the Setup Review Cycle button on the Action Bar. Notes opens a very smart-looking dialog box that delights you with a picture of the Middle East from space as you decide how you want your document reviewed.

2. Choose a system or style for reviewing your document. Your review style options are:

> **Serial Review** This sends your document in sequence, one step at a time, to each of the reviewers whose names you soon will provide. Notes makes all changes to the same copy of the document, but also keeps an unedited copy in the database.

> **Serial (Keep All Revisions)** This form of serial review still passes on a single document, but all older versions (and the original) are also stored in the database as responses to the latest edited version.

> **Document Reservations** This review style sends requests to all reviewers at the same time. When one reviewer opens the document, Notes "locks" the document at the server and warns anyone else who wants to edit the document that a review is in progress. Reviewers edit a single copy of the original document, while Notes also keeps a clean copy.

> **Response Review** This works like the document reservations system, except that the file is not locked. Reviewers edit their own copies of the document, which become responses to the original.

3. Then you need to choose whether you want to place a time limit on the review process. If you do, you can choose whether to send automatic reminders after a certain number of days, or to just move the document on to the next reviewer. You can also choose to have Notes notify you when each reviewer finishes looking at your document, or just when the whole process is complete.

4. A final checkbox lets you save these settings for the next time you want a document to be reviewed.

5. Click on OK and Notes will add a whole new section called Review Cycle Information to your document. This section confirms the review options you've chosen, names you as the Originator of the document, and lets you enter the names of your document's reviewers.

6. Once you have set up the review cycle to suit you, click on Submit for Review. Notes presents a dialog box confirming the names of the people it has asked to review your document. You can change the review parameters by clicking on Setup Review Cycle again. If you decide against sending your document for review, click on Clear Review Cycle.

Reviewers receive a mailed notification asking them to review the document. (If you choose either style of Serial review, Notes doesn't send a reviewer a notification until it is his or her turn.) This notification Bookmark contains a DocLink that the reviewer can use to open the document. The Review Cycle Information section remains in the document as it is reviewed—your reviewers can see who asked for the review, who has already reviewed the document, who is reviewing it now, and who has yet to review it.

TIP	If your workgroup frequently uses the Serial Review or Document Reservations styles of reviewing, you may want to have each member adopt a distinctive style of Permanent Pen to make it easier to identify the author of each comment. How to use Permanent Pen is described in Chapter 6.

When reviewers finish editing your document, they click on the My Review Is Complete button. Notes displays a dialog box telling them who it is notifying that the review is complete. Notes also adds a Reviewer Log section at the bottom of the document, showing who has reviewed it and when.

When the last reviewer finishes editing your document (and at intermediate times if you choose that option), Notes sends you a notification. The Review Status view lets you see where documents are in the review process.

Suite-Specific Document Libraries

As well as the standard Document Library template, Lotus also provides two special versions with Notes 4.5 that are specifically designed to be used with two popular office software suites: Lotus SmartSuite 96 and Microsoft Office.

The principal difference between standard document libraries and databases based on these two special templates is that the suite templates let users automatically create documents in any of that suite's applications. This allows a workgroup to use a Notes document library as a central repository for documents created in other applications and also to use Notes' reviewing functions to manage workflow.

Each template has extra options on the Create menu that let users start a new document in any one of the suite's applications. When users finish working on these new documents, Notes asks them for a name and category to use for the document library.

The Lotus SmartSuite 96 Library template works with Lotus 1-2-3 worksheets, Lotus Freelance presentations, and Lotus WordPro documents. The template is not backward-compatible with earlier versions of SmartSuite.

The Microsoft Office Library template works with Microsoft Excel worksheets, Windows Paintbrush pictures, Microsoft PowerPoint presentations, and Microsoft Word documents. Excel users can choose between creating a full worksheet (which is linked to the Notes document) or just a Quick Sheet (which is embedded instead).

> **NOTE** For a general discussion of object linking and embedding, see Chapter 7.

Personal Journals

 The Personal Journal database template is new in Notes 4.x. You can use it to create your own database in which to store personal documents. You can use a personal journal in whatever way suits you. For example, it can be a scratch pad for ideas or a place to work on documents before adding them to another database.

NOTE Creating a database from a template is covered in Notes Help.

The structure of personal journals is quite simple, with a single view—All Documents—and just two forms. The basic form is the Journal Entry, which contains only a Title field and a Body field. Place whatever you like in the Body field, and give the document a title to identify it in the view.

Sometimes you may want to create a document in which the title isn't displayed, such as when you anticipate printing out the document as a business letter or proposal. For these occasions, use the Clean Sheet form. It's just the same as a Journal Entry, except that the Title field doesn't display on the form. Use the Doc Info button on the Action Bar to provide a title, or just wait for Notes to ask you when you close the document.

You can use the Doc Info buttons displayed above any personal journal document, view, or folder to find out more about the document that's open or highlighted. If you use your journal extensively, you may want to create folders to organize your work.

One clever feature of the personal journal is an automatic "versioning" system. If you're working on a long or important document, you may want to save a copy of it before you make a major change. To do this, choose Actions ➤ Save As New Version before you make the changes. Notes saves the old version as a response to the newer one. Then, if you change your mind about the alterations, you can always go back to the old version.

Resource Reservation Databases

Organizations can use the Resource Reservations template to provide a central means of booking meeting rooms, electronic equipment, or any other type of resource. It works with Notes 4.5's calendaring and scheduling features to let users book rooms and resources at the same time they schedule a meeting.

NOTE Notes 4 included a Room Reservations database template. Although the Resource Reservations database template is an outgrowth of that, it has been extensively modified to work with the new scheduling capabilities available in Notes 4.5. As a consequence, you can't automatically reserve rooms in a Notes 4 room reservations database when you schedule a meeting in Notes 4.5. Ask your Notes administrator about creating a Notes 4.5 resource reservations database instead.

You may not need to open the resource reservations database at all, as you can book, reschedule, and cancel rooms and resources from any Calendar Entry in your mail database. However, if you frequently book rooms, you may find it useful to scan the actual reservations database occasionally. The resource reservations database you use may cover a small group of Notes users or the whole organization, depending on how Notes has been set up.

The person setting up the database creates a Site Profile for each location that will be using this copy of the database. Then designated people create Resource documents that detail particular rooms and pieces of equipment. Each resource is named and described; rooms are also given a capacity. The person creating a resource also selects the days of the week and times of day when the room or item is available.

The Resources view shows all the resources that have been defined for the database.

To Reserve a Resource

You can reserve rooms and resources at the same time you invite people to your meeting. Chapter 17 covers these advanced scheduling functions. You can also reserve rooms and resources independently of Notes' scheduling functions. To do this, open the resource reservations database to one of these three views: Calendar, Reservations by Date, or Reservations by Resource. Each shows you precisely which rooms have already been booked and for when.

Reservations by Date and Calendar are the views to look in when you know the date and time of your meeting but need to find a free room or piece of equipment. Reservations by Date categorizes existing reservations by month and then by day; Calendar shows reservations on the same styles of calendar as you use in your mail database.

Look in Reservations by Resource when you want to book a particular room or resource but have some flexibility in scheduling. This view categorizes reservations first by the room or resource booked and then by month and by day.

When you have found a workable combination (or even if you can't) here's how to reserve a room or resource:

1. Click on the Create Reservation button on the Action Bar, or choose Create ➤ Reservation. Notes opens a new Reservation document.

2. Notes places your name in the Reserved By field. If you're booking a resource for someone else, enter his or her name instead. Enter a contact phone number and choose whether you want to book a room or resource. Then click on the Continue button.

3. Tell Notes whether you are more concerned to find a free time for a particular room or resource, or a free room or resource at a specified time. Click on the Continue button again.

4. If you chose to find an available room or resource at a specific time, do the following:

   • Enter a date for the reservation and select start and end times and the site where the meeting will take place.
   • For a room, enter the number of attendees; for a resource, choose the resource category you require.
   • Then click on the Find Available Room/Resource button to find out which rooms or resources are free during the period you've specified.
   • Choose a room or resource from the dialog box that Notes displays.

   If you chose to find an available time for a specific room or resource, do the following:

   • Click on the Choose Specific Room or Choose Specific Resource button. Notes opens a Rooms/Resources dialog box listing all bookable rooms or resources.
   • Select an entry and click on OK.
   • Tell Notes the date and duration of the booking.
   • Now click on yet another button, labeled Find an Available Time. Notes opens a Free Time dialog box (see Chapter 17 for more information on using this dialog box) that you can use to track down a workable time.
   • Select a time and click on OK to confirm it.

5. If you're reserving a room or resource for someone else, enter a few words in the Purpose field. Notes includes your explanation in the notification it sends to the person in whose name you are making the reservation.

6. Close and save the reservation; Notes automatically sends a notification to the person you named as reserving the resource.

If you find later that you need to alter the details of a resource reservation, you can't simply edit the Reservation document as you would in most Notes databases. Instead, you must delete your original reservation and compose a new one.

My Reservations is a public view that becomes private the moment you open it. From then on, it just shows in order of date and time which resources you have reserved.

WARNING **If you reserve a room or resource for a meeting directly from the resource reservations database, rather than making the reservation from the meeting's Calendar Entry, Notes will *not* automatically reschedule or cancel the resource reservation if you reschedule or cancel the meeting.**

Other Database Templates

As well as the four types of databases we've looked at in this chapter, there are many other possibilities within Notes. Personal and Public Name & Address Books, Mail, Database Library, and Database Catalog are templates available to all Notes users. The principal uses for these databases are explained elsewhere in this book, and you're not likely to be creating your own databases from these templates.

You will probably see a number of databases that have been designed by people in your own company. Obviously, these databases will have their own structure of forms, views, and actions, and this book can't give you specific instructions on their use.

Notes 4.5 is supplied with a number of other templates besides the four described in this chapter. Some are available to Lotus Notes Mail users and others aren't. Almost all these other templates deal with behind-the-scenes administration and management functions that would put you to sleep were you to start reading about them.

One template, Approval Cycle, is classified by Lotus as an application template for non-Mail Notes users. Really, though, it's more of a component that database designers can incorporate into other databases to provide approval functions.

Users of Notes Desktop and the full version of Notes can make use of the Search Site database to make full-text searches of multiple databases. You can find more information on this database in Chapter 15.

Another database you may commonly see is InterNotes News. This database lets Notes and Notes Desktop users subscribe to USENET newsgroups on the Internet, and read and reply to newsgroup articles. The database is available to download from `http://www.notes.net/`.

There is only one other standard Notes database that most Notes users will come into contact with: the Web Navigator. The Web Navigator lets you use Notes to browse pages from the World Wide Web. It's a powerful tool and the subject of Chapters 11 and 12.

Chapter 11

USING THE WEB NAVIGATOR

- **Connecting to the Internet with Notes**
- **The Personal and Server Web Navigators**
- **Setting up the Web Navigators**
- **Getting around in Web pages**
- **Web Navigator views**

You know how easily Notes lets you find information within your company, but how much can it help when you need to look further afield? The past few years have seen the rise of the Internet (and the World Wide Web in particular) to become a ubiquitous information resource. For almost any question you might have, the answer is out there on the Web. Notes 4.5 functions as a full Web browser, allowing you Internet access from your own computer or via a Domino server connected to the Internet. And Notes documents can contain hotspots that allow readers to jump automatically to related Web pages.

Connecting to the Internet with Notes

You probably want to start surfing the Web right away, but there are a few checks to make and details to explain first of all. Don't panic: I promise to keep the technical stuff to the minimum you'll need to launch yourself into cyberspace.

About the World Wide Web

The World Wide Web is a global system containing millions of interlinked pages of information. The Web Navigator database provides a straightforward way to view these pages in Notes, translating each Web page into a Notes document.

You can also use the Web Navigator as an interface to several other facets of the Internet, such as Gopher and File Transfer Protocol (FTP) file exchanges. However, the World Wide Web is the bit of the Internet that everyone's excited about, as you've no doubt read.

> **NOTE** To find out about sending mail via the Internet, read Chapter 18.

This chapter does not provide a guide to the Web (there's a whole shelf full of books that do in your local bookstore). In fact, you'll probably find that you don't need any special guidebook to explore the Web using the Web Navigator. Several straightforward search "engines" let you find relevant Web pages; well-constructed Web pages are self-explanatory and contain their own links to items of related interest.

Your principal resources for information on using the Web Navigator are the Web Navigator User's Guide database and booklet. The booklet duplicates the content of the database; which one you use depends on which you have available and your personal preference.

About the Web Navigators

Why is the heading for this section plural? Ah... there are actually two Web Navigators, one to use when you have your own Internet connection and one to use when you don't. The best way to know which version of the Web Navigator to use is to ask your Notes administrator.

If you are lucky, your Notes administrator will already have set up and configured the correct Web Navigator when Notes 4.5 was installed for you. In that case, you only need to skim this section and the one on Setting up the Web Navigator that follows. If, however, you are left to choose and set up the correct Web Navigator on your own, here's what you need to know:

- The *Server Web Navigator* (sometimes called the InterNotes Web Navigator) is a shared Notes database that gives a group of Notes users access to the Internet through a connection at the server level. Use this database if you know that your company has designated an InterNotes server for your group, and provided an Internet connection for the server.
- The *Personal Web Navigator* is a local Notes database that lets you connect to the Internet directly from your own computer without having to go through a Domino server. Use this database if you know that your computer has its own Internet connection (probably a dial-up connection via a modem) and has been set up to use the TCP/IP network protocol. Ask your network administrator whether TCP/IP has been installed and configured on your computer. You will need a fairly large hard disk (500MB or more is recommended) if you plan to make much use of the Personal Web Navigator.

When you retrieve a page from the Web, it is automatically converted into a Notes document and stored in whichever Web Navigator database you are using. Then, when you need to look at the page again, Notes just shows you the copy in the database, which is much faster than getting the page from the Internet again. Storing Web pages within Notes also means that you can browse the Web even when you aren't connected to the Internet!

As you may already have realized, the choice of which version of the Web Navigator to use is unlikely to be yours to make. More likely, some senior systems administrator has already decided whether to set up InterNotes servers for your organization (along with the quite large Web Navigator databases they require), or to support the TCP/IP protocol for individual computers, allowing you to connect to the Internet more directly.

It is very possible that your company has not yet chosen either method of providing Web access within Notes. It may instead have chosen to provide network or dial-up access outside of Notes, perhaps just to certain employees. In general, Internet access through Notes is more convenient for the user. However, supplying the necessary disk space and communications capacity to provide universal access can be expensive and require a fair investment of time from already busy Notes support staff. If you feel there's a compelling reason to have Internet access through Notes, start some gentle-but-insistent lobbying.

Navigators, Navigators, and more Navigators

One of the problems of new technology is adapting old words to fit it. The past decade has seen an explosion in the number of different types of software that has left software developers struggling for meaningful vocabulary. One symptom of the confusion this causes is the burgeoning number of things called *navigators*. The word has obviously been chosen to inspire confident visions of masterful direction, but the sheer number of different navigators out there only adds to the confusion.

If you are using Notes and the Internet, there are several navigators to bear in mind:

- The *Web Navigators*, in personal and server versions, are your interface to the World Wide Web. They are Notes databases that translate Web pages into a form best suited to Notes.
- A Notes *navigator* is a graphical guide to a Notes database, providing an easy means of switching views and folders. The Server Web Navigator database itself uses three graphical navigators of this sort.
- The *Navigation Pane* is one of the three panes in the three-pane window that you met in Chapter 2; if it hasn't been hidden, you can find it at the top left of any view window. The navigation pane can display either the standard arrangement of folders and views, or a graphical navigator.
- The *Navigational Bar* is a Web browsing aid that appears above the Action Bar. It is described in more detail later in the chapter.
- *Netscape Navigator* is one of the most popular commercial Web browsers. The Notes Web Navigators perform a similar function for Notes users.

Setting Up the Web Navigators

Once you have established whether you will be using a Server or Personal Web Navigator, you can get started setting up your copy of Notes to use the correct database. The set-up procedure for each version is broadly similar:

1. If you are going to be using the Personal Web Navigator, make sure your computer meets these requirements:

    - It is configured to run the TCP/IP network protocol.
    - You have arranged a connection to an Internet Service Provider.
    - If you are using a dial-up connection, you have installed a modem and appropriate software.
    - You have a substantial amount of free hard disk space (a 500MB disk drive is recommended).

    If you are going to be using the Server Web Navigator, make sure you know the name of the InterNotes Server you will be using. For either version, if your Notes administrator has told you that you will be using a "proxy server" over a LAN, make sure you have the proxy server's name or IP address.

2. Choose File ➤ Mobile ➤ Edit Current Location, choose Edit Current from the pop-up location indicator on the status bar, or click on the File Mobile Edit Current Location SmartIcon. This opens the current location document, which will look something like the one in Figure 11.1.

> **NOTE** **Location documents let you maintain different settings for each place you use Notes. Mobile users can find out in Chapter 13 how to configure several different location documents. Desk-tethered Notes users will probably only need to bother with one.**

3. In the Retrieve/Open Pages field, choose "from InterNotes server" to have Notes use the Server Web Navigator, or "from Notes workstation" to have Notes use the Personal Web Navigator.

4. If you are using the Server Web Navigator, enter the name of the server that hosts the Web Navigator database in the InterNotes server field. If your company names servers hierarchically, you'll need to include all components of the server's name.

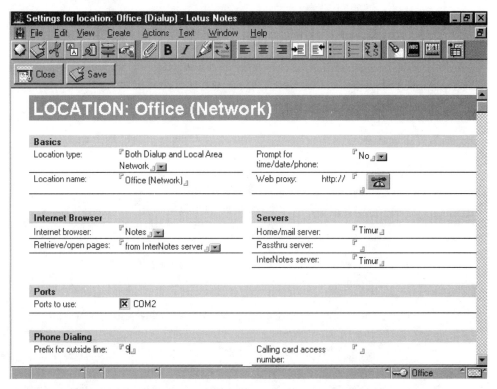

FIGURE 11.1: Use your Location document to tell Notes how you want to connect to the Internet.

5. If you were told that you will be connecting to the Internet via a proxy server, enter its name or IP address in the Web proxy field.

6. Click on the Close button to exit and save the Location document.

7. Choose File ➤ Open URL, press Ctrl+L, or click on the Open URL SmartIcon to have Notes display the Open URL dialog box.

> **NOTE** URL stands for uniform resource locator. It is a standard format for identifying Web pages and other Internet features. The URL for a page on the World Wide Web always begins `http://`.

8. Enter the URL of a Web page, such as `http://www.lotus.com` for the Lotus home page, or `http://www.sybex.com` for the Sybex home page, and click on the Open button. Notes adds the appropriate Web Navigator database to your workspace and opens the Web page you specified.

TIP

For both Web Navigators, the default URL protocol is `http://`.
So if you enter `www.lotus.com`, Notes assumes you mean
`http://www.lotus.com/`.

Using the Web Navigators

If the Web Navigator that you will be using was chosen and set up by someone else, then simply follow steps 7 and 8 above to have Notes open a Web page in the Web Navigator database. If you just set up one of the Web Navigators yourself, you will now be looking at whatever Web page you chose in step 8 of the set-up process.

Your screen will now look something like the one in Figure 11.2, which shows the Lotus home page within the Personal Web Navigator. Notice the new Navigational Bar (the extra line of buttons above the Action Bar), which is detailed later in the chapter.

FIGURE 11.2: A typical Web home page offers links to more specific information.

If you are using the Server Web Navigator, then the page itself will appear similar to the one in Figure 11.2, but the buttons on the Action Bar will be those in Figure 11.3.

FIGURE 11.3: The Server Web Navigator displays slightly different buttons than the Personal Web Navigator.

Finding Your Way around Web Pages

So, now that you've finally made it to a Web page, what can you do here? The possibilities are almost as diverse as the imaginations of computer users around the world. You can check stock prices, research information on markets or competitors, keep up with news in your professional field, and order products and services, much of which probably persuaded your company to give you Web access. And, of course, you can also play games, send electronic Valentine's Day cards, tune in for online soap operas, and find yourself a better job, which might not have been part of your employer's justification. The choice, and responsibility, is yours.

I can't hope to tell you anything much here about what you can find on specific Web pages, but I will show you how Notes lets you move around the Web, and the kinds of things you can expect to see on your screen. The next few sections should make you feel at home with navigating the Web. If you need to find specific information now, you may want to skip ahead to "Searching the Web" in Chapter 12 and return to this section later.

Following Links

The most common way to move from one Web page to another is to follow hypertext links. These are highlighted pieces of text or graphics that you can click on to tell Notes to jump to another Web page. Link text is displayed in blue and underlined, by default. If you are using the Personal Web Navigator and would like it to show up differently, see "Personal Web Navigator Options" in Chapter 12. Often link text is displayed next to a graphical icon that you can click as an alternative.

As you move the cursor over a hypertext link of any sort, Notes changes the cursor to a pointing finger like the one next to this paragraph. To find out where the link will take you, look on the status bar, where Notes displays the destination URL.

To follow the hypertext link, click once on the link text or graphic. One special type of graphical link is called a "clickable map." Basically this is a graphic (usually quite large) in which clicking on different sections takes you to a variety of Web pages. Clickable maps are commonly used for contents pages or to present geographical information on an actual map.

Moving to the Previous (or Next) Page

 Click on the Previous button on the Action Bar to move back to the previous page.

 If you then need to move forward again, click on the Next button on the Action Bar. Obviously, you can only use the Next button when you have previously followed a link—otherwise Notes won't know which link to follow.

Using the History List

When you click on the Previous and Next buttons on the Action Bar, Notes knows which page to go to because it keeps a sequential list of pages you have visited, which it calls the History list. You can use this list yourself to go to an earlier page without having to flip back page by page with the Previous button. You can choose Actions ➤ History to display the History dialog box shown in Figure 11.4. Alternatively, if you are using the Server Web Navigator, you can click on the History button on the Action Bar.

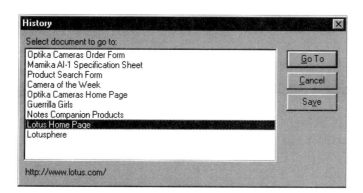

FIGURE 11.4:
The History dialog box lets you skip back and forth among Web pages you have looked at in the current session.

> **NOTE** To store a History list so that you can later reload it and run through the sequence of pages again, read "Creating and Using Web Tours" in Chapter 12.

> **TIP**
>
> When you follow a normal Notes link, Notes opens a new window for each new page. Because navigating through the Web often involves following many links, you could end up having dozens of windows open at once. Instead, when you follow a link from one Web page to another, Notes opens the new page in place of the old one. If you want to jump back to a page you already looked at, you can use the History list to find it.

Reloading a Page

If you suspect that the information on the current Web Page may have changed recently, you will want to make sure that you are looking at the most recent version. You can have Notes reload the page from the Internet (rather than showing the copy stored in the Web Navigator database already) by clicking on the Action Bar's Reload button. This button looks a little different in each version of the Web Navigator.

If you experience problems retrieving a page (maybe certain graphics are displaying partially or not at all), you may also want to try reloading a page from the Internet.

> **TIP**
>
> When you use the Open URL dialog box to open a Web page, you can check a box to force Notes to reload the page from the Internet rather than from the Web Navigator database.

Canceling the Retrieval of a Web Page

If you start to retrieve a Web page from the Internet and then change your mind, you can cancel the retrieval without having to wait for the page to finish loading. Either press Esc or click on the "flowing pages" graphic on the Navigational Bar (described next). You can also cancel a slow or stalled retrieval in this way.

The Navigational Bar

Above the Action Bar on each Web page Notes displays the Navigational Bar, as shown in Figure 11.5. This gives you a quick way to get move through Web pages.

FIGURE 11.5: The Navigational Bar helps you tackle Web pages.

The most prominent part of the Navigational Bar is the long white box into which you can type a Web page's URL. Click on Open to have Notes open the Web page you have specified. The graphic between the URL listing and the Open button plays an animation of billowing documents as Notes retrieves a page; you can click on it to cancel the retrieval. Click on Reset to clear the URL listing and on History to open the History dialog box.

When you are looking at other Notes documents and views, you can display the Navigational Bar by choosing View ➤ Search Bar. In fact, Notes may display either the Navigational Bar or the Search Bar at this point. The Search Bar helps you make full-text searches and is described in Chapter 15. Clicking on the leftmost button on either bar toggles to the other bar. Choosing View ➤ Search Bar again hides the bar.

Your Home Page

Notes also gives you a Home button that you can use as a shortcut to a frequently used Web page. Again, this button will look different depending on which version of the Web Navigator you are using. The Home button may already be set up to take you straight to your company's or department's home page. If not, then you will probably find that it takes you to `http://notes.net/`, a Lotus Web page that gives you lots of information on Notes. See "Personal Web Navigator Options" in Chapter 12 to find out how to tell Notes which URL you want it to use as your home page.

Special Web Items and Other Internet Features

As you wander through the Web you may come upon a whole variety of special pages and other quirks that each have their peculiarities. This book is not the place to look at these items in detail, but here's a quick summary of the more common items:

> **Web forms** Web forms let you provide information to a Web site. They let you search a database, provide address information, and so on. Older Web forms are not guaranteed to keep the information you provide secure from prying, so you should not use them to provide personal or financial information.

> **SSL pages** Newer Web forms use the Secure Socket Layer (SSL) to let you submit information securely. These pages have URLs that begin `https://`, and information you provide is encrypted so that it cannot be read if intercepted in transit.

Password protection Some pages require you to enter a user name and password the first time you retrieve them and then supply the name and password on subsequent visits.

Java applets These are miniature programs embedded in a Web page. Notes includes a Java interpreter to run Java applets.

Netscape plug-ins These are add-on programs that extend the functionality of a Web browser to allow multimedia viewing and similar capabilities. Notes supports Netscape plug-ins, but you must first tell Notes that you want to use them. See "Changing Your User Preferences" in Chapter 14 for more information.

Multimedia objects This technology, supported by Notes, allows the inclusion of such weird and wonderful items as ActiveX controls, components, applets, plug-ins, and media handlers within a Web page.

FTP sites These three letters stand for file transfer protocol, a standardized way of exchanging computer files over the Internet. The URL for an FTP site always begins `ftp://` and points to a particular directory on an Internet-connected computer. If you open this URL, Notes shows you the contents of the directory. Double-click on any of the files listed to download it.

Gopher pages Gopher is an older Internet protocol that is principally used to arrange text information in hierarchies. The URL for a gopher resource always begins `gopher://`. There are relatively few gopher sites still actively maintained.

Mailto You may see URLs in the form `mailto://user@domain.com` on some Web pages. If you click on one of these URLs, Notes opens a new memo that you can use to send a message to the Internet address listed. To send the message, your company needs to have an Internet mail connection (see Chapter 18).

Finger URLs in the form `finger://user@host` let you find information about Internet users or computers connected to the Internet.

USENET newsgroups You won't find these on Web pages, but they are another facet of the Internet that you can access through Notes. If your company has chosen to make newsgroups available, you can find out a little more about Lotus's InterNotes News server add-on in Chapter 10.

Web Navigator Views

Although you'll spend most of your browsing time looking at Web pages, it is useful to understand the view-level structure of the Web Navigator you have chosen. The views and navigators differ quite substantially between the two Web Navigator databases, and so the next two sections look at each in turn.

When you open a Web page by entering its URL in the Open URL dialog box, Notes goes straight to that page without opening a view-level window for the database. If you then follow hypertext links to other Web pages, Notes opens them in the same window. This means that you need to open the database from the workspace in order to see the views and navigators that you can use to organize and browse Web pages.

As with any other Notes database, you can open your chosen Web Navigator by clicking on the appropriate icon in your workspace. The upper icon next to this paragraph is for the Server Web Navigator and the lower icon is for the Personal Web Navigator. If you are using the Server Web Navigator, read the next section to find out about the views and navigators available. If you are using the Personal Web Navigator, skip the next section and read "Views in the Personal Web Navigator," which follows.

Views in the Server Web Navigator

When you open the Server Web Navigator database, you will always see a screen like Figure 11.6, the Home navigator. This provides a convenient starting point for most of your Web work.

The Home navigator has three sections. At the left, the Our Home button gives access to your company's own World Wide Web home page. If your company does not have its own Web page, or has not modified the Server Web Navigator template, you may find that this button takes you to Lotus's home page.

To the right, the Sampler section lets you quickly open selections of Web pages on 10 broad topics.

Along the base of the Home navigator, you'll find five buttons that control special features of the Server Web Navigator. Here's what they do, from left to right:

Database Views Click on this button to open the View navigator, which gives you access to the various views of pages already stored in the Server Web Navigator.

Recommended Click here to open the Recommended navigator, which lets you see which Web pages your colleagues have rated the best.

FIGURE 11.6: The Home navigator is a good jumping-off point for browsing the Web.

Directory Search Use this button to open a form that you can use to search for information in three major World Wide Web indexes. You type the words you want to find, separated by plus signs (+), and click on the icon for the index you want to search: Yahoo!, Lycos, or the Securities and Exchange Commission.

Open URL Click here to bring up the Open URL dialog box and retrieve a specific Web page.

User's Guide Clicking on this button opens the Web Navigator User's Guide.

> **TIP** You can jump straight to Lotus' own home page by clicking on the Lotus logo in the graphic at the top of the Home navigator.

The View Navigator

In contrast to the Home navigator, which offers a quick way to jump to all sorts of Web pages, the View navigator is more focused on the type of Web pages you need to use in your job. That's because it lets you look at views of all the Web pages that you and your colleagues have already retrieved into the Web Navigator database. You can see the View navigator in Figure 11.7.

FIGURE 11.7:
The View navigator lets you view and organize the Web pages already stored in the database.

From top to bottom your choices here are:

My Bookmarks Click on this button to open a folder of bookmarks you have stored to mark Web pages you use frequently. To create a bookmark, drag a Web page listing from the view onto the My Bookmarks button. Bookmarks are explained in more detail in Chapter 12.

Folders Clicking on this button switches to the familiar form of Notes navigator, with the standard type of view and folder hierarchy. Action Bar buttons allow you to return to the Home, View, and Recommended navigators.

All Documents This button opens the main view, showing all the public Web pages in the database. This is the default display when you open the View navigator.

By Host This button switches to a view that categorizes all the public Web pages by the Web site where they can be found.

File Archive Click here to display only those pages with attached files.

Web Tours Click this button to view a list of Web browsing sequences your colleagues have thought worth saving.

Recommended Clicking this button switches to the Recommended navigator.

Back to Home Clicking this button switches back to the Home navigator. You can also return to the Home navigator by clicking on the Lotus InterNotes logo at the top of the Navigation Pane.

The Recommended Navigator

This confusingly named navigator shows you which Web pages your colleagues rate most highly. Figure 11.8 shows the Recommended navigator as you will see it. To find out about rating Web pages yourself, see "Sharing the Fruits of Your Web Browsing" in Chapter 12.

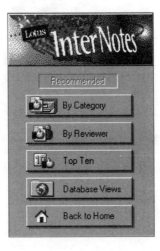

FIGURE 11.8:
Find out how your colleagues rate Web pages by browsing in the Recommended navigator.

Here, the choices are:

By Category Click on this button to see a view of recommended pages organized into 15 predefined categories.

By Reviewer Clicking on this button categorizes recommended pages by the person who suggested them.

Top Ten This button shows you the 10 Web pages your coworkers have rated most highly.

Database Views Clicking on this button switches to the View navigator.

Back to Home Clicking on this button switches back to the Home navigator. Again, you can also click the Lotus InterNotes logo at the top of the Navigation Pane.

Views in the Personal Web Navigator

By default, if you have never used the Personal Web Navigator before, Notes will open it to the All Documents view with a large preview pane on the right-hand side of the screen, as shown in Figure 11.9. Subsequently, when you open the database, Notes will show whichever view of the database you were last using.

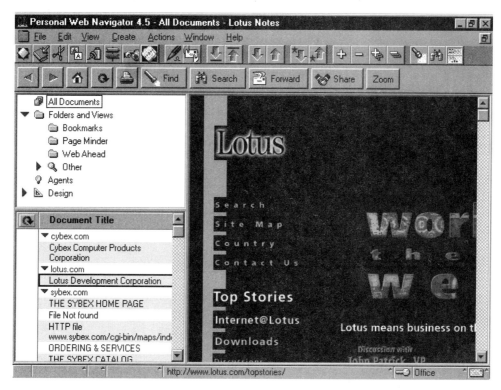

FIGURE 11.9: The Personal Web Navigator's All Documents view shows you all the Web pages already stored in the database.

The default arrangement of this view lets you use the view pane in the lower left corner to select Web pages already in the database, and see the pages displayed in the preview pane on the right. As with any other Notes database, you can use View ➤ Arrange Preview to manipulate the arrangement of the panes in this view to best suit you.

In the Navigation Pane you will find three folders listed in the Folders and Views section. The Bookmarks folder lets you see frequently used Web pages that you have marked for easy access. To create a bookmark, drag a Web page listing from the view into the Bookmarks folder. Bookmarks are explained in more detail in Chapter 12.

The Page Minder folder lets you keep tabs on a Web page that you expect to be updated. Notes keeps a watch on all pages you drag into this folder and notifies you if they change. Placing a Web page in the Web Ahead folder tells Notes to preload all the pages to which this page links. Both Page Minder and Web Ahead are described in more detail in Chapter 12.

Below these folders, you can click on the Other heading to see three extra views. The File Archive view shows all Web pages in the database with file attachments. The House Cleaning view ranks Web pages by the amount of storage space they consume, to help you keep the size of the Personal Web Navigator in check. The Web Tours view shows any Web browsing sequences you have chosen to store in the database.

Creating Web Tours is one of the many advanced features of the Personal and Server Web Navigators covered in Chapter 12.

Chapter 12

DOING MORE WITH THE WEB NAVIGATOR

FEATURING

- **Searching the Web**
- **Using Bookmarks**
- **Sharing Web pages**
- **Web Ahead and Page Minder**
- **Web Tours**
- **Using other Web browsers**
- **Internet options**

Once you become a keen Web user, you will be glad to pick up a few extra skills to help you find the pages you want and incorporate the Web into the way you use Notes. In this chapter you can discover all about keeping track of your favorite Web pages and pointing them out to your colleagues, using Notes to scan for changed and linked pages, customizing the Web Navigators, and searching for and within Web pages.

Searching the Web

It will not have escaped you that the World Wide Web contains a massive amount of information. Obviously, you could benefit from any means of cutting through this encyclopedic breadth and finding the information you seek. To do this you can use any of several different search methods.

Standard Notes Search Methods

Because both Web Navigators are Notes databases, you can apply all the same search methods to the Web as you would elsewhere in Notes. Specifically, you can:

- Use text searching to find words or phrases in a single Web page.
- Use Quick Search to find the next occurrence of a piece of text in a Web Navigator view.
- Use the Search Bar to select documents in a Web Navigator view that contain a particular piece of text.
- Make complex full-text searches of Web pages in a Web Navigator view.

NOTE You can find out more about full-text searching in Chapter 15 and about other text searches in Chapter 14.

Providing a full-text index for a Web Navigator can add greatly to the database's usefulness. However, there are two potential drawbacks. Web Navigator databases already tend to grow in size very quickly, and a full-text index can increase that size by a large fraction. The contents of a Web Navigator also change frequently, requiring frequent reindexing.

If you use a Personal Web Navigator, the choice of whether to add a full-text index is likely to be your own. However, Server Web Navigator users will probably have to live with whatever decision their Notes administrator has made.

Using Web Search Engines

You can also search the Web beyond Notes. A number of third-party Web indexes have sprung up to meet the growth in Web use. These sites constantly survey the entire Web firmament and distill it in their proprietary, but comparatively comprehensible indexes. Notes is set up to provide access to several of these by default.

Web Searches in the Server Web Navigator

To access these indexes from the Server Web Navigator, click on the Directory Search icon in the Home navigator, or choose Actions ➤ Directory Search in the View or Recommended navigator. Notes opens an Internet Directory Search form.

Enter the subject for which you want to search in the box provided. If there is more than one word, separate them with plus (+) symbols. Then click on one of the three search buttons provided: Yahoo! and Lycos are virtual industry standards in Web searching; the Securities and Exchange Commission is an obviously sensible place to look for information on U.S. companies.

Web Searches in the Personal Web Navigator

To perform a Web search from the Personal Web Navigator, click on the Search button on the Action Bar, or choose Actions ➤ Search. Notes opens whichever Web search engine is set as the default for the database (initially it is Yahoo!). Follow the conventions of the individual search engine to compose and submit your search.

To change the default search engine, choose Actions ➤ Internet Options. The second section on the form, Search Options, gives you a choice of four popular search engines: AltaVista, Excite, Lycos, and Yahoo! You can also select Other to provide the URL for a different search engine, if you prefer.

Using Web Sites' Own Indexes

Many Web sites have their own indexes and search mechanisms, and Notes is programmed to recognize these and alert you. If you retrieve an indexed Web page, Notes displays a Search button on the Action Bar. The Web page itself will most likely draw attention to the fact that it is indexed.

If you click on the Search button, Notes opens a Search Internet Server dialog box. Enter your search text and then click on OK to have Notes relay the search to the Web server and retrieve the results.

More Web Navigator Features

Both types of Web Navigator boast an assortment of additional features that, while not central to Web browsing, you may find very useful. You can make Bookmarks for pages you use often, share pages with your colleagues, have Notes preload pages and check pages for updates, transfer files with FTP, and use Gopher. First, however, we'll look quickly at the multitudinous ways to open Web pages.

50 Ways to Open a Web Page

You have seen some ways to get to Web pages in Notes, but there are surprisingly many (though perhaps not 50). Here they are in summary:

- If you know a Web page's URL, you can open the page directly from anywhere in Notes. To enter a URL, you can click on the Open URL SmartIcon, or on the Open button at the top of any Web page. You can also choose File ➤ Open URL, or press Ctrl+L. Notes displays a dialog box in which you enter the Web page's URL. A checkbox lets you choose whether you want to force Notes to reload the page from the Internet or just use the one in the database.
- In the Server Web Navigator you can also open a specific Web page by choosing Actions ➤ Open URL in the View navigator or Recommended navigator, or by clicking on the Open URL icon in the Home navigator.
- You can browse the views in either type of Web Navigator, double-click on a row to look at a Web page that takes your fancy, and mark your favorites with Bookmarks.
- In the Server Web Navigator, you can take a Web Tour to see a sequence of pages suggested by a colleague. You can also use the 10 sampler lists in the Home navigator as a quick way to find Web pages of a particular type.
- You can click on text and graphical hypertext links on Web pages to jump to other Web pages.
- You can set an option in your User Preferences (see Chapter 14) to have Notes display URLs that occur in documents other than the Web Navigator as green, underlined text hotspots on which you can click to jump straight to the relevant Web page.
- You can enter a URL in the Quick Search dialog box that appears when you start typing in *any* view of *any* database. Normally Notes looks for an item in the view that begins with the text you type, but if you enter a URL, Notes will open the Web page instead.
- You can enter URLs in the Navigational Bar above each Web page. In other views and documents, choose View ➤ Search Bar to display the Search/Navigational Bar.

Using Bookmarks

As you find yourself using the Web more frequently and more confidently, you may want to mark your favorite locations for easy reference. Of course, Notes already makes it easier to find Web pages you have used before by storing them in the Web Navigator database. But most popular Web browsers allow you to create Bookmarks for your favorite pages, and Notes is no exception.

If you are using the Server Web Navigator, Notes stores marked pages in the private folder My Bookmarks; in the Personal Web Navigator the pages are stored in the Bookmarks folder. Server Web Navigator users should be aware that any private folders in the database (including your My Bookmarks folder) may be purged periodically by routines designed to perform housekeeping in the database.

To place a Web page you are looking at in the My Bookmarks folder, click on the Bookmarks button on the Action Bar (the folder button in the Personal Web Navigator) or choose Actions ➤ Move to Folder. Notes opens the Move to Folder dialog box, in which you select the My Bookmarks folder (just called Bookmarks in the Personal Web Navigator) and click on Add. You can also drag and drop Web pages from the View Pane into the Bookmarks and My Bookmarks folders, or onto the Bookmarks icon in the Server Web Navigator's View navigator.

> **TIP**
> The Bookmarks folder works just like any other folder in Notes. If you want, you can use Create ➤ Folder to set up other folders in which to organize Web pages. You can even create subfolders within the Bookmarks folder. In the Server Web Navigator, of course, these folders are private.

Importing Bookmarks from Another Web Browser

If you have switched from using another browser to using the Personal Web Navigator to access the Internet, Notes may be able to convert Bookmarks you have created in the other browser. Notes can import Bookmarks from Netscape Navigator and favorites from Microsoft Internet Explorer. Here's how to do it:

1. First of all, find out the full location of your Netscape Bookmarks file or Microsoft Favorites directory.

2. From the view level of the Personal Web Navigator, choose Actions ➤ Import Navigator Bookmarks or Actions ➤ Import Microsoft Favorites.

3. Notes displays the Import Bookmarks or Import Favorites dialog box as appropriate.

- For Netscape Navigator, enter the filename of your Netscape Bookmarks, such as `c:\netscape\navigator\bookmark.htm`. You can use the Browse button to help locate your Bookmarks file.
- For Microsoft Internet Explorer, enter the directory name of your Microsoft Favorites, such as `c:\win95\profiles\username\favorites`.

4. Click on OK.

> **NOTE** Later in this chapter you can find out how to use Netscape Navigator or Microsoft Internet Explorer as an alternative to the Notes Web Navigators.

Sharing the Fruits of Your Web Browsing

As you trawl the oceans of good, bad, and (quite often) indifferent information available on the World Wide Web, you may find some pages that you would like to bring to the attention of your coworkers. Each of the Web Navigator databases gives several means of doing this. The various methods divide broadly into those that rely on Notes mail and those based on sharing pages in the Server Web Navigator.

Forwarding a Link to a Web Page

Perhaps the least fancy and most convenient means of sharing your Web findings is to send someone a link to the page. There are two easy ways to do this:

- In either Web Navigator you can choose Edit ➤ Copy As Link ➤ Document Link from a Web page or with a page highlighted in a view. This puts a link to this page on the Clipboard. Then choose Create ➤ Mail ➤ Memo to start a new memo, and use Edit ➤ Paste to place the URL in the memo's body field. You can use this same technique to place a URL link in any rich-text field in any document.

- In the Personal Web Navigator you also have another means of forwarding a URL. Open the Web page whose link you want to forward, or highlight it in a  view. Then click on the Share button on the Action Bar. Notes opens the Share Options dialog box (this doesn't mean that you are going to get rich quick on company stock). Select the radio button marked Forward Only the URL and enter the name or names of those to whom you want to send this message. You can look up the names in your Notes address books if necessary. Then click on OK.

Forwarding a Web Page

If you want to send information from a Web page to someone who doesn't have access to the Web Navigator databases, or you want to include part of a Web page, you can forward the actual content of a Web page, rather than a link. To forward an open Web page or one highlighted in a view, click on the Forward button on the Action Bar or choose Actions ➤ Forward. Notes copies the contents of the page into a new memo that you can address and edit as you wish.

> **WARNING** If you plan to forward a Web page to someone who doesn't use Notes, you should consider whether the recipient will be able to view the page in the same form that you send it. See Chapter 18 for more details on sending mail beyond Notes.

Copying Web Pages to the Server Web Navigator

If you use the Personal Web Navigator but many of your colleagues use the Server Web Navigator, you can let them know about useful Web pages by copying them to the server database. Click on the Share button on the Action Bar and choose the radio button marked Copy Page to Shared Web Navigator Database. Notes informs you of the server and filename of the database to which it will copy your page. Use Actions ➤ Internet Options to change this location.

Recommending Web Pages to Others

Users of the Server Web Navigator (and those Personal Web Navigator users whose colleagues use the Server Web Navigator) can also rate Web pages as a means of recommending them to their colleagues. If you come across a Web page that you would like to review for your coworkers, here's how to do it:

1. 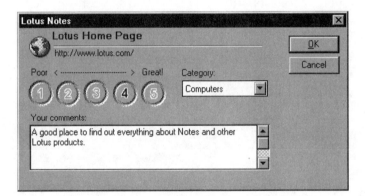 In the Server Web Navigator, click on the Recommend button or choose Actions ➤ Recommend. Notes displays the dialog box in Figure 12.1. In the Personal Web Navigator, click on the Share button, or choose Actions ➤ Share, and then select the radio button marked Create Rating in Shared Web Navigator Database. The Share Options dialog box now looks quite similar to Figure 12.1.

FIGURE 12.1: Rate Web pages from 1 to 5, and add your comments for others to read.

2. Choose a rating between one and five, and assign the page to one of 15 broad categories available. Then enter any comments you would like to add in the box below.
3. Click on OK. If you are using the Personal Web Navigator, Notes will copy the page to the Server Web Navigator.

You can then see the page in the views available through the Server Web Navigator's Recommended navigator.

Creating and Using Web Tours

If you like the idea of recommending Web pages to your colleagues, another feature you may find useful is the Web Tour. Users of both types of Web Navigator can create Web Tours, which are really just a way of storing History lists to replay later on. If you use the Personal Web Navigator, any Web Tours you create will be for your own benefit. However, Web Tours created in the Server Web Navigator are available to all the database's users.

To set up a Web Tour:

1. Browse the Web, opening all the documents that you want to include in your Web Tour.
2. Choose Actions ➤ History, or click on the History button on the Navigational Bar, or click on the History button on the Server Web Navigator's Action Bar. Notes opens the History dialog box.
3. Click on the Save button. Notes opens a new Web Tour document containing your History list.
4. Enter a title for your Web Tour.
5. If you want, you can edit the Web Tour, perhaps to change the sequence of pages. Each page in the tour takes two lines in the list. The first gives the page's name as you see it on the title bar; the second gives the page's URL.
6. Describe your tour in the Comments field.
7. Close the new Web Tour document.

If you are using the Server Web Navigator, you can view the available Web Tours by clicking on Web Tours in the View navigator. In the Personal Web Navigator, you will find the Web Tours view under Other in the list of views and folders. Double-click on the name of a tour in the view and Notes opens the Web Tour document so you can see where the tour will take you.

From the Web Tour document, you can click on the Load Tour button on the Action Bar to place the tour in your History list and load the first Web page. Then use the Previous and Next buttons and the History list to advance through the tour.

Using Page Minder

The content of many Web pages is relatively static, changing only when someone decides to work on revising it. Many others, however, are either regularly updated manually, or are linked dynamically to a changing source of information. These types of changing pages include such information as stock quotes, status reports, and schedules of upcoming events.

If you use the Personal Web Navigator, you can use a feature called Page Minder to have Notes automatically monitor pages of this sort and notify you when they change. Once you have set up Page Minder, all you need to do to keep tabs on a particular Web page is to drag it into the Page Minder folder.

To set up Page Minder:

1. Choose File ➤ Tools ➤ User Preferences and check Enable Scheduled Local Agents in the Startup Options sections on the Basics tab. Chapter 14 tells you more about setting your user preferences. Click on OK.

2. In the Personal Web Navigator, choose Actions ➤ Internet Options. Notes opens the Internet Options document. The Page Minder Agent Preferences section is towards the bottom of the screen.

3. Click on the Enable Page Minder button. Notes opens a dialog box that asks you to specify a server on which to run Page Minder. Choose Local and click on OK. Notes warns you to make sure you have changed your user preferences to allow local background agents—don't worry, you just did that.

4. Choose the frequency with which you want Notes to check for updates. Your options are hourly, every four hours, daily, or weekly.

5. Choose what you want Notes to do if the page has changed. You can have Notes mail you just a notification or the entire page.

6. By default Notes will send *you* notifications of any changes. To send them to someone else, enter the recipient's name in the box or use the Address button to choose from a list.

7. Close the Internet Options document.

Now you can drag pages to the Page Minder folder to have Notes track them for updates. If you want to turn Page Minder off, return to the Internet Options document and click on the Disable Page Minder button.

Using Web Ahead

Web Ahead is a special feature of the Personal Web Navigator that lets you tell Notes to preload all the links that extend from Web pages you have chosen. It works similarly to Page Minder in that you enable and configure a local background agent first of all. Then Notes automatically preloads the links for any pages you have dragged to a special folder.

To set up Web Ahead:

1. Choose File ➤ Tools ➤ User Preferences and check Enable Scheduled Local Agents in the Startup Options sections on the Basics tab. Chapter 14 tells you more about setting your user preferences. Click on OK.

2. In the Personal Web Navigator, choose Actions ➤ Internet Options. Notes opens the Internet Options document. The Web Ahead Agent Preferences section is towards the bottom of the screen.

3. Click on the Enable Web Ahead button. Notes opens a dialog box that asks you to specify a server on which to run Web Ahead. Choose Local and click on OK. Notes asks you to make sure you have changed your user preferences to allow local background agents—you did that in step 1.

4. Choose the number of levels down you want Notes to search to preload links. Choosing just one level loads all the linked pages specified by URLs on the page you nominate. Choosing two levels loads all the pages specified by URLs on the linked pages already preloaded, and so on. Notes offers a maximum of four levels of preloading, which should be enough for most mortals.

5. Close the Internet Options document.

Now you can drag pages to the Web Ahead folder. Every half hour while you are running Notes on your computer, Notes will retrieve linked pages to the depth you specified. If you want to turn Web Ahead off, return to the Internet Options document and click on the Disable Web Ahead button.

Using a Different Web Browser

If you have become familiar with the *modus operandi* of a particular Web browser and are loath to switch to this new-fangled Notes Web Navigator, you can tell Notes to open Web pages with your preferred browser instead.

Choose File ➤ Mobile ➤ Edit Current Location and select your favorite alternative browser in the Internet browser field. Notes offers you two popular choices—Microsoft Internet Explorer and Netscape Navigator—or you can select Other to choose another browser.

If you chose Other in the Internet Browser field, Notes displays a new Internet Browser Path field and a button that opens a file dialog box in which you select your Internet browser's path and filename.

Disconnected Web Browsing

Your Web access doesn't have to stop when you go on the road. If you travel with a notebook computer, you can bring along your Personal Web Navigator or a local replica of the Server Web Navigator and view Web pages even if you don't have an Internet connection. Chapter 13 contains full details of this and everything else for the mobile Notes user.

From Notes to the Web

As well as bringing Web information into Notes, you can also place Notes documents on the Web. Lotus' Domino server technology, provided with Notes 4.5, provides an interactive means of publishing Notes databases on the Internet. That level of database and application development is beyond the scope of this book. If you are interested in Domino and Domino.Action, you may want to take a look at *Mastering Lotus Notes 4.5 and Domino*, also from Sybex.

Setting Internet Options

Notes lets you set options relating to the Internet in several different places. Some options are set in your user preferences. You can read about these in Chapter 14. Other options are set in your current Location document, some of which are described in the text of this chapter and Chapter 11. All these options are the same for users of either type of Web Navigator.

As well as the Web Navigator options you have already encountered in the Location document, there are many others in the Advanced section that impact your Web browsing. Most of these options are well beyond the scope of this book, and you should turn to the Notes Help 4.5 and the Lotus Notes and the Internet databases for more information.

If you have an older, slower computer or modem, you may want to have Notes display images only after it has loaded and displayed the rest of the page. To set this option, enter the database or highlight its icon in the workspace, choose File ➤ Database ➤ Properties, and click on the Basics tab. Check the box marked Display Images after Loading.

If you choose to display images after loading, then you can also choose whether Notes always loads graphics in Web pages, or only on request (that is, when you click on them). You will find this option in the Advanced section of your Location document (File ➤ Mobile ➤ Edit Current Location).

Personal Web Navigator Options

For Personal Web Navigator users, many options that relate to Web use are set in the database's Internet Options document. You may have already used this several times to control such features as Web searches, Web Ahead, and Page Minder. This section summarizes your other Internet options in this document.

Open the Internet Options document by choosing Actions ➤ Internet Options. You should see a screen like the one shown in Figure 12.2.

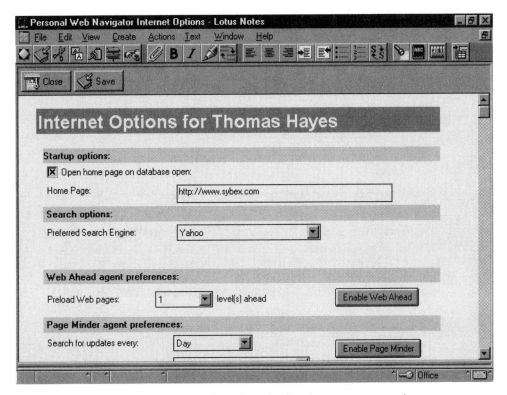

FIGURE 12.2: Customize the Personal Web Navigator by changing your Internet options.

Changing the options in each section of this document produces the following effects:

> **Startup Options** Here you can enter a URL that Notes will regard as your home Web page. If you want, you can also tell Notes to open this page automatically every time you open the Personal Web Navigator.

The next three sections—Search Options, Web Ahead Agent Preferences, and Page Minder Agent Preferences—were discussed previously, and let you specify your preferred Web search engine and allow you to enable Web Ahead and Page Minder.

Database Purge Options This section lets you tell Notes to keep down the size of the Web Navigator database by certain means. You can choose to reduce fully stored Web pages to URL links (or remove them from the database entirely) if they haven't been read within the past 15, 30, 60, or 90 days. If you choose this option, you need to click on the Enable Housekeeping button and make sure that you have enabled local background agents in your user preferences (see Chapter 14). You can choose instead to adopt a less interventionist approach, and merely have Notes warn you when the database exceeds a certain number of megabytes.

Collaboration Options Use this section to specify the location of a Server Web Navigator to which you wish to sometimes transfer Web pages (rated and unrated).

Presentation Preferences Here you can choose the style, font, and size that Notes should use in displaying six key components of Web pages. A checkbox tells Notes to additionally store the entire text of a Web page in its native HTML format in each corresponding Notes document.

Network Options This section contains just a single button, giving you a quick means of editing Internet options in the current location document.

Short of becoming a Notes developer, you have come as far as you can in learning about Notes and the Web. If you still seek greater challenges in Notes, may I suggest leaving your office… and using Notes on the road, the subject of Chapter 13.

Chapter 13

MOBILE NOTES

Most of this book has assumed that you're using Notes at an immobile, network-connected computer in a stuffy office. One of the most useful things about Notes, however, is that it lets you keep in touch with the office without having to show your face. You can run Notes on a notebook computer or a home computer, or from a branch office that has computers but no network.

To use Notes without being connected to a network, you need to pay a *little* more heed to the mechanics of getting your computer to talk to a Domino server. Don't worry, though. This process is relatively painless.

How Are You Using Notes?

First of all, it's useful to establish just how your remote computer is going to communicate with your company's Notes network. These are the most likely scenarios:

- You're using Notes on a notebook computer and connecting to your company's Domino servers via a modem and a phone line. This is probably the most common scenario for Notes users who have to travel at least some of the time in their jobs.
- You're using Notes on a notebook computer that is sometimes directly connected to a network (perhaps through a docking station) and sometimes dials in to a Domino server. With this configuration, your computer sometimes acts as a regular network-connected workstation and sometimes as the notebook computer in the first example.
- You're using Notes on a home computer or at a remote office where your connection to a Domino server is through a modem and a phone line. In practice, this is a lot like the first example. The main difference is that you are more likely to always call the same server.
- You're using Notes on any kind of computer, but you have *no* need to exchange mail or use *any* shared databases. Occasionally, you might end up in this situation—you might be working at home putting together a reference documentation database that isn't yet available as a shared database. If you're sure you don't need access to Notes mail or any shared databases, then you needn't worry about any of the information in the rest of this chapter. Of course, once you're done putting the database together, you still need to transfer it to a Domino server.

The first three scenarios all require you to get Notes to communicate with a server through a modem and over a phone line. They only differ in a few niceties, such as the need to dial different servers at different times or to switch from modem to network communications.

In most of this chapter, I'll assume that you're using a notebook computer to connect to your company's Domino server via a modem, but the procedure would be the same for a desktop computer that connected via a modem.

All about Replication

Before we can get you exchanging e-mail from a moving train, we need to look at how Notes lets users throughout a company have access to the same information. This process is called *database replication*. Although it sounds like something from a 1950s science fiction movie, database replication is actually quite manageable.

Replication is a special way of copying a database so that the copy always contains the same information as the original database. Actually, the replica doesn't always contain exactly the same information. Instead, Notes compares the two databases at scheduled intervals and brings each one up to date with changes that have been made to the other.

Replication allows a company's offices in Seattle and El Paso to share the same customer tracking database. Each office actually has its own replica of the database. The company's Domino servers call each other (perhaps every hour, perhaps just once a day) and exchange additions, modifications, and deletions between the database replicas that they have in common. Thus, the people in El Paso have access to changes made by the people in Seattle, and vice-versa.

"Great," you're thinking. "Now I know how Notes allows people in different parts of my company to work with the same information. But what's that got to do with my notebook computer?" The answer is that the same replication process makes sure that you're working with the same information as the people back at the office.

In a nutshell, you set up replicas on your notebook for the databases that are most important to you. Then, each time you have your computer call your Domino server, Notes replicates the databases to keep you abreast of your deskbound colleagues' antics and to update them with changes you have made to the databases.

So much for the information-sharing part. How do you get your notebook to talk to your Domino server?

Getting Started

Most of the rest of this chapter tells you how to set up Notes so that you can make your first remote connection to your Domino server. After you've made the first connection successfully, the procedure for subsequent ones is much simpler.

The general outline of the setup procedure is:

1. Tell Notes what sort of modem you have.
2. Tell Notes which server to call and what phone number to use.
3. Tell Notes how to reach a server from each location at which you'll be working.
4. Set up and populate local replicas of the server-based databases to which you want access.

Once this setup is complete, you can take your notebook on the road and dial in for mail and database updates.

> **NOTE** Most mobile Notes users should be able to get set up by working through this chapter from start to finish. However, many factors affect the successful mobile use of Notes, and you may run into problems that aren't covered in detail in this chapter. If you do, you can try to resolve them yourself with the aid of the Mobile Notes section in the Notes Help and Help Lite databases (choose Mobile Notes from the Navigator, or Contents ➤ How Do I...? and then Do Everyday Tasks ➤ 08 Use Mobile Notes), or you can enlist the support of your Notes administrator.

Telling Notes about Your Modem

Maybe I've implied this pretty strongly already, but just in case there's any confusion, I'll spell it out right now: For you to connect to a Domino server without a direct network connection, your computer needs to have a modem and you need to have access to an analog phone line.

Most modern modems work fine with Notes. Modems are rated by the number of bits per second (bps) of information they can transmit. The most common speeds are 2,400bps, 9,600bps, 14.4Kbps (14,400bps), 28.8Kbps, 33.6Kbps, and 57.6Kbps. If you have a 2,400bps modem, replicating databases and exchanging mail takes a long time. If you are lucky enough to have a 57.6Kbps modem, you'll save a bundle on hotel telephone bills.

An *analog phone line* is just another term for a regular phone line. The other type of phone line is a digital line. The problem is that both types tend to use the same style of connectors (called RJ-11), and you usually can't tell which type of phone line you have by looking at the jack.

Here are two clues that suggest your phone is plugged into an analog line:

- Pick up the handset and dial a few numbers, listening to the tones the phone makes as you dial. If the pitch (the note) varies with each number, you should have an analog line.
- Look at the underside of the phone. If it has a sticker on its underside listing its FCC ringer equivalence number (REN), you can be pretty sure that the line it's plugged into is analog.

> **WARNING** Many notebook modems can sustain severe damage if they are plugged into a digital line, so it pays to check whether the telephone line you're connected to is digital or analog.

Enabling a Port for Your Modem

Once you've established that you do indeed have a modem, you need to tell Notes about it. The first step is to let Notes know that you even have a modem. Choose File ➤  Tools ➤ User Preferences and then click on the Ports icon, or click on the File Preferences Ports SmartIcon, and you'll see the Ports panel of the User Preferences dialog box, shown in Figure 13.1.

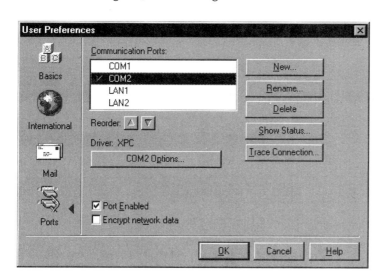

FIGURE 13.1:
The Ports panel in the User Preferences dialog box lets you tell Notes that you do indeed have a modem.

NOTE

It goes without saying (but not without writing) that you should be using the copy of Notes that's on your notebook computer and not the one on your regular network computer (if you have one). Telling Notes about the modem in your desktop computer won't help you dial in from the notebook. If Notes isn't installed on your notebook computer or it hasn't been set up for you, turn to Appendices A and B.

All you have to do in this dialog box is select the name of the port to which your modem is connected and check the Port Enabled box. The difficult part is knowing to which port your modem is connected.

- In Windows or OS/2, it will be one of the COM ports and almost certainly either COM1 or COM2. If you have a serial mouse (which plugs into your computer with a connector that has nine pins in two rows), the mouse is probably connected to COM1 and your modem to COM2.
- Similarly, in Unix, your mouse is usually connected to Serial1 and your modem to Serial2.
- On the Macintosh, you've got it easy. You have a choice of ports with labels like Modem and Printer (and maybe AppleTalk and MacTCP). As you've already guessed, you want to enable the Modem port.

When you've selected the correct port, verify that the Port Enabled box is checked and the XPC driver is listed.

If you don't know what port your modem is connected to, you probably will have to ask someone to find out for you. Who that might be varies from one company to another, but your Notes administrator would be a good person to try first. If you are going to ask for outside help (and there's no need to feel bad about it), you might as well get answers to as many of the following questions as you can, because you are going to need this information later.

- What port is my modem connected to?
- What make and model of modem do I have?
- What is its top speed?
- What dial-in servers are available for me to use?

- What are their phone numbers?
- If my home server isn't among the dial-in servers I can use, can I use a Passthru server or hunt group to reach it? If so, what is the name and phone number of the Passthru server or hunt group?

TIP

If you have more than one port enabled (for example, you have network and dial-up connections), Notes assumes that your preference is to use the first enabled port in the list. To change the order of ports in the list, use the pair of arrow buttons marked Reorder.

Telling Notes What Kind of Modem You Have

Notes now knows that you have a modem and which port to use to talk to it. Now you need to tell Notes what kind of modem you have so that Notes can communicate at the right speed and adopt a dialect that your modem understands.

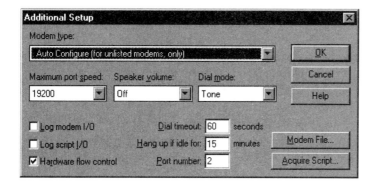

FIGURE 13.2:
It's named "Additional Setup," but this dialog box should really be called "Tell Me about Your Modem."

Click on the button marked *Port* Options (the exact text on the button depends on which port you selected) on the Ports panel. This brings you to the Additional Setup dialog box shown in Figure 13.2. Yet again, there's a profusion of list boxes, push buttons, and checkboxes for you to play with. Actually, you only need to do two or three simple things here to tell Notes about your modem.

Modem Type

Your first step is to look in the Modem Type list for the name of your modem. Most modems use the same basic language, but each manufacturer has its own interpretation. Notes comes with profiles of about 150 of the most popular modems. If yours is named in the list, select its name and advance to Go (or at least to the next step).

If your modem isn't listed by name, look for a modem with a very similar name (perhaps the same manufacturer and speed, but a slightly different model). Your next resort is the line labeled Auto Configure near the bottom of the list. If you try the Auto Configure setting and it doesn't work for your modem, try Generic All-Speed Modem File. If none of these choices work for your modem, it's time to call your affable Notes administrator.

Maximum Port Speed

Your second action in the Additional Setup dialog box is to select a Maximum Port Speed for your modem. You should select the top speed at which your modem is capable of communicating. If your modem's top speed isn't listed (14.4Kbps and 28.8Kbps modems, for example), choose the next higher speed that is listed (19,200bps or 38,400bps). Unfortunately, if you have a slow modem, you can't make it any faster by choosing a higher maximum speed setting here.

Speaker Volume

You may also want to change the Speaker Volume setting. This governs whether or not you hear the characteristic squeaky warbling sound of the modem at the beginning of each call you make to the server, and if so, how loud the sound is.

It's a good idea to have the speaker on for the first few calls you make, until you know for certain that your modem is connecting to the server. If you have been experiencing problems connecting to your Domino server, turning this setting on and listening to the sounds may help your Notes administrator or a technician diagnose the problem. If you do choose to listen to your modem, you can decide whether to believe the technical explanation that the sound is the two modems negotiating a handshake, or my editor's contention that it is a mermaid in a blender.

Once you've chosen a modem type, speed, and warbling volume, click on OK to save your selection and on OK again to close the User Preferences dialog box.

Telling Notes Whom to Call

Next you're going to tell Notes which servers you want to call and their phone numbers. If you didn't already find out what dial-in servers are available to you and what their phone numbers are, now is the time to do so.

If Your Domino Server Isn't a Dial-In Server

Not every Domino server is a dial-in server, and it's entirely possible that your home server (the one you normally use) isn't among those that you can dial into. If it's not, you have two options:

- Use Notes 4.5's "server Passthru" (perhaps with a hunt group) to dial a different server and then connect to your home server.
- Move your mail file to a server that you can dial into (that is, change your home server).

This decision is likely to be made by your Notes administrator, but to begin using Notes via a modem you will need to know if you will be using a Passthru server.

Specifying a Server Phone Number

You tell Notes the details of how to call each server by creating a Server Connection document for each one in your Personal Name & Address Book.

NOTE This is just one use of your **Personal Name & Address Book.** Chapter 18 shows you how to use it to draw up your own groups, record external e-mail addresses, and make shortcuts for the people you write to most.

To open a new Server Connection document, choose File ➤ Mobile ➤ Server Phone Numbers. Notes opens your Personal Name & Address Book. Then click on Add Connection and you'll see a new connection document like the one in Figure 13.3.

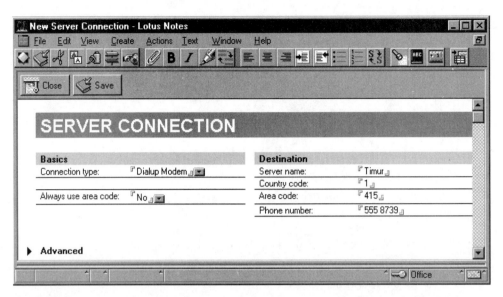

FIGURE 13.3: Server Connection documents in your Personal Name & Address Book tell Notes how to get in touch with your favorite dial-up servers.

There are just three items to enter here:

Connection Type Choose Dialup Modem.

Server Name Type in the name of the Domino server that you're calling.

Phone Number Type in the server's phone number, with a country code and area code if necessary. For the moment, don't include any numbers you need to dial to get an outside line or to make a calling card call—there's a place for those later.

> **TIP**
>
> If you have more than one phone number for a particular server, you can enter them all, separated by semicolons. Then, if one number is busy, Notes will try the others.

Save this new document and close the window. Then create similar documents for any other servers you will need to call directly. If you are going to connect to servers via a hunt group, read the next section to dial a single number to connect with one of several servers; you don't need to create separate server documents for each.

Notes summarizes the servers for which you've created connection documents in the Server ➤ Connections view of your Personal Name & Address Book.

Passthru Servers and Hunt Groups

If your home server is not equipped to let you dial in with a modem, Notes 4.5 lets you dial a connected server and then make a "Passthru" connection to your home server. If your Notes administrator has told you that you should use a Passthru connection to your home server, you need to tell Notes how to make the connection. You have two options:

Using the same Passthru server Most people will always use the same Passthru server from any particular location (while traveling, at home, at a branch office, etc.). These people only need to set a default Passthru server for the location and tell Notes how to call that server. When they try to connect to a server for which there is no Server Connection document, Notes automatically dials the default Passthru server instead. If this situation applies to you, see the next section, "Setting Up a Default Passthru Connection."

Using more than one Passthru server A few people will need to use more than one Passthru server from any one location. These people must tell Notes which Passthru server to use to connect to each Domino server. They still should set up a default Passthru server for each location, but in addition, they need to tell Notes when to use Passthru servers other than the default one. If you are in this special category, see both of the following sections.

Setting Up a Default Passthru Connection

To tell Notes how to contact the default Passthru server that you will use:

1. Create a dial-up Server Connection document (as in "Specifying a Server Phone Number" above) for the Passthru server.

   - Select a connection type of Dialup Modem.
   - Enter the Passthru server's name and phone number.

2. Your only remaining step is to name the default Passthru server in your Location document (see "Telling Notes Where You Are" later in this chapter).

TIP   If you set up multiple remote locations, such as Home, Travel, Milwaukee Office, etc., you can choose to use a different default Passthru server in each. Set up each one as described in this section.

Setting Up Special Passthru Connections

In addition to defining a default Passthru server for each location, you can also tell Notes when to use other Passthru servers. For instance, when you work at home, you might dial the Passthru server Andromeda to reach your home server, Zeus. But when you need to update databases from the sales server Mercury, you use the Passthru server Bacchus. In this case, you would set up Andromeda as your default Passthru server (as above), and tell Notes to dial Bacchus each time you need to connect to Mercury.

For each of these additional Passthru servers, you must create two different Server Connection documents.

1. First create a Server Connection document (as in the previous section) that tells Notes how to call the Passthru server.

    • Select a connection type of Dialup Modem.
    • Enter the Passthru server's name and phone number.

2. Then create a Server Connection document that tells Notes which Passthru server to use to reach which other server.

    • Select a connection type of Passthru Server.
    • For the Passthru server name, enter the name of the server you will dial.
    • For the Destination server name, enter the name of the server you want to reach.

TIP   You can make use of Notes' hierarchical naming conventions to set up a single Passthru connection document that lets you connect to all the servers in a department or organization. To do this, you use an asterisk as a "wildcard" character in the Destination server name field. For example, you might enter */Sales/Optika Cameras to specify all servers in Optika Cameras' sales department. Your Notes administrator can tell you more about how servers in your company are named.

Setting Up a Hunt Group

If the organization you work for has many mobile Notes users, then it may have set up several Passthru servers in what Notes calls a *hunt group*. The benefit for your company is that it can balance the communications workload of many simultaneous dial-up connections among several Passthru servers. The benefit for you is that you only have to set up Notes to call a single telephone number for the hunt group, and you will be automatically connected to a free server.

If your Notes administrator has told you that you will be using a hunt group, here is how to set up your connection:

1. Create a hunt group Server Connection document that tells Notes how to dial the hunt group.

   - Select a connection type of hunt group.
   - Enter a name for the hunt group. You can use any name you like.
   - Enter the phone number (and the country and area codes if necessary) for the hunt group.

2. Create a Passthru Server Connection document for each destination server to which you will connect through the hunt group.

   - Select a connection type of Passthru Server.
   - Enter in the Basics section the name that you gave the hunt group.
   - Enter in the Destination Server field the name of the server to which you want to connect via the hunt group.

Telling Notes Where You Are

So far, you have told Notes what kind of modem you have and which server you want to use. The remaining link is to create one or more Location documents in your Personal Name & Address Book to tell Notes when and where you want it to use the modem to dial this server. If you always use Notes in the same place—say, dialing the server from a branch office—then you'll probably just need one Location document. If you use Notes in a variety of different places—at the office, at home, from a hotel—then you can use Location documents for each place to tell Notes how to get in touch with a server.

Depending on how Notes was set up when it was installed for you, you may already have appropriate locations such as Home and Travel defined for you. To see what locations are available, choose File ➤ Mobile ➤ Locations. This opens the Locations view in your Personal Name & Address Book, which lists all the locations that are currently defined.

You don't need to have a separate Location document for every single place you use Notes, just one for each distinct set of circumstances. If you use a dial-up connection in one place and a network connection in another, you should use separate Location documents. If you travel a lot and dial in with a calling card from various hotels, one Location document that you can modify as necessary will suffice.

Double-click on a location name to view its settings. Figure 13.4 shows settings for the location Travel. Depending on how you use Notes, you may also want to use locations such as Home, Office, Hotel, and Internet. If there is no suitable location already available, click on Add Location to create a new one.

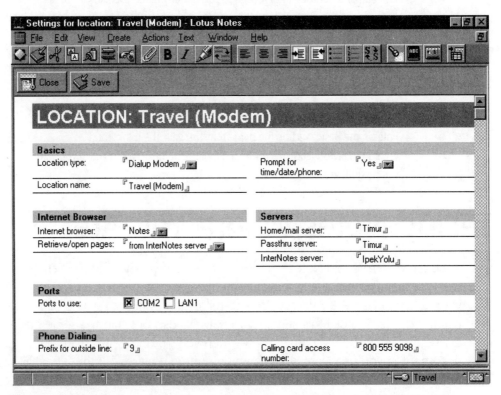

FIGURE 13.4: Multiple Location documents let you quickly switch from using Notes in the office to using it on the road.

You can specify many different settings for a particular location, but for now we'll stick to those most closely linked to using Notes remotely. If you already have a location such as Travel or Home defined, most of the settings should be correct.

Basics

Use Location Type to tell Notes what kind of connection you have to your Notes network: Dialup Modem, Local Area Network, both, or neither. The type of location you select affects the other options that Notes presents. Then give your location a name.

You can choose to have Notes prompt you for time, date, and phone number each time you use this location. Select Yes here if you expect to change the time zone, country, or area code regularly, or the number to dial to get an outside line.

Internet Browser

You can use this section to tell Notes which Web Navigator database or other Web browser to use at this location. See Chapters 11 and 12 for more details.

Servers

Enter the name of the home server you want to use and, if appropriate, a Passthru server and InterNotes server (for Web access). Using the InterNotes Web Navigator is covered in Chapters 11 and 12.

Ports

Select one or more ports to use at this location. If your server connection at this location is just a dial-up connection, make sure the only box that is checked is the one for the serial port to which your modem is attached.

Phone Dialing

For a location with either a dial-up or dial-up and LAN connections, Notes provides a section titled Phone Dialing. The items you can enter here are:

- A prefix to dial to get an outside line. From many business phones this is 9.
- The prefix to make an international call. If you are within the United States, this is 011, but other countries use different prefixes.
- The location's country code. This is the code *at* the location, not the code for any server you will be dialing. The code for the United States is 1; codes for other countries are listed in the phone book.

- The area code (so Notes knows whether to use it when dialing a server)
- A calling card access number and card number. Fill in these fields if you want Notes to use your calling card when dialing a server. The access number is the number you dial to reach the calling card company and indicate you want to use your card. You dial this before you enter the phone number you want to reach. The card number is the number of the card itself.

WARNING If the line you use has "call waiting," you need to disable it for the duration of your modem call because you lose your connection if another call comes in while you are communicating with a Domino server. On most U.S. phone systems you can suspend call waiting temporarily by dialing *70 from a touch-tone phone or 1170 from a rotary phone. You can include this as part of the dialing prefix.

TIP You can place one or more commas in any part of the phone number to have Notes pause during dialing. Each comma causes a two-second delay. You can also include parentheses and hyphens to make phone numbers more readable; Notes ignores them when dialing.

For advanced users, the Dialing Rules button lets you choose a different prefix, phone number, or suffix to use for a particular server at this location.

Mail

If you are going to be using dial-up access at this location, check that Notes is set to look for your mail file locally. If you are using local mail, you may also want to adjust the setting for the number of messages Notes allows to accumulate before automatically dialing your server to send them. The default is five.

Replication

For the moment, make sure the replication schedule is set to Disabled.

Advanced

As the name implies, you won't need to alter the settings here very often. One pair of settings you might need to change are the Local Time Zone and Daylight Savings fields. Although you can tell Notes to prompt you to select a time zone when you change to certain locations, you may find it more convenient to define a particular default time zone for some locations.

Administration

You should have no need to change the settings in this section.

Once you have set the correct options for this location, save the document. If you expect to be using Notes in other circumstances, check that Location documents exist for these, too.

Choosing a Location

Once you've defined settings for one or more locations, you need to choose one of them to use. You have two ways to tell Notes where you are:

- Choose File ➤ Mobile ➤ Choose Current Location to open a dialog box that lets you select your location.
- Choose a location from the pop-up list from the status bar's location indicator (the second item from the right).

The status bar's location indicator also has an option to edit the settings for the current location. Other ways to do this are by clicking on the File Mobile Locations SmartIcon or choosing File ➤ Mobile ➤ Edit Current Location.

If you need to change the time, time zone, dialing prefix, or country or area code quickly, choose File ➤ Mobile ➤ Edit Current Time/Phone to see a dialog box with these parameters.

NOTE See Chapter 14 to find out how to get Notes to ask you for a location every time you start the program.

Making Replicas of the Databases You Want

The next step in the setup procedure is to create replicas on your notebook computer of the databases you want to use. To start with, you may want to choose just a few key databases to replicate. When you're more comfortable with replication, you can choose whether you want to add larger or less frequently used databases to your selection of replicas.

If it's at all possible, you should create your replica databases (and perform the initial replication) when your computer has a direct, network connection to the Domino servers you want to dial into later. In the initial replication, Notes copies the documents from the original database to the replica. This happens quite quickly with a network connection but very slowly over a dial-up connection.

If you have a notebook that you sometimes use remotely and sometimes connect to the network, you are in luck. If you don't have any obvious means of connecting your remote computer directly to your company's Notes network, talk the matter over with your Notes administrator.

If you have to, you can perform the entire process via a dial-up connection. For the initial replication of a database, however, Notes has to exchange *most or all* of the database's documents and *all* of its forms and views. Even for a few moderately sized databases replicated over a reasonably fast modem connection, this could take an hour or more. If you *absolutely must* do this initial replication remotely, try to do it at a time when your phone charges are going to be lowest.

Which databases you replicate varies from person to person, but one database you are bound to want in some form is your mail database. If Notes was set up on your remote computer (when the program was installed) to have either a dial-up connection or network and dial-up connections to your company's Notes network, you should automatically have received in your workspace a replica stub of your mail database.

A *replica stub* is like a placeholder for a database. It tells Notes that at some time later on you're going to want to replicate documents between the stub and a database on a server. Until you perform this initial replication, the stub is just an icon without any forms, views, or documents. If Notes was set up on your dial-up computer to think it was going to have only a network connection, you need to create the replica stub for your mail database yourself by following the procedure in the next section, "Creating Replicas." You also have to create replicas for any other databases you want to use on the road.

Creating Replicas

To create a replica of a database, follow these steps:

1. Go to your workspace and highlight the icon for the server version of the database. Then either choose File ➤ Replication ➤ New Replica or click on the File Replication New Replica SmartIcon. This opens the New Replica dialog box shown in Figure 13.5. If you make one of these actions without first selecting a database icon, Notes will ask you to choose the database of which you want to make a replica.

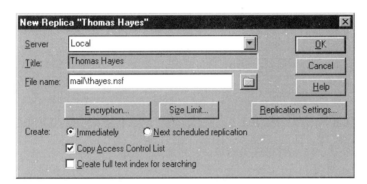

FIGURE 13.5:
Replica databases begin life in the New Replica dialog box.

> **NOTE** You need to have access to a database to make a replica of it. If you've established that there's no way you can connect your computer directly to your company's Notes network even once, read "Connecting Directly to a Server" at the end of this chapter.

2. Notes assumes that you're going to create a local replica of the server database with the same title, so it doesn't let you alter this field. It also suggests you use the same filename as the server database, and there's not much reason to change this setting.

3. Your next choice is whether to create the replica database immediately or to have Notes wait until the first time you choose to replicate it. You will usually want to create the replica immediately, which tells Notes to copy all the documents from the original database.

4. If you do not have a direct network connection to your server, you may want to click on the button marked Replication Settings to restrict the range of documents that Notes copies into the new replica. Read "Selective Replication" later in this chapter for an explanation of your choices.

5. Take a careful look at the two checkboxes at the bottom of the dialog box. Generally, you want to replicate the Access Control List for the database. You won't usually want to create a full-text index at this point (more on these in Chapter 15).

6. Click on OK to create the replica and start the initial replication.

Notes adds an icon for the new replica to your workspace and begins copying documents to it. Once it has finished, you can repeat this process to make replicas of other databases you want to use while traveling.

If you would prefer to create all the icons first and then copy documents for all your replica databases at the same time, choose the Next Scheduled Replication option in the New Replica dialog box. Then you can use the instructions in "Using the Replicator Tab to Manage Replication" later in this chapter to replicate a group of databases at once.

If you *do* choose not to have Notes create a new replica's documents right away, Notes creates something it romantically calls a *replica stub*—a database with no structure or documents. Replica stubs don't even have graphic icons, so the icon you'll see in your workspace will merely be plain gray. Notes tells you on the status bar, "Created OK - Initialization will occur next replication."

TIP

If Notes displays the message "Access control is set to not allow replication" when you try to replicate documents to your new replica, there may be a problem with the Access Control List (ACL) for your new replica. In order to copy documents to the replica, the server from which you are replicating needs to have sufficient access rights. Modifying ACLs is covered in Notes Help. Your new replica's ACL should be set to allow Manager access to the server with which you want to replicate.

Stacking Replica Icons

As a mobile Notes user, you'll start accumulating multiple copies of database icons, one for each replica of a particular database. Initially you'll probably just have databases on your home server, along with their local replicas, but if you travel much you may later have to add replicas from other servers, and the number of icons will grow.

Notes offers a way to control this icon proliferation. Choose View ➤ Stack Replica Icons, and Notes keeps just one icon for each database, no matter how many replicas of it you use. You can tell if there's more than one replica available for a database by a small triangle at the top right of the icon. Click on this triangle and Notes pops up a small menu, as in Figure 13.6, listing the locations of available replicas and an option to replicate your local copy.

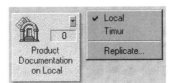

FIGURE 13.6:
If you choose to view replicas as stacked icons, Notes provides a pop-up menu that lets you choose which to use.

The *most* convenient aspect of stacking replica icons, however, is that Notes knows to use different replicas of a particular database in different locations. You needn't think about which replica to use—just double-click on the database icon. If you are at a network-connected location, Notes will open a server replica; without a network connection, Notes will open a local replica.

NOTE Choosing to stack replica icons automatically turns on the option to display server names on icons. The section "Getting Information about a Database from Its Icon" in Chapter 14 covers this in more detail.

Using the Replicator Tab to Manage Replication

The best way to coordinate database replication is to use the Replicator tab, the farthest right of the tabs in your workspace. Click on the Replicator tab and you should see something like Figure 13.7.

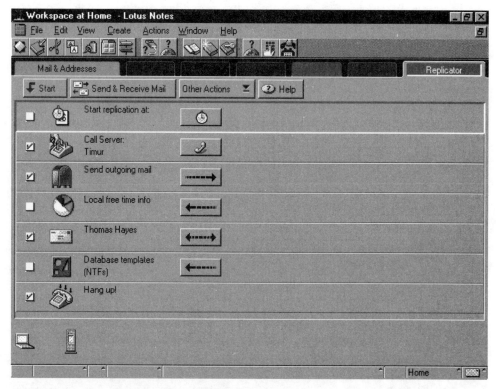

FIGURE 13.7: Notes' Replicator tab provides an intuitive interface to the process of replication.

Notes lists a variety of items on the Replicator tab:

Start Replication At Lets you choose to replicate your databases automatically, on a schedule you set. See "Scheduling Replication" later in this chapter for details.

Call Server Tells Notes to dial a particular server.

Send Outgoing Mail Tells Notes to take any mail that's waiting to be sent and place it on the server to be delivered.

Local Free Time Info Lets you replicate Freetime Schedules for the people with whom you most often need to coordinate meetings. With an up-to-date copy of their Freetime Schedules, you can arrange meetings without a permanent network connection. There's more information on Freetime Schedules in Chapter 17.

Database Entries Notes provides an entry for every local replica you have (Figure 13.7 has room for just one entry: the user's mail database). For each entry, you can choose whether and how to replicate documents.

Database Templates Lets you choose to update the design of any local template-based databases from templates on the server. Unless you have reason to expect that a database's template has changed, you usually won't need to use this option.

Hang Up! Tells Notes to end the call to the server.

The checkboxes on the left-hand side tell Notes whether to perform the associated action or not. When you want to replicate databases, click on Start, which will prompt Notes to work through the checked items in order.

Notes keeps separate settings for the Replicator tab for each location you use. This lets you check different boxes to choose a different set of local databases to replicate when you are using a network connection at the office, a local phone line from home, or a transpacific toll call.

Most items on the Replicator tab also have an action button you can click to provide settings for that item. For databases, the button lets you choose the direction of replication (send changes, receive changes, or both), the server to replicate with, and the amount of each document to exchange. The arrow on the button indicates the direction setting.

You can't change the direction of transfer for outgoing mail, but you can use the button on the Start Replication At item to set a replication schedule for this location. The button on the Call Server item lets you choose which server to call. The button for Local Free Time Info lets you tell Notes whose schedules you want to replicate locally, how many weeks or months to keep these schedules, and how frequently to replicate the schedule.

You can click on items in the Replicator list and drag them to new positions to change the order in which Notes replicates your databases. The schedule item is always first and Hang Up! is always last.

If you need to call more than one server, you can use Create ➤ Call Entry and Create ➤ Hangup Entry to add extra server connections. To delete a call or hang-up entry, highlight it and press Delete. If you accidentally delete a database replica's entry or find that Notes has inexplicably failed to add it, you can add the database to the Replicator list by dragging its icon from the workspace onto the Replicator tab.

> **TIP**
>
> **When you're working in Replicator, you can quickly go to a database's icon in the workspace by double-clicking on its entry in the Replicator list.**

Several options let you perform restricted parts of the normal replication process. The Send & Receive Mail button does just what it says. Under Other Actions, you'll also find Send Outgoing Mail and Replicate Selected Database.

During replication, the indicator at the bottom of the Replicator tab shows you how the transfer is going. You can stop the whole process by clicking on the Stop button, or halt replication of the current database and move on by clicking on Next. Once you've replicated a database successfully, its entry in the Replicator list displays the date, time, and server of the replication.

> **NOTE**
>
> **Notes creates your Local Free Time Info database the first time you use a location in which you have a local mail file. If you don't see the Local Free Time Info entry in the Replicator, switch to a mobile location and use File ➤ Mobile ➤ Edit Current Location to make sure that your local mail file is specified.**

Other Ways to Replicate Databases

As well as using Replicator, there are other ways you can replicate databases. However, they aren't really any more flexible than Replicator and have the distinct disadvantage of working in the "foreground."

When you use Replicator to connect to a server and exchange changes, Notes starts a separate mini-program that runs in the "background" performing the replication. This means that you can carry on working in other parts of Notes while the exchange takes place. If you don't use Replicator, however, the replication takes place in the foreground and you have to wait for it to complete before you can carry on with other work. About the only reason to replicate in the foreground is if you need to perform a replication quickly that's not part of your regular Replicator process (say, updating a single database from a different server than the one you would usually use).

To perform foreground replication, select the icons of the databases you want to replicate in the workspace and then choose File ➤ Replication ➤ Replicate or click on the File Replication Replicate SmartIcon. You can also choose the Replicate option from the menu available on a stacked replica icon. Then choose Replicate with Options and select a server with which to replicate, a direction for the exchange, and the document portions you want.

Disconnected Web Browsing

Because both types of Web Navigator databases (see Chapters 11 and 12) store Web pages as Notes documents, you don't even need to have an active connection to the Internet to browse the Web. Instead, you can read pages in the Personal Web Navigator or a local replica of the Server Web Navigator at your convenience.

This approach can be useful for mobile Notes users, who can't always rely on finding a telephone connection. Of course, pages in a disconnected Web Navigator database will only be as recent as the last time they were refreshed, and you are limited to pages already stored in the database, but it is better than having no access at all.

If you usually use the Server Web Navigator, you will need to set up a replica of that database on your mobile or remote computer first. Then you should replicate the local copy of the database with the server immediately before you leave on a trip. That way, if you are unable to make a dial-up connection to your home server while you are away, you can still view copies of pages in the Web Navigator that were current just before you left.

Telling Notes to Look for Web Pages Locally

When you want to use the Web Navigator but can't make a dial-up connection, you have to tell Notes to look for Web pages locally instead. The procedure is the same whether you are using a local replica of the Server Web Navigator or your own copy of the Personal Web Navigator:

1. Choose File ➤ Mobile ➤ Edit Current Location to open the current Location document.
2. In the Internet Browser section of the Location document, set the Retrieve/Open Pages field to No Retrievals.
3. Close and save the Location document.

Now, when you open the Web Navigator database, Notes understands that it can only provide pages already stored in the database. When you next have a network connection available, you can change the Retrieve/Open Pages field to reflect the type of connection you have. If you are using the Server Web Navigator, you can also replicate your local copy with the server to update the stock of Web pages.

> **TIP** If you know in advance where you will not have Web access, you can use File ➤ Mobile ➤ Locations to edit each Location document to specify using stored Web pages only.

How Remote Mail Works

So far I haven't really explained how Notes handles your mail when you're not at the office. Although you can use remote Notes mail without understanding how it works, you may find it helpful to have some understanding of the procedure.

When desk-tethered Notes users send memos, the copy of the program on their workstation sends the memo straight to the Domino server program. From there it is distributed to all its recipients. However, when you don't have a direct network connection, Notes can't send your mail immediately. Instead, it stores it in a special Mailbox database with the filename MAIL.BOX. This database isn't to be confused with any version of your mail database.

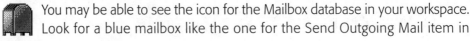 You may be able to see the icon for the Mailbox database in your workspace. Look for a blue mailbox like the one for the Send Outgoing Mail item in Figure 13.7.

The only reasons to know about the Mailbox database are so that you don't have to wonder where your mail goes or what that strange icon in your workspace is. You don't ever need to do anything with the Mailbox database yourself.

> **NOTE** Each time you change from a remote location to a networked location, Notes checks your Mailbox database for unsent messages. If it finds messages you haven't yet sent, it will offer to send them rather than let them languish in your Mailbox database.

Most things about Notes mail work the same way whether you are connected to a network or not, but there are a few key differences:

- You won't have access to your company's Public Name & Address Book to help you address messages, because it's stored on the server. You can use your Personal Name & Address Book, however.
- When you send mail from your mail database, it doesn't actually start its journey until you dial up your server and exchange mail.

> **NOTE** Most mobile users don't keep a local replica copy of their company's Public Name & Address Book because it is usually very large and takes a long time to replicate. Another reason is that unless it is absolutely up to date, you risk having your messages sent to the wrong people or not delivered at all because of changes to the personal names and groups in the Public Name & Address Book.

Your other databases are also going to work much as they would if you had a direct network connection. A couple of points to remember are:

- The information they contain is only going to be as up-to-date as the most recent time you replicated each database. Similarly, your colleagues are going to be in the dark about any changes you make until you replicate them to the server.
- Any databases that use Notes mail will have their mail messages stored in your outgoing Mailbox database just like the messages you send.

Scheduling Replication

Sometimes you may want to have Notes replicate your databases at a particular time—when phone rates are cheap, or when your dial-in server is least busy. Notes lets you schedule replication in advance.

1. On the Replicator tab, click on the action button next to the Start Replication At entry (the one with a picture of a stopwatch). Notes opens the Location document for the current location.

2. Move to the section marked Replication. Here you have several options to set:

   - You can enable or disable scheduled replication. This corresponds to checking the checkbox on the Start Replication At entry in Replicator.
   - You can set a time to call (e.g., 3:00 AM), or a range of times during which to call (e.g., 8:00 AM - 5:00 PM).
   - You can choose how often to call (in minutes) or enter 0 to have Notes just call once per day.
   - You can choose which days of the week Notes should call.

3. Once you've set your replication schedule, save and close the Location document. Notes returns you to the Replicator.

To have Notes perform replication on a schedule, you need to have the schedule item checked in the Replicator's list. If you want Notes to replicate your databases unattended, remember to leave Notes running and your modem plugged into a phone line.

| TIP | If you don't want to replicate free time information every time Notes performs a scheduled replication, you can click on the action button on the Replicator's Local Free Time Info entry and set a maximum replication frequency. |

Selective Replication

Once you have replicated your databases a few times, you'll be keen to make sure you only exchange the information you're going to need. If you have to pay a lot for a phone connection (maybe you're staying at a hotel) or your modem is not screamingly fast, then you have a particular incentive to make replication as efficient as possible. If your notebook computer has limited storage capacity or a pedestrian processor (this describes most notebook computers), you may also be thankful for anything that helps keep the size of your database replicas down.

Choose File ➤ Replication ➤ Settings (or click on the File Replication Settings SmartIcon) to display the Replication Settings dialog box. Two of the panels in this dialog box have options you may want to set. The Space Savers panel in this dialog box is shown in Figure 13.8.

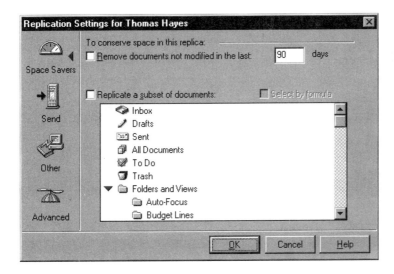

FIGURE 13.8:
The Replication Settings dialog box offers several settings that can speed up replication and cut down on the size of replica databases.

Space Savers

One way to reduce the size and replication time for a long-standing database is to remove documents that haven't been modified recently. To use this feature, check the first box on the Space Savers panel and specify a number of days beyond which you don't want to keep unmodified documents.

You can be even more precise about what to replicate by checking the option to replicate only a subset of documents. Then you can either select folders and views to define the documents you want to exchange or use a Notes formula. Providing this kind of formula is a good idea when you are interested in replicating the part of a large database that relates to you. Say you have a Customer Tracking database on your home server that keeps information on every customer with whom your company works. You could replicate the same database with a formula like this:

```
Select AssignedSalesRepresentative = "Thomas Hayes" or
Form = "Contact" : "Customer"
```

You would receive all the Contact and Customer profiles plus any other documents in the database that relate to the accounts with which you work. This might exclude call reports and correspondence on most of the accounts and cut down the replication volume considerably.

If you think a formula like this might be useful, you may want to enlist the help of the database's designer or manager, or your Notes administrator, in constructing the appropriate syntax.

> **NOTE**   Remember that you can use the options available for each database in Replicator to choose whether to import full documents, a summary and the first 40KB of full text, or just a summary. If you do choose to shorten documents, Notes displays the legend "(TRUNCATED)" as part of the document's title. You can then use Actions ➤ Retrieve Entire Document to have Notes contact the server and get the full version. You can't edit truncated documents or use agents on them.

Send

The Send panel tells Notes which types of changes in your replica it should pass on to other replicas. The only one of these options you might need to change is whether or not to send deletions made in your replica to other replicas.

Other

The panel named Other offers several useful settings. The first of these is a checkbox that lets you turn off replication for this database for the moment, if necessary.

You can mark this database as low, medium, or high priority for replication. High priority databases are marked with a red exclamation point on the Replicator tab, and you can use Options ➤ Replicate High Priority Databases to update them independently of your other databases.

TIP
> A quick way to mark a database as high priority for replication is to right-click on its entry in the Replicator and choose High Priority from the shortcut menu that Notes displays. Repeating this action returns the database to medium priority.

The third item lets you specify a cutoff date for replication. Notes won't bring in documents from the server that were last saved or modified before this date.

Unless you are publishing your own Notes databases on CD-ROM, you can safely ignore the CD-ROM publishing date option.

Advanced

You'll have little reason to alter the settings in the Advanced panel. They let you specify which subset of documents to replicate when connected to a particular server, and they let you choose which elements of a database's design to exchange.

Connecting Directly to a Server

Now that I've spent an entire chapter telling you how to set up an elaborate system of replicas, I'm going to let slip the fact that, if you wish, you can actually use the databases on the server from your notebook computer. Before you throw this book out of the window (if you're reading this in-flight, please be careful), here are two good reasons why you're not going to be doing this much:

- You need a pretty fast modem to get any kind of acceptable performance from a server database that you're looking at over a direct dial-in link. Even so, opening views and documents would be much slower over a direct dial-in link than opening them would be with a local replica or a direct network connection.
- The extra time it takes to open views and documents, plus the fact that you would always need to have a phone connection to use any database, would make you one of Ma Bell's best customers. More likely, your employer would just say no to running up so many hours of long-distance phone calls.

At times, however, nothing beats a direct connection to the server (perhaps to add a new replica when you're far from a network connection), so here's how to do it:

1. Choose a location that is set up to use a modem connection.
2. Choose File ➤ Mobile ➤ Call Server or click on the File Mobile Call Server SmartIcon. Notes opens the Call Server dialog box.
3. Select a server and click on Auto Dial.

Once you're connected, everything works as if you were connected directly to the network—except very slowly. When your call is finished, remember to choose File ➤ Mobile ➤ Hang Up or click on the File Mobile Hang Up SmartIcon.

That's all most Notes users will need to know about the Replicator, Passthru servers, hunt groups, and similar beasties. The next couple of chapters return to much more comprehensible subjects: how to search for text and documents in Notes, getting Notes to scan for unread documents, using collapsible views, and changing your user preferences. Take a look.

Part 4

Advanced Notes Features

Chapter 14

NOTES TOOLS

- **Text searches**
- **Unread marks and selection checkmarks**
- **Scanning for unread documents**
- **Collapsible views**
- **Navigators**
- **Your user preferences**

By now you should be getting comfortable working with a range of Notes databases. However, there are still times when you'll find it difficult to track down quite the right document, or when you would like to have Notes work a little differently. Finding what you want and setting up Notes to work the way you want are the main subjects of the next two chapters. Here, you'll find instructions on everything from finding textual needles in the database haystack to a clever mouse shortcut that closes Notes windows.

Searching for Text

Notes offers a variety of search techniques to help you find a particular document and find particular information within that document. You have the following options:

- Search for words and phrases in a single document.
- Search for text in the rows of a view.
- Search for words in several documents in a view.
- Perform full-text searching within a view.

Full-text searching is a powerful and flexible tool, worthy of a chapter to itself: Chapter 15. Here, we'll look quickly at the three types of word searching you can do in Notes and a way to keep track of the right document once you have found it.

Searching for Words or Phrases in Documents

Notes' word searches work a lot like the kinds of searches you may do in your word processor. If you are reading or editing a Notes document and want to see where a certain word or combination of words is located, you can use Notes' Find and Replace function. Any of the following actions opens the Find and Replace dialog box, as shown in Figure 14.1:

- Choose Edit ➤ Find/Replace.
- Press Ctrl+F.

- Click on the Edit Find/Replace SmartIcon.

In the dialog box, enter the word or words you are looking for in the Find text box. Click on Find Next to look for the next occurrence of the word or phrase. If you are in edit mode, Notes starts looking at the insertion point and continues until the end of the document. If you are in read-only mode, Notes starts at the top of the document and works down. If you want to search from the bottom of the document towards the top, click on Find Previous.

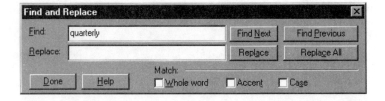

FIGURE 14.1:
The Find and Replace dialog box lets you search for a particular word.

If Notes finds the word, it highlights it and lets you decide what action to take. If it can't find the word, it tells you so and gives you the opportunity to enter a new word in the Find text box.

Three checkboxes at the bottom of the dialog box allow you to modify the way Notes searches:

Case If you check Case, Notes looks for the exact combination of upper- and lowercase letters you typed.

Accent If you check Accent, you can search for *résumé* as distinct from *resume*.

Whole Word If you check Whole Word, your search for *twee* won't turn up *between*, for example. Notes will only find complete words, not letters within words.

Your other options in this dialog box depend on whether you are in read-only mode or in edit mode. In read-only mode, you can search again, or click on Done to leave the dialog box.

Searching for and Replacing Text

In edit mode you can also type in a word or phrase in the Replace text box to replace the highlighted text Notes has found. Then your options are:

Replace Click on the Replace button to have Notes substitute the new text for the old.

Replace All Click on the Replace All button to have Notes substitute the new text for every occurrence of the old text in your document.

Once you have performed a search, Notes gives you the option to repeat it if necessary. These three actions all tell Notes to find the same text again:

- Choose Edit ➤ Find Next.
- Press Ctrl+G.
 - Click on the Edit Find Next SmartIcon.

If Notes was able to find the text you were looking for the last time you used Find, clicking on the Find Next SmartIcon tells Notes to find the next occurrence of the word or phrase. But if your last search failed, Find Next knows not to look again and instead opens the Find and Replace dialog box so you can redefine your search.

Searching for Text in a View

You can use the same Find command when you are looking at a view to have Notes search for the next occurrence of a particular word or phrase. To use Find in a view, press Ctrl+F, click on the Edit Find/Replace SmartIcon, or choose Edit ➤ Find/Replace. Notes opens a Find dialog box like the one for searching in a document, but without the options to replace text.

Type the text you want to search for and click on either Find Next or Find Previous to have Notes search the columns of the view. Again, you can repeat your search by pressing Ctrl+G, by choosing Edit ➤ Find Next, or by clicking on the Edit Find Next SmartIcon.

Using Quick Search

If you're using an alphabetical view and just want to move to the first row that begins with a particular piece of text, use Notes' Quick Search feature. Here's how it works:

1. Click in the View Pane.
2. Type the first few letters of the name of the item to which you want to move.
3. Notes opens a Quick Search dialog box containing the text you typed.
4. When you've typed enough to identify the item you're searching for, press Enter or click on OK.
5. Notes searches in the first column of the view for an entry that begins with the text you typed. Its possible responses are as follows:

   - If there's only one occurrence of the text, Notes highlights it.
   - If there's more than one occurrence of the text, Notes highlights the first.
   - If there's no entry that begins with the text, Notes beeps and displays a message on the status bar.

> **TIP**
>
> You can type the URL for a Web page into the Quick Search dialog box to have Notes open that page in your Web Navigator database. For more information, see "50 Ways to Open a Web Page" in Chapter 12.

Searching for Words across Several Documents

Alternatively, you can have Notes look for text in a group of documents. Notes then searches the whole content of the documents, not just the data displayed in the view. This starts to come close to the type of search you can do with Notes' full-text searching, and indeed Notes uses the same interface for you to compose your search.

Choose View ➤ Search Bar or click on the View Show/Hide Search Bar SmartIcon to have Notes insert a blank text box and some buttons between the SmartIcons and the Action Bar, as in Figure 14.2. This is the Search Bar.

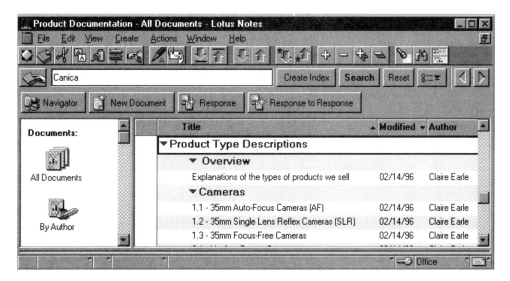

FIGURE 14.2: The Search Bar lets you search more than one document for a piece of text.

Then type the word or phrase you want to find in the text box and click on Search. Notes will scan each document in the view and place a checkmark next to each one that contains the text you typed. If you already had some documents checked, Notes will just scan those documents and leave checkmarks on only those that contain the search text.

When the search is complete, Notes sets the view to show only the selected documents. To see all the documents in the view again, click on the button marked Reset.

Once you have found a document that contains the word for which you are searching, you can open it and then choose Edit ➤ Find Next to see where the word occurs in the document.

TIP

When you are searching a large number of documents without the benefit of a full-text index (see Chapter 15), Notes may take a long time to produce results for your search. The speed with which Notes searches depends a lot on the computer you are using. If you decide that you want to abandon a search, press Ctrl+Break to return to the view.

Finding the Same Document in Another View

This tip doesn't fit neatly into any section on using views, but if you have to switch between views often, you'll be glad to learn about it.

You may already have noticed that when you switch from one view to another, Notes usually opens the new view the way it was when you last used it. Sometimes you'll find this behavior useful, but sometimes you'd prefer to be able to switch views while keeping the same document highlighted. For example, you might have found a customer listed in an alphabetical view of a sales database and want to switch to view the same customer in the Customers by Sales Volume view, to see how this customer ranks against your others.

To switch to the new view and keep the same document highlighted, hold down Ctrl (⌘ on the Macintosh) and then choose the new view from the View menu or a navigator. Of course, it's possible that the document isn't listed in the new view. If that happens, Notes beeps to alert you.

NOTE

Unfortunately, Notes won't allow you to use this technique when switching to or from Calendar-style views.

Selecting Documents in a View

Selecting documents in a view is an easy and powerful way to quickly find, analyze, and compare information. Notes offers a variety of commands to select, deselect, and manipulate documents.

As you saw in the last section, you can use the Search Bar to select only those documents in a view that contain a particular word or phrase.

In Table 14.1 you'll find two SmartIcons that help you move from one selected document in a view to another. These SmartIcons work at both the view and document levels. If you are looking at a view, they just move the highlighting bar onto the previous or next selected document. If you are looking at a document, they close it and open the previous or next document selected in the view.

Table 14.1: Navigation SmartIcons for Views and Documents

Next	Previous	Moves to
		Any document
		Main documents only
		Unread documents only
		Selected documents only

Notes also lets you single out the selected documents in a view. The menu choice View ➤ Show ➤ Selected Only removes everything from the view except the documents with checkmarks next to them. Choosing this option again returns the view to normal.

You can place a checkmark next to every document in the current view with any of these three actions:

- Choose Edit ➤ Select All.
- Press Ctrl+A.
 - Click on the Edit Select All SmartIcon.

To remove all selection marks, choose Edit ➤ Deselect All.

Another way you can use selection marks is to move documents between databases. Notes lets you use the standard commands for cut and copy at the view level to place selected documents on the Clipboard. If there are no documents selected, Notes will just cut or copy the highlighted document. You can then move to a view in another database and paste the documents from the Clipboard.

> **WARNING** If the new database does not contain the same forms and views as the old database, you may have trouble finding the pasted documents in any view and reading them once you find them. Unless you have a detailed knowledge of the structure of the databases with which you are working, try *copying* documents in small numbers at first. This way you can check to see that your copied documents work as intended.

Working with Unread Documents

Notes also offers a variety of ways to manipulate unread documents. Some of them are very similar to the commands that work with selected documents.

Table 14.1 shows a pair of SmartIcons that you can use to move from unread document to unread document at either the view level or the document level. (The table also shows a pair of SmartIcons that takes you to the next document, regardless of its type, up or down in the view. Another pair only takes you to main documents and not responses.) There's also a View ➤ Show ➤ Unread Only command that lets you restrict the current view to include only unread documents.

Four more SmartIcons with corresponding menu choices let you tell Notes which documents it should regard as read or unread. These are summarized Table 14.2.

Table 14.2: Working with Unread Marks

SmartIcon	Menu Command	Action
	Edit ➤ Unread Marks ➤ Mark Selected Read	Marks every selected document as read
	Edit ➤ Unread Marks ➤ Mark All Read	Marks every document in the view as read
	Edit ➤ Unread Marks ➤ Mark Selected Unread	Marks every selected document as unread
	Edit ➤ Unread Marks ➤ Mark All Unread	Marks every document in the view as unread

With these commands, you can use unread marks in whatever way suits you: as strictly an indication of which documents you have opened and which you haven't, or as a more flexible notation as to which documents you have evaluated for a particular purpose and which you are still considering.

Getting Information about a Database from Its Icon

Notes gives you several options to put different kinds of information on the database icons in your workspace. Whichever option you choose, Notes applies it to all the icons in the workspace. Figure 14.3 shows you the four ways you can choose to have Notes display database icons.

A standard database icon looks something like the first icon in Figure 14.3. It displays just the name of the database and a graphic to help you identify it.

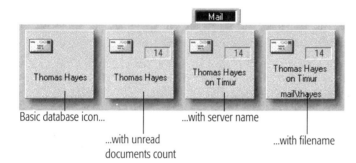

Basic database icon...

...with unread documents count

...with server name

...with filename

FIGURE 14.3: Use Notes database icons to find out how many documents in a database are unread, on which server the database is stored, and in which file.

Choose View ➤ Show Unread or click on the View Show Unread SmartIcon to have your database icons look like the second example in Figure 14.3. The number (in red on color screens) tells you how many documents in this database are marked as unread.

> **TIP**
>
> The number of unread documents is updated each time you close the database or tell Notes to update the count. You can update the count by choosing View ➤ Refresh Unread Count or one of the unread document scanning commands, all of which are described later in this chapter. Because the count is generally updated only when you close a database, there may be more unread documents when you open your mail database, for example, than the number indicated on the database icon. This is because documents have been added to the database since the last time you opened it (for example, you have received new mail).

If you also choose View ➤ Show Server Names or click on the View Show Server Names SmartIcon, your database icons will look like the third example in Figure 14.3. Notes lists the name of the server after the database name for each shared database. See Chapter 9 for an explanation of Domino servers and shared databases.

If you hold down Shift while choosing View ➤ Show Server Names or while clicking on the View Show Server Names SmartIcon, your database icons will look like the final example in Figure 14.3. As well as the name of the server, Notes now lists the filename (and directory) in which the database is located.

> **TIP**
>
> For local databases on the Macintosh, the filename and database name are the same. If you choose Shift+View ➤ Show Server Names on the Macintosh, Notes will only display filenames for databases that are stored on Domino servers.

Another command that you may find helpful in working with database icons is View ➤ Refresh Unread Count, or F9. There is a corresponding View Refresh Unread SmartIcon. This command is only available when you are looking at the workspace (you've already met its counterpart in a view). View ➤ Refresh Unread Count tells Notes to go into each database on the current workspace page and update the number of unread documents it lists. You can use this command to make a quick check to see if anything new has arrived that you might want to see.

Scanning for Unread Documents

Notes also provides three other ways to look for unread documents. One option helps you scan your mail database. The second option lets you scan within a selected group of databases. And the third option lets you define a group of databases that you regularly want to check for unread documents. Here's how to use them.

Looking for Unread Documents in Your Mail File

At any time, you can use either of the following options to see if there are any unread documents in your mail file:

- Choose Scan Unread Mail from the Mail item at the far right end of the status bar.
- Click on the Edit Scan Unread Mail SmartIcon.

If you have read all your mail, Notes tells you on the status bar, "There are no unread documents in your mail file." If there is unread mail, Notes opens the first unread message it can find. When you are done reading the message, you can press Enter or Tab to move to the next unread message or close the window to browse your mailbox at the view level.

Looking for Unread Documents in Several Databases

As well as looking for unread mail, you can check for unread documents in one or more other databases. Just select their icons in the workspace (to select several, hold Shift while clicking) and choose Edit ➤ Unread Marks ➤ Scan Unread. As shown in Figure 14.4, Notes announces each database in turn in the Scan Unread dialog box. It also tells you the number of unread documents the database contains.

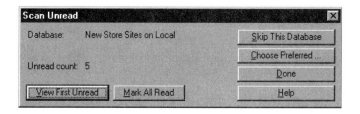

FIGURE 14.4:
The Scan Unread dialog box lets you decide into which databases with unread documents to dip.

Your options in the Scan Unread dialog box are as follows:

View First Unread Opens the first unread document in the database. You can then press Tab or Enter to move from one unread document to the next, or close the document window to see the database at view level and close the view window to return to the Scan Unread dialog box.

Mark All Read Marks all documents in this database as having been read. This option is useful if you discover that you don't need to bother with the unread documents in a database.

Skip This Database Moves to the next database without altering the number of unread documents in this database.

Choose Preferred Lets you set up a list of databases to scan. This option is described in the next section.

Done Tells Notes that you are finished and want to return to the workspace.

Maintaining a Short List of Databases to Scan

Once you get to be comfortable with scanning databases this way, you'll find that scanning is a pretty powerful tool. You may want to scan your favorite databases regularly for unread documents.

Notes can maintain a short list of databases that you can scan with a simple command. To compose the list, click on the Choose Preferred button in the Scan Unread dialog box or click on the Edit Scan Choose SmartIcon. Either way, Notes displays the Scan Unread Preferred Setup dialog box shown in Figure 14.5.

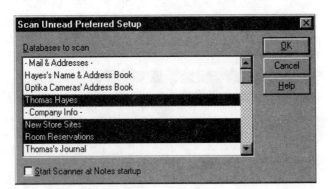

FIGURE 14.5:
The Scan Unread Preferred Setup dialog box lets you select a group of databases that you want to regularly scan for unread documents.

The Databases to Scan box lists all the databases in your workspace in alphabetical order by workspace page. Selecting a database in this box adds it to Notes' list of your preferred databases to check for unread documents. Lines in the Mail & Addresses format are the names of your workspace tabs, which are listed to help you identify databases.

If you want, you can have Notes automatically scan for unread documents each time it starts up. To choose this option, check the Start Scanner at Notes Startup option. Once you have chosen your list of preferred databases, click on OK. If you liked the list better before you started fussing with it, click on Cancel.

To have Notes actually scan your preferred databases, choose Edit ➤ Unread Marks ➤ Scan Preferred or click on the SmartIcon shown here (confusingly, it's called the Edit Scan Unread *Choose* Preferred SmartIcon). While you have to be looking at your workspace to scan selected databases, you can scan your preferred databases at any time. Notes will open a Scan Unread dialog box like the one in Figure 14.4 so you can work your way through the databases you listed.

Using Categorized and Hierarchical Views

One convenient way that information is often displayed in Notes is in a *categorized view*. You've probably seen at least one of these views in Notes' own Help database; as you use more Notes databases, you'll see others.

In databases based on the Discussion template and those where people respond to others' comments, you may see *hierarchical views.* In hierarchical views, main documents have responses indented below them, and the responses have their own responses.

These two types of views work very similarly, letting you expand categories to view the documents they contain, or expand main documents to view their responses. Each view displays twisty triangles to indicate which items you can expand and collapse.

You'll generally find that using these views is straightforward—the main technique you need to know is that double-clicking on any item with a twisty toggles it between its collapsed and expanded states. However, there are a few special commands that you may find helpful. The instructions that follow for categorized views apply equally to hierarchical views.

Collapsing Categories

Any one of the following methods will *collapse* a category or a main document so that only the heading is listed, with no subordinate documents:

- Double-click on the category name.
- Click on the category's twisty once.
- Highlight the category name and press Enter.
- Highlight the category name and press the minus (−) key.
- Highlight the category name and choose View ➤ Expand/Collapse ➤ Collapse Selected Level.
 • Click on the View Collapse SmartIcon.

You can collapse as many categories as you like, so that the view lists just the documents you want.

If you want, you can collapse all the categories in a view with one of the following methods:

- Choose View ➤ Collapse All.
- Press Shift and the minus (−) key on your keypad. (You need to have the number keypad lock turned off on your computer. Press the key marked Num Lock at the top left of the keypad until the corresponding light is off.)
 • Click on the View Collapse All SmartIcon.

Expanding Categories

Naturally, as well as collapsing categories and main documents you can also *expand* them. To expand a single category or main document:

- Double-click on the category name.
- Click on the category's twisty once.
- Highlight the category name and press Enter.
- Highlight the category name and press the plus (+) key on your keypad.
- Highlight the category name and choose View ➤ Expand/Collapse ➤ Expand Selected Level.
- Click on the View Expand SmartIcon.

You probably noticed that three of the options (pressing Enter, double-clicking on the category name, and clicking on the category's twisty icon) work either to expand or collapse a category.

To expand all the categories in a view, your options are:

- Choose View ➤ Expand All.
- Press Shift and the plus (+) key on your keypad. (Again, you need to have Num Lock turned off.)
- Click on the View Expand All SmartIcon.

Often, a categorized view will have more than one level of categorization, or a hierarchical view will have more than one level of responses. In these cases you can use the usual expand methods to expand an item by one level, or you can choose instead to fully expand all the subcategories or responses below a category or main document. To expand all levels below a document, use the asterisk (*) key on the numeric keypad or choose View ➤ Expand/Collapse ➤ Expand Selected & Children.

Viewing Just Categories

When you are looking at a view that contains many documents and categories, it can be difficult to find out what your category choices are. Choosing View ➤ Show ➤ Categories Only shrinks the view so that only category names are showing. This can be particularly helpful in views that use cascading or nested categories (categories within categories).

With this option selected, you can expand and collapse categories, but Notes won't display any documents. Once you find the category you want, you need to go back to the regular view (choose View ➤ Show ➤ Categories Only again) to open a document.

> **NOTE** One more type of view you may see is a calendar view. These views look a lot like the Calendar view in your mail database, but can display information other than just appointments and meetings.

Using Navigators

A navigator is the general term for anything that sits in the top left pane when you're looking at a view. Navigators are supposed to help you find your way around a database, and they should be designed so that you can use them without instructions.

Categorizing, Your Way

Sometimes you might want to use more than one level of categorization where a database provides just one. An example might be a documentation database that offers a single Category field, and you would prefer to use main categories and subcategories.

One way around this problem is to alter the database's forms and views to add extra fields that you can use to categorize documents. The disadvantage of modifying a database in this way is that it may render the database unusable to Notes Mail users.

If the database needs to remain accessible to people with Notes Mail licenses, there is an alternative. Notes treats a backslash character (\) as a category separator. For example, enter **Vendor Documentation\Press Releases** in a categorized field and Notes will interpret Press Releases as a subcategory of Vendor Documentation. The "Document Libraries" section in Chapter 10 shows how this technique can work in practice.

This brief section is just for your reference in case you find a navigator that isn't straightforward to use.

For any database, you can display a standard Notes navigator showing views, folders, and agents by choosing View ➤ Show ➤ Folders. This navigator is structured similarly to the one in your mail database, with views and folders listed in an expandable hierarchy.

Special Navigators

Often a database will offer specially designed navigators as well. If there are any special navigators available, they are listed below the Folders item on the View ➤ Show submenu. If there are more special navigators than Notes has room to list on the menu, use View ➤ Show ➤ Other to see a complete list.

Special navigators can work in a wide variety of ways. At their simplest, they may work like some of the special navigators in the Notes Help database, giving you access to the database's main views and perhaps a few special features such as the Visual Index.

An example of more complex navigators is the Visual Index itself. Each screen of the Visual Index is a navigator, with hotspots that can take you to documents in the Help database or to other parts of the Visual Index.

The most complex navigators provide a completely new way to work with Notes, such as letting you use maps to home in on geographical data. The interface for the InterNotes Web Navigator database uses several complex navigators.

Because special navigators are so flexible, it isn't possible to predict in what forms you'll encounter them. A navigator can include text, graphics, and hotspots. Navigator hotspots can perform a wide variety of actions, including opening a view or folder, running an agent, and opening another navigator.

In some navigators you'll see folder icons with labels such as My Favorite Documents. These icons let you open the folder that is named. You can also add documents to the folder by dragging them to the icon in the navigator.

Changing Your User Preferences

Would you prefer Notes to ask you first instead of automatically saving a copy of every memo you send? Would you rather have Notes prompt you to choose your location every time you start the program? You don't always have to put up with the way Notes does things. In a number of areas, Notes lets you choose how the program operates through your user preferences.

To view and change your user preferences, choose File ➤ Tools ➤ User Preferences. Notes opens the User Preferences dialog box, displaying the Basics panel, as in Figure 14.6. The rest of this chapter covers the settings on the Basics, International, and Mail panels. The Ports panel is covered as part of the discussion of mobile Notes in Chapter 13.

Basic Settings

The Basics panel, shown in Figure 14.6, lets you customize many aspects of Notes' appearance and behavior. With several of these settings, once you close the dialog box, Notes will tell you that your changes won't take effect until the next time you start the program.

The first four checkboxes let you tell Notes that each time it starts up it should:

- Scan your list of preferred databases for unread documents.
- Prompt you to select a location (useful if you are using Notes on a notebook computer).
- Run any scheduled agents on your computer.
- Update local full-text indexes in the background.

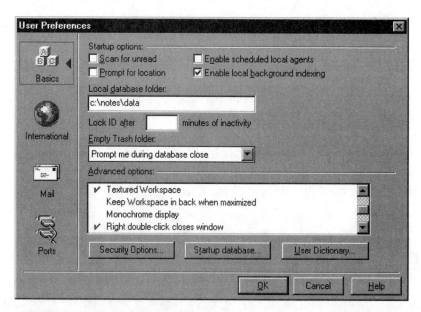

FIGURE 14.6: Most often, when you need to change your user preferences, the setting you want to alter will be on the Basics panel.

Notes needs to know the location of your local database folder or directory to function properly. This is the place in which Notes stores your own databases, your workspace and personal folder information, and a large number of other critical files.

 **WARNING** You probably shouldn't change the location of your local database folder except under the direction of your Notes administrator.

As a security measure, you can set Notes to lock your User ID if the program hasn't been used for a certain number of minutes. That way, if people walk up to your computer while you're away from your desk, they'll need to supply your password to use shared databases or send mail in your name.

You have three choices of how Notes should decide when to empty databases' trash folders. You can have Notes ask you every time you close the database, have Notes empty the trash without asking, or have Notes leave emptying the trash to you.

Next on the Basics panel is a scrolling list of up to 12 advanced options that you can check. Here's the effect of each:

Mark Documents Read When Opened in Preview Pane   Normally an unread document stays unread if you only open it in the Preview Pane at the bottom of a view. Check this option to regard previewed documents as read.

Typewriter Fonts Only   Tells Notes to display text in a monospaced font, in which every character has the same width. You're unlikely to need this unless you're designing views or forms.

Large Fonts   If the text for Notes commands is difficult to read on your monitor, try using this setting to increase the size of the fonts Notes uses in the workspace, views, and documents.

Make Internet URLs into Hotspots   If you check this option and have either version of the Web Navigator available, Notes underlines in green any occurrence of an Internet uniform resource locator (such as a Web page address) in rich-text fields in other databases. You can click on these hotspots to open the item within the Web Navigator.

Textured Workspace   Checking this option tells Notes to make your workspace look more like it is made of three-dimensional marble slabs than the usual gray blocks. This option is only available if your computer is using a suitable display driver.

Keep Workspace in Back When Maximized   Notes normally treats the workspace as just another window when you switch between windows. If you check this option, Notes behaves as it used to in Notes 3 and will always try to avoid displaying the workspace when you close other windows. This option is not available for Macintosh users.

Monochrome Display   If you're using a color monitor but want to see how a document would look to a user with a monochrome screen, this option is for you. It tells Notes to display everything in shades of gray. This option is not available for Macintosh users.

Right Double-Click Closes Window   Choose this option to have Notes interpret your double-click of the right mouse button as a command to close the current window. This was the standard way Notes behaved in earlier versions. Macintosh users won't see this option as their mice have only one button.

Keep All Windows within Main Notes Window (MDI) This setting appears only for Windows users of Notes. With this option checked, Notes uses Windows' Multiple Document Interface, keeping all windows within the main Notes window and showing only one set of SmartIcons, one status bar, and so on. Unchecked, this tells Notes to use the Single Document Interface. You can move windows where you like, and each window has a full set of controls.

Enable Plugins Plugins are miniature programs stored on your computer that allow Web pages to provide extra features, such as the ability to play sound files or video clips.

Enable Java Applets Java Applets add extra features to certain Web pages. Users of Windows NT, Windows 95, and certain versions of Unix can tell Notes here that they want to use Java applets in the Web Navigator database. Unlike plugins, Java applets are loaded afresh each time you click on a Web page that uses them. This poses greater potential security risks. The Advanced section of each Location document provides more detailed control of Java applets.

Dither Images in Documents Choosing this option doesn't mean you will suddenly see illustrations of procrastination in your memos. Instead, it refers to a technique that improves the quality of 16- and 24-bit images on 256-color displays. Users of other types of displays won't see this option.

At the bottom of the Basics tab are three buttons that you can click to make further settings. Here are your options:

Security Options Click on this button and Notes opens the Workstation Security: Execution Control List dialog box. This new feature extends Notes' network security structure to your own computer. You can set up Notes to only allow specified people access to certain functions. These users are identified by their Notes user IDs and must enter their passwords before they can use Notes on your computer. Your company will probably have decided who should be allowed to perform which actions on particular computers, so you should not need to change these settings yourself.

Startup Database If you use one database frequently, you may want to have Notes open the database automatically every time you start the program. Click on this button to open a dialog box in which you can select any database already in your workspace.

User Dictionary This button opens the User Spell Dictionary dialog box shown in Figure 14.7. Here, you can edit the supplementary dictionary Notes uses for spelling checks. When you define a word during a spelling check, Notes adds it to this list. There are three ways to change the list. To delete a word, select it in the upper list box and click on Delete. To add a new word, type it in the bottom text box and click on Add. To change the spelling of a word in the list, select it in the list box, then type the corrected spelling in the text box and click on Update. Once you've made all the changes you need, click on OK to approve them or on Cancel to abandon them.

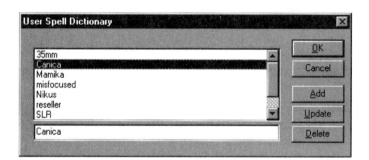

FIGURE 14.7:
This dialog box lets you fine-tune the supplementary dictionary.

International Settings

The International panel in the User Preferences dialog box lets you change a number of settings relating to the language in which you are using Notes. Most settings relate to foreign languages, but you can also choose the variant of English you want to use for spelling checks, and even choose to use a medical dictionary.

The three options under Collation/Casing let you choose how Notes sorts letters and numbers in views. Normally, Notes regards numbers as coming before letters, and accented letters as coming after their unaccented cousins. With Scandinavian collation checked, Notes sorts certain accented characters after unaccented characters. French Casing removes the accents on uppercase characters. Numbers Last collation sorts numbers after letters. If you change any of these settings, you'll need to restart Notes for the changes to take effect. Then move to the view you want to resort, and use Shift+F9 to rebuild the view according to the new sorting rules.

> **TIP** You can use Shift+F9 to have Notes rebuild any view that does not appear to be working properly. Notes completely reconstructs the view from the documents on which it is based, so this may take a while.

Cutting to the Chase in Windows 95

If you are using Notes on a Windows 95 workstation, you can go one step beyond just naming a database for Notes to open each time you start the program. You can also create shortcuts on your Windows 95 desktop that take you straight to a particular database, view, or document in Notes. The procedure is similar to the one for creating DocLinks, described in Chapter 8:

1. Open the database, view, or document that will be the destination for the shortcut you are going to create.
2. Choose Edit ➤ Copy As Link and then select Document Link, View Link, or Database Link as appropriate.
3. Go to the Windows 95 desktop (you may need to minimize the Notes window to make the desktop visible).
4. Right-click on the desktop and choose Paste Shortcut from the pop-up menu that Windows 95 displays. Windows 95 will create your shortcut.

Double-clicking on the shortcut opens the relevant database, view, or document. You can use Windows 95 shortcuts whether or not Notes is already open; if the program is already running, Windows 95 will switch to it rather than open a second copy.

If you find the shortcut labels Notes provides too wordy, highlight the shortcut and then click once on it again. You can then edit the label to make it more concisely descriptive.

The Measurements setting lets you choose between the Imperial system of measurements used in the United States, Myanmar, and the Central African Republic, and the Metric system used everywhere else.

Two buttons in the center of the panel open dialog boxes that allow you to make language-specific settings. You're unlikely to need to alter the Import/Export Character Set unless you're heavily involved in translating data from other computer systems. However, you may want to change the Spelling Dictionary that Notes uses.

Your choices of Spelling Dictionary depend on the version of Notes you are using. When Notes is sold outside North America, it is usually provided with several alternative dictionaries. You can then choose to check your spelling in many major languages. Among them are the American, Australian, and British variants of English (including both -*ise* and -*ize* conventions for British English). Medical professionals will welcome the ability to choose to use a medical dictionary (also available in American, British -*ise*, and British -*ize* versions).

Your last option on this tab is to choose the day that Notes should regard as the beginning of the week. This lets companies set Notes to match their internal and regional conventions. However, you would be well advised not to make a unilateral decision to start your own work week on, say, a Wednesday.

Mail Settings

You can get straight to the Mail panel of the User Preferences dialog box by clicking on the File Preferences Mail SmartIcon, or you can use File ➤ Tools ➤ User Preferences and then choose the Mail panel. Either way, what you see looks like Figure 14.8.

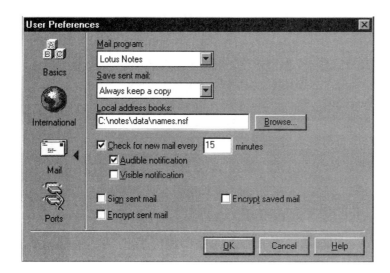

FIGURE 14.8:
The Mail panel of the User Preferences dialog box

Your first choice here is deciding what mail system to use: Lotus Notes, cc:Mail, another VIM-compliant mail package, or no mail at all. This option is set when Notes is set up for you, and it's unlikely that you'll need to change it.

You have three choices of how Notes should deal with mail you send: to have Notes always save a copy, to never save a copy, and to have Notes always ask you if it should save a copy.

The Local Address Books field contains the locations of your Personal Name & Address Book and any other name and address books you have stored locally. You can specify more than one address by separating the locations with commas; Notes treats the first as your main name and address book. If there's no location specified, Notes assumes you're using an address book called NAMES.NSF in your Notes data directory. You're unlikely to need to change this setting yourself.

The next group of settings determines when Notes looks for new mail and how it lets you know when new mail has arrived. Make sure the first box is checked to ensure that Notes does indeed check for new mail. The next setting lets you determine how often you want Notes to check. If you have a permanent connection to a network, you may want to check as frequently as every five minutes.

You probably remember that Notes changes the mail icon at the right of the status bar to an inbox icon when you have new mail waiting. You have another couple of options for how Notes notifies you of new mail. Check Audible Notification to have Notes beep when it finds new mail for you; check Visible Notification to have Notes place a message on the status bar and display a dialog box that lets you open your mailbox.

The final three checkboxes deal with encrypting and signing mail, subjects that are covered in detail in Chapter 18. They allow you to place an electronic signature automatically on every message you send, and to encrypt every message you send and/or every message you save.

Having molded Notes to your whims, collapsing and expanding every view within reach, you may be looking for some other core Notes skills to learn. Perhaps you've tried the text-searching techniques described at the beginning of this chapter and decided that you really need something more powerful to find the information you want. In fact, Notes offers some of the most heavy-duty text-searching techniques available, letting you quickly find just the right information from one or more databases. How to use these powerful features is the subject of Chapter 15.

Chapter 15

FULL-TEXT SEARCHING

FEATURING

- **Using operators and wildcards**
- **Simple searches with the Search Bar**
- **Complex searches with the Search Builder**
- **When to use a full-text search**
- **Stored searches**
- **Searching multiple databases**
- **Creating full-text indexes**

In Chapter 14, I told you about several ways to search in Notes. You saw how to search for text within a single document, how to search the whole contents of a view, and how to search across multiple documents in a view. Full-text searching is the one remaining way to search for text in Notes, and it is so flexible that it merits its own chapter: this one.

What Is Full-Text Searching?

Full-text searching is a very quick way to find all the documents in a view that contain a particular word or combination of words. If you have been using the word searching method we looked at in Chapter 14 to search in views, you've probably discovered that the time it takes to search a database increases quickly once the database starts to get big. In contrast, full-text searches take just a couple of seconds, even in large databases.

With full-text searching, you can specify the particular combinations of words you are looking for more accurately than you can by word searching. And you can tell a full-text search to look only in a particular field in a document. Full-text searching can also be set up to search for words in encrypted fields and in files attached to documents. You can even search several databases at the same time.

Notes gives you two main ways to use full-text searching:

- You can accomplish most searches by typing the terms to search for in the Search Bar.
- You can click on the Add Condition button to construct more complicated searches in a Search Builder dialog box.

Why You Shouldn't Use Full-Text Searches All the Time

As you might expect, full-text searching is a very good way to cut through a large database and quickly find the documents you want (or at least reduce the number of documents you have to sift through). So why would anyone bother with the slower, less flexible word search?

Full-text searches have two disadvantages:

- The index for the search must be created first and then kept up to date. The index is a separate series of files that tell Notes what words occur where in the database. Indexes for shared databases can only be created by people who have at least Designer-level access to the database (see Chapter 9 for an explanation of access levels). *You* must create and maintain the index for a local database in which you want to use full-text searching. (You can find out how to do this at the end of this chapter.)

- The index can be quite large. It may eat up storage space on the Domino server (for shared databases) or on your own computer (for local databases). Depending on how much information in a database is made up of text, the database's full-text index can consume from 1 to 50 percent as much space as the database itself.

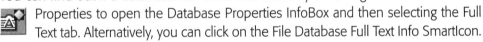

NOTE **If you have been using Notes 3.x on a Macintosh, you probably know that you couldn't create full-text indexes of local databases. In Notes 4.x, that drawback has been removed: You can use full-text searches on both local and shared databases.**

Finding Out If a Database Has a Full-Text Index

If you want to search a shared database for which you don't have Designer access, you have to rely on the database designer having established a full-text index already. You can find out if a database has a full-text index by choosing File ➤ Database ➤ Properties to open the Database Properties InfoBox and then selecting the Full Text tab. Alternatively, you can click on the File Database Full Text Info SmartIcon.

If the first line of the Full Text tab lists the last time the index was updated and its size, you know the database is indexed already. You can go ahead with your search. But if it reads instead, "Database is not full text indexed," then you can't perform a full-text search—at least not yet.

If you feel the database should have a full-text index, then there are two circumstances in which you can create it yourself:

- The database is a local database, stored either on your own computer or on another computer on the network to which you have access.
- The database is a shared database, stored on a Domino server, but you have at least Designer-level access to it.

If you *do* want to create an index, you should read "Creating a Full-Text Index" at the end of this chapter.

Most of the time, you won't have the necessary access to create a full-text index for a database. If you click on the Create Index button on the Full Text tab, Notes displays a message telling you that it is sorry it can't create an index for you. If you think an unin-dexed database is crying out for full-text indexing, you will need to petition the database manager to set up an index.

Searches from the Search Bar

Once you have determined that your database has a full-text index, you can go ahead and search it. Full-text searches only look at documents in the current view, so make sure you have opened a view that contains all the documents you want to search.

Choose View ➤ Search Bar or click on the View Show/Hide Search Bar SmartIcon to have Notes display the Search Bar at the top of your view. One is shown in Figure 15.1. You may have seen the Search Bar briefly in Chapter 14 when we looked at searching for text in multiple documents when a database *isn't* full-text indexed. The Search Bar in a database that does have a full-text index looks very simi-lar except that the button that was marked Create Index now says Add Condition.

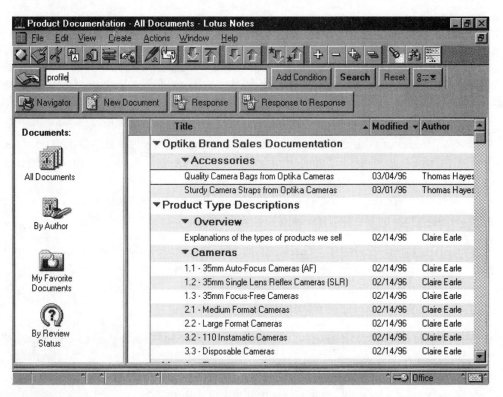

FIGURE 15.1: The Search Bar sits on top of your view and lets you quickly compose full-text searches.

In some ways, the Search Bar works like the Ruler Bar. You don't have to get rid of it once you're done searching. If you want, you can leave it displayed while you move in and out of documents in this view and even switch to other views. If at any time you want to see a couple more rows of the view, you can choose View ➤ Search Bar again to hide it.

In Notes 4.5, the Search Bar can also be exchanged for a Navigational Bar that helps you get around in Web pages (see Chapter 11). To switch to the Navigational Bar, click on the pointing-finger-and-book button on the Search Bar. To return to the Search Bar, click on the pointing-finger-and-globe button on the Navigational Bar.

To perform a straightforward full-text search, you only need to use two items on this bar:

1. Type the word or words you want to search for into the empty white text box.
2. **Search** Click on the Search button to tell Notes to look for your words.

As Figure 15.1 shows, I'm looking for any occurrences of the word *profile* in the documents in the current view. Clicking on the Search button produces something like Figure 15.2. It looks like a regular view except that it has fewer documents, no categories (assuming you had categories to start with), and a weird black and gray bar along the left-hand margin.

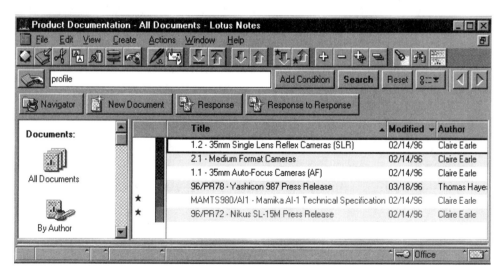

FIGURE 15.2: Once Notes finds the documents that contain the search terms, it ranks them by the frequency with which they occur in each document.

I assume you're not surprised that there are fewer documents. The category names are removed to help you focus on the documents your search has found.

What about the shaded bar? It indicates how "relevant" to your search Notes thinks the document is. Notes lists the documents in order from the one with most occurrences of the search terms to the one with the fewest. The bar helps you tell how many occurrences to expect in a particular document.

If you would prefer to have Notes display the search results as selected documents in a view, choose View ➤ Show ➤ Search Results Only. This option toggles between the regular and relevance-ranked views.

Reading the Documents You've Found

You read documents in relevance-ranked views just as you would normally. Once you open one of the documents in the view, you'll see that Notes has placed a red box around each occurrence of the words you were searching for (on a monochrome screen, the red box will be a delicate shade of gray). Notes even provides a couple of commands to help you skip from one search "hit" to the next:

- Press Ctrl and the + key or click on the Navigate Next Highlight SmartIcon to move from one highlighted word to the next in the document. Notes shows the current highlighted text with a green box. (Unfortunately, users of monochrome screens will find it difficult to pick out the gray box around the current highlighted text from the gray boxes around other words highlighted by the search.)

- Press Ctrl and the – key or click on the Navigate Previous Highlight SmartIcon to move back up the document from one highlighted word to the previous one.

Performing Another Search

To try another search in this view, type the words you want to search for into the Search Bar and click on the Search button again. To make changes to the search that you just performed, edit the text on the Search Bar and click on the Search button. To show all the documents in the view again, click on the Reset button.

Using Search Builder for More Complex Searches

If you want to look for a combination of words, then your best choice is to click on the Add Condition button. This opens the Search Builder dialog box shown in Figure 15.3.

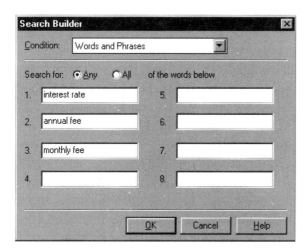

FIGURE 15.3:
The Search Builder lets you easily construct more complex searches, such as combinations of words.

The Words and Phrases search option shown in Figure 15.3 is only one of a number of possible types of searches you can perform in Search Builder. You can choose others from the drop-down list labeled Condition. The following is a brief description of each possible search type.

Searching for Words and Phrases

The Words and Phrases Search Builder helps you search for combinations of words. Type one of the words you want to look for into each of the numbered boxes, and then choose whether to search for Any of the words or All of them.

Once you have constructed your search, click on OK to have Notes place a "search token" on the Search Bar. This is a gray rectangle with a brief identification of your search. Later, you'll see how combining search tokens lets you construct more complex searches. For now, you want to perform the search you've defined, so click on the Search button.

Of course, you only have to fill as many boxes as you need for your search. And you can even put more than one word in a box. For example, placing the phrases **interest rate**, **annual fee**, and **monthly fee** in the first three boxes and selecting Any will find any document that contains one or more of these three phrases. If you select All, and then type **35mm** in the first box and **zoom lens** in the second, Notes will find only documents that contain both phrases.

Searching by Author

The By Author Search Builder lets you find documents written by a certain person. You can type the person's name in the box provided or click on the person icon to open a Names dialog box that lets you select names from an address book.

You can search for documents written by one of several people by separating their names with commas. If you don't know the full name, you can type just a first or last name. You can even choose to search for documents *not* written by a certain person.

Searching by Date

With the By Date Search Builder, you can find all documents written or edited on, before, or after a date, or within a range of dates. Choose first whether you're interested in the date on which the document was created or the date on which it was modified. Then choose one of the 10 types of date search. The first four relate to a particular date, and the next four relate to a particular number of days in the past or future. The last two options let you specify a range of dates.

Searching by Field

Choose the By Field Search Builder and you can restrict your search to looking in a particular field in the document. You could look for documents where the Address field contains the words *Paris, Texas* or where the Priority field does not contain the word *Urgent*.

First, choose a field name from the drop-down list. Without knowing the detailed structure of the database (and unless you have at least Designer-level access, you won't), it can be difficult to know which field you want to search. A field's name is not usually listed on forms or documents. Good database designers give their fields descriptive names, but there's no guarantee that, say, the address field on two different forms in the same database will have the same name.

TIP
If you have trouble working out the name of the field you wish to search, you should read the next section to see whether a Search by Form might be more productive. If you still want to search by field, try opening a document that contains the field. Then open the Fields tab of the Document Properties InfoBox. By scrolling through the field choices in the left-hand list, you should be able to work out which field contains the information you want.

Once you've determined in which field to look, the other items should be familiar: a choice of contains vs. does not contain, and a box to enter the text for which you're searching.

Searching by Form

There is a big difference between this type of search and the similarly named Search by Form Used. A Search by Form lets you type the text you want to search for directly into the fields of one of the database's forms. A Search by Form Used looks for documents created with a particular form.

Your first task in a Search by Form is to choose the form to use from the drop-down list. Then type the terms you wish to search for into the form's fields. Notes searches for documents that contain all the terms you specify (in their appropriate fields).

NOTE
You may find that in some databases (such as mail databases) there are many forms from which to choose. This is usually because there are many subforms and letterheads defined. Notes includes these in the Form list even though they are of little use for searching.

Searching by Form Used

This type of search differs from a Search by Form, as explained previously. In the By Form Used Search Builder, Notes provides a list of forms available in the current database. Place checkmarks next to the ones you want Notes to search for. When you perform the search, Notes finds every document composed with one of these forms.

Editing Searches

You will not always get the results you want on your first search. You can edit a search (before or after you perform it) by double-clicking on the search token on the Search Bar. Alternatively, you can highlight the token on the Search Bar and click on the Edit Condition button.

Notes opens the Search Builder dialog box again, where you can now edit the terms of your original search or even use the Condition box to change to a different type of search entirely. To delete a search token from the Search Bar, highlight the token and press the Delete key.

Searching with Operators and Wildcards

Once you've used Search Builder to add one search token to the Search Bar, you can click on Add Condition again to define a new search. Notes then separates the second search token from the first with the word AND, as in Figure 15.4. When you click on Search, Notes searches for documents that match *both* sets of criteria.

FIGURE 15.4: Click on the Add Condition button a second time and Notes lets you combine two search tokens.

Notes lets you use operators such as AND to combine search terms into more complex searches. You can combine one piece of search text with others, one search token with others, and even text with tokens. There are four operators that you can use with either text or tokens:

- As you've seen, AND tells Notes to search for documents that contain the text or tokens on both sides of it. You can also type this operator as and or &.
- OR, or, and | are different ways of telling Notes to search for either one of the search terms (or both).
- Place NOT, not, or ! before a search term to tell Notes to search for documents that don't contain the term.
- The operator ACCRUE works like a special version of OR. Notes finds documents that contain either term, but accords a greater relevance ranking to those that contain both.

Notes also offers three "proximity operators" designed for working with text.

- The operator `near` tells Notes to rank documents as having greater relevance when the terms separated by `near` are closer together.
- The `paragraph` operator works like `near` but only finds documents where the words occur in the same paragraph.
- The `sentence` operator works like `near` but only finds documents where the words occur in the same sentence.

To further manipulate the relevance ranking, place a `termweight` operator before each of your search terms. This lets you assign a weighting to each of the words for which you are searching. Here's an example:

```
termweight 25 Seattle or termweight 75 Tacoma
```

This search will find documents containing the name of either city but rank those containing mentions of Tacoma before those with mentions of Seattle.

As well as the previously mentioned operators, there are a number of other ways to manipulate text searches:

- Wildcards are special characters that you can use to match one or more letters in a word in order to conduct searches. Notes offers you two wildcard characters:

Character	Matches
?	Any one character in a word
*	One or more characters, or none at all

- You can use either wildcard character as many times as you want in a single word, with the exception that you can't use two asterisks in a row. You also can't use wildcards in date or number fields.
- If you hyphenate a word, Notes finds documents that contain the text as a hyphenated word, as two words, or that run it together as a single word.
- If you place parentheses around part of a search term, Notes calculates that part of the search expression before the part outside the parentheses.
- If you place quotation marks around a phrase, Notes looks for the exact combination of words you specify.
- If you place the operator `exactcase` before a search phrase, Notes only finds documents that contain the text in the same combination of upper- and lowercase characters.

The following list gives some examples of searches using these techniques and the kinds of words and phrases they would select in documents:

Search	Selects Documents Containing
?otes	Notes, motes, totes
??tes	Notes, bites, metes, hates
note*	note, Notes, notebook
n?t*s	Notes, nuts, notaries
note-book	note-book, notebook, note book
"war and peace"	war and peace (*the complete phrase*)
exactcase Lotus Notes	Lotus Notes is a fine groupware package, *but not* Lotus notes rise in demand for e-mail.

> **NOTE**
>
> **Most of these operators and wildcards can also be used in the fields of a Search Builder dialog box. For example, you could search for an Author named *(Dmitry Makarov OR Carol Simpson) AND NOT Kevin Johnson.***

Setting Search Options

When you type a search at the Search Bar or construct one in the Search Builder, you can take advantage of a few additional settings to tweak the searching process. To do so, click on the Options button on the Search Bar to display a menu of search options.

When Include Word Variants is checked, Notes finds variant forms of the word for which you are searching. For example, a search for *close* would also find *closed*, *closes*, and *closing*.

If you check Use Thesaurus, Notes will look for synonyms of the search terms you specify. Thus a search for *money* might also produce documents containing the word *currency*.

You have three options for displaying the result of your search. Sorted by Relevance is the standard for full-text searching, with the graded relevance bar in the margin. You can also display your search results Sorted by Oldest First and Sorted by Newest First.

If you perform full-text searches of large databases, you will frequently find that searches that are not sufficiently specific return far too many documents. You can keep this from happening by selecting Maximum Results and entering a number in the dialog box that Notes displays. When Notes finds the number of documents that match the search (the default is 250), it stops the search and tells you, "More than *xxx* matching documents were found."

The final two options on this menu are covered in the next section.

Saving Searches

Once you become comfortable with the process of full-text searching, you may find that you would like to repeat a particular search at fairly regular intervals. One case might be with a news database in which you've created a fairly intricate search that looks for documents that contain certain key words of interest to you.

Choose the Save Search option from the Options menu and Notes will prompt you for a name for this search. If you are using a shared database and would like this search to be available to other users, check the Shared Search box. Then click on OK and Notes will store your search. You can use the search any time you return to the database by choosing its name from the bottom of the Options menu.

You can get rid of a saved search by selecting Delete Saved Search from the Options menu, choosing the name of the search, and clicking on Delete.

Searching Multiple Databases

Notes offers you two methods of searching for text across several databases at the same time:

- Search site databases provide a single index for a group of named databases within a company or department (or even on your own computer). They need a fair amount of preparation and can take up significant disk space, but let Notes users find information more efficiently.
- *Ad hoc* searches let individuals scan a group of databases of their own choosing at short notice. The results of these searches are less integrated than those from search site databases.

Using Search Site Databases

Companies that use Notes can create whatever search sites they choose. You may find that you have access to more than one site, each covering key databases in a particular department or on a particular subject. Equally, if you work for a smaller company or if you only have access to a limited number of Domino servers, you may be able to use only one search site or none at all. Chapter 9 discusses various techniques you can use to track down a search site database. Alternatively, enlist the help of your Notes administrator.

Once you have added the database icon to your desktop and opened the search site, you will see the Search form shown in Figure 15.5.

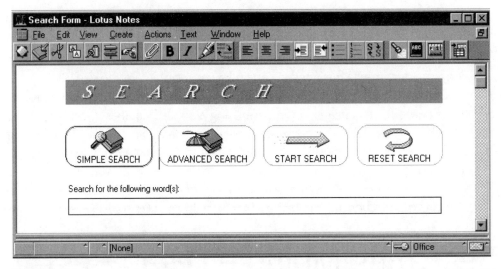

FIGURE 15.5: Use a search site database to scan multiple databases for the information you want.

There are two search types you can use in a search site database:

- Choose Simple Search to enter one or more words for which you want to search.
- Choose Advanced Search to compose more complex queries that can find word combinations and dates. You can limit your search to a maximum number of documents and to documents in certain named categories. You can also choose how Notes sorts the results it displays.

Once you have composed your search, click on the Start Search hotspot. Notes then displays the search results, with document titles, percentage relevance, and a

DocLink you can use to open the full document. If the search did not produce the document you are seeking, click on Reset Search to clear the form and try again.

> **NOTE** You can even create your own search sites for local databases. Bear in mind that you will need to have several local text-rich databases to make this worthwhile, and that search sites can consume considerable disk space. If you feel that a local search site might prove useful, you can find more information in the Notes Help database.

Searching Multiple Databases Yourself

If you don't have access to a search site database, or if you want to scan databases that are not included on it, you have another option. You can open a Navigation Pane that contains documents from several databases and then perform a regular full-text search on all the databases at once.

The first step is to open all the databases you want to search in the same navigator:

1. Go to the workspace.
2. Click *once* on the icon for the first database you want to open.
3. Hold down Shift and click *once* on the icon for each additional database you want to open.
4. Still holding down Shift, double-click on the icon for the last database you want to open. Notes opens the first database you selected. The titles of the other databases are displayed at the bottom of the Navigation Pane.

You can collapse and expand databases in the navigator just as you do when you work with views and folders in a hierarchy. If you compose a full-text search, Notes will display the documents it finds in the current view of the current database. However, you can switch between views and databases to find other occurrences of your search expression. Figure 15.6 shows a search across three databases.

> **TIP** You can even combine databases with and without full-text indexes in this type of search. Remember, though, that those databases without full-text indexes will take longer to search and won't display a relevance ranking.

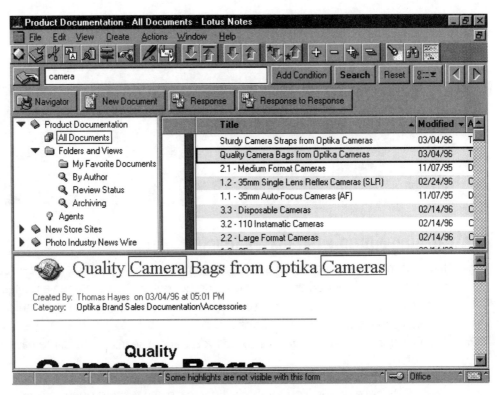

FIGURE 15.6: The view displays search results from one database, but the navigator shows that two others were searched.

Creating a Full-Text Index

The countless hours you have saved by using full-text searching have convinced you to index every database you can lay your hands on. How do you do it? First, you have to consider the two main drawbacks to full-text indexing that we touched on at the beginning of this chapter.

The index may take up to 50 percent as much disk space to store as the database itself. If the database is a local one, it's probably the disk space on your own computer you have to worry about (and it's probably your own decision what to use it for). If the database is shared (like your mail database), the index will consume space on a Domino server. You should therefore abide by whatever policy your company may have regarding consuming storage space on Domino servers.

The index needs to be maintained to be useful. Database indexes on a Domino server are maintained automatically, but for local databases the responsibility is yours. If you add new documents to a local database or modify existing ones, your changes won't be included in the index until you update it. Consequently, if you search the database, you won't find the new information you added. If you've deleted stuff, you may find documents that no longer contain the terms you searched for. You should update a local database's index at least every time you run a new search and when you have made substantial modifications.

Constructing an Index

To create an index for a database, you need to highlight the database's icon in the workspace or have a view or document in the database open on the screen. Choose File ➤ Database ➤ Properties to open the Database Properties InfoBox. You can also choose Database Properties from the shortcut menu that appears when you click the right mouse button. Then switch to the Full Text tab and click on Create Index to open the Full Text Create Index dialog box, shown in Figure 15.7. Two other options are to click on the File Database Full Text Create Index SmartIcon, or to click on the Create Index button on the Search Bar.

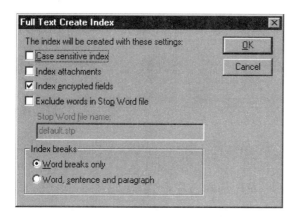

FIGURE 15.7:
The Full Text Create Index dialog box is where you tell Notes what kind of full-text index you want.

You can usually accept the default selections Notes makes in this dialog box, but if you're curious, here are your options:

> **Case Sensitive Index** Choosing a case-sensitive index lets you use the index to search for "Notes" and "notes" separately, for example. Case-sensitive indexes take up 5 to 10 percent more disk space.

Index Attachments Choose this option to have Notes include in the index words that appear in attached files. If a search retrieves a document because of a word contained in an attachment, you'll need to launch or view the attachment to find the search term. Notes can't highlight text in attached files.

Index Encrypted Fields If your database stores some information in encrypted fields, you can choose whether to include these in the index. The argument in favor of this is that your searches will look at the whole document. The argument against this is that even if unauthorized people can't read the field itself, they could use the information from a full-text search to see which documents contain what text.

Exclude Words in Stop Word File You can tell Notes not to index any occurrences of the words in a *stop word file*. The stop word file is an ASCII file that contains a list of common words, such as articles, prepositions, and conjunctions, that you don't want to waste space indexing. Notes provides a default file called DEFAULT.STP that contains 50 common words and all numbers. If you want to exclude additional words (say you work for a poultry producer and almost every document contains the word "chicken"), you can use a text editor to write your own stop word file. Using the default stop word file reduces the size of the average index by 15 to 20 percent.

Index Breaks You can choose to have Notes record sentence and paragraph breaks, which lets you search for words occurring in the same sentence or paragraph. Even without these breaks indexed, you can still rank documents depending on how close together the search terms are.

Once you have chosen precisely what to index, click on OK to start the indexing process.

If the database is stored on a Domino server, Notes will take over the process. The index is created by the server once the server has time to get around to it, and in 10 minutes or so you can start performing full-text searches.

If you're indexing a local database, you may see a notice that asks, "This is a local database and must be indexed manually. Do you want to index it now?" Notes is being both polite and confusing at the same time. The confusing part is the bit about "manual indexing." This doesn't mean getting your hands dirty or even typing indexing terms yourself. Instead, *manual indexing* means that you can't do anything else with your computer while Notes is indexing your database. The polite part is that Notes is trying to tell you this before it starts.

Of course, you want to index the database. You wouldn't have come this far by accident. So click on Yes and get a cup of coffee. Unless you have a *very* slow computer and a *very* big database, building the index shouldn't take more than 10 minutes.

NOTE Chapter 14 shows you how to set your user preferences to index local databases in the background.

Updating and Deleting Indexes

If your database is stored on a Domino server (your mail database, for example), the index is maintained by the server according to parameters set by your Notes administrator. Indexes for shared databases can be updated hourly, daily, or every time the database is altered.

If you're dealing with a local database, you have to remember to update the index. You do this by clicking on the Update Index button on the Full Text tab in the Database Properties InfoBox or by clicking on the File Database Full Text Update Index SmartIcon. The update process runs about as quickly as the initial indexing, but usually only a small number of documents have changed, so updating generally takes only a few seconds.

Even if you've forgotten to update a full-text index for a while, you should make a point of updating it before you do a new full-text search in the database. Otherwise, the search won't take account of any of your changes. You can find out how many documents have been changed since the last index by clicking on the Count Unindexed Documents button on the Full Text tab.

If you index a database by accident or decide that you could use the disk space for a new flying wombat screen saver, go to the Full Text tab in the Database Properties InfoBox and click on Delete Index.

Have you enjoyed the taste of power that full-text indexing gives you? If you want to further indulge your megalomania, the next step is to unleash an army of Notes agents upon your favorite databases. Chapter 16 shows you how to put together agents that can automate humdrum Notes tasks such as copying, deleting, and updating documents.

Chapter 16

GETTING AGENTS TO DO THE WORK

FEATURING

- **Agents you know and love**
- **Planning an agent**
- **Copying existing agents**
- **Creating a new agent**
- **Using the Agent Builder**
- **Testing and using your agent**

You've probably already found that Notes can save you a lot of time in your work, but you may also have run into some Notes tasks that are just tedious.

Maybe you are tired of filing the frequent notifications you receive from a work-flow-tracking database. Perhaps you often scan a Notes-format news service for articles relevant to your work.

Notes agents allow you to automate almost any type of tedious task in Notes. Beyond that, they can even make possible tasks that would take so long for you to do yourself that they would be impractical.

What Are Agents?

An *agent* is just a set of instructions that tells Notes what to do. You create an agent by telling Notes when you want to run the agent (on a schedule or triggered by an event), which documents it should act on, and what it should do with those documents.

> **NOTE**
>
> In earlier versions of Notes, agents were called macros. Changes in Notes 4.*x* mean that agents are now much easier to create and use than the old macros were. If you were put off by the complexity of creating macros in Notes 3.*x*, give them a second chance in Notes 4.*x*.

Notes divides agents into two types: personal agents, which can be used only by the person who created them, and shared agents, which are available to all users of a database and can be created by anyone with Designer-level access. Both types of agents are stored as part of the database. Once created, agents can't be changed from shared to personal or vice versa. In this chapter we look mainly at creating personal agents, but the process of creating shared agents is similar.

Notes agents can perform three sorts of actions. The simplest type can be chosen from a list of 14 actions provided by Notes. Here we will concentrate on agents that use one or more actions of this type. If you need to manipulate documents at a greater level of detail, you can use formulas composed from the 190 Notes @Functions. For ultimate sophistication, agents can also run LotusScript programs.

Some Familiar Agents and the Agent List

You may already have used several Notes database features that rely on actions for their operation. Here are some examples.

In your mail database, emptying the trash is performed by an agent. In addition, all the options on the Actions ➤ Mail Tools menu, covered in Chapter 18, launch agents. These let you archive your older mail, send automatic replies to colleagues when you're out of the office, and customize the appearance of your messages. A scheduled agent keeps track of your To Do list items.

The Discussion database uses several agents to manage the process of creating and editing personal interest profiles and sending out newsletter summaries based on the profiles. The Document Library template contains an agent to deal with documents that aren't reviewed by their due dates. Resource Reservations databases use a scheduled agent to purge reservations once they have expired. Among the scheduled agents in the Server Web Navigator database is one that updates the Top Ten selection of Web pages every hour. The Personal Web Navigator uses agents to set your Internet options and to manage the Web Ahead and Page Minder functions. Many Notes databases provide archiving agents.

You can see what agents exist for any database by choosing View ➤ Agents or by clicking on the Agents icon, which appears after the list of Folders and Views in the standard database navigator. What you'll see will be something like Figure 16.1, which shows the standard agents provided with the Mail database template.

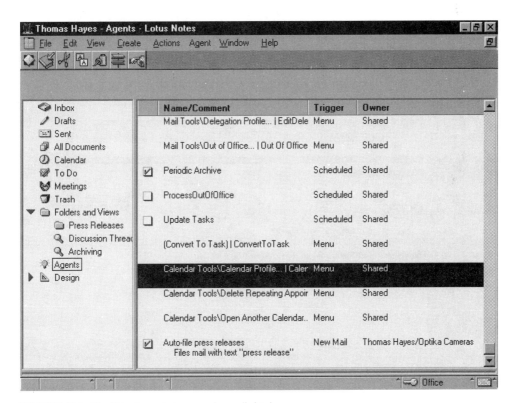

FIGURE 16.1: The list of agents in a regular mail database

Notes lists shared agents first, followed by hidden shared agents (which can only be run from this agent list) and personal agents. Agents that are defined to run on a schedule display a checkbox in the left-hand column. This checkbox determines whether or not the agent is currently enabled.

The second column lists the agent's name and, beneath that, any comment its creator has provided to explain its purpose. The last entry in the agent list in Figure 16.1 is a personal agent that includes a comment. Then comes the agent's trigger—the event that starts its operation—and the owner's name (for personal agents).

You can double-click on any agent's name in this view to edit its structure in the Agent Builder, a screen that asks the questions that tell Notes what you want the agent to do. Figure 16.2 shows the Agent Builder screen for a typical personal agent that files incoming mail. The sections that follow take a more detailed look at the options available in each part of the Agent Builder.

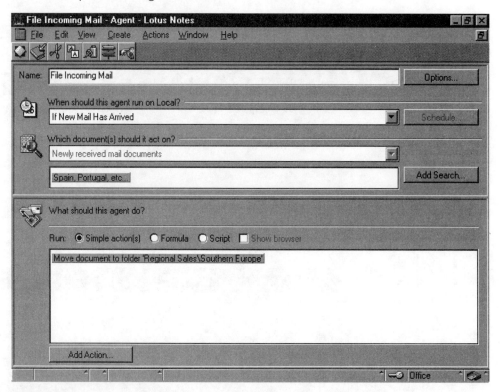

FIGURE 16.2: The Agent Builder takes you step by step through the process of making an agent—here it's an agent to file your incoming mail.

Planning an Agent

If you feel that an agent might be able to automate a particular task, you may want to sketch out specifications for it on a notepad. Decide whether your agent should be scheduled (acting every hour, day, week, or month) or triggered by an event (such as new mail being received or you choosing the agent's name from a menu).

Work out how you want Notes to determine on which documents the agent should act. Maybe you want to deal with every document in the database or every document in a particular view; maybe you'd rather have the agent work only on documents that you select or on those that have been added or modified since the last time you ran the agent. You may also want to further refine your selection by adding the same kinds of search conditions that you can use to define a full-text search.

Then define the action or series of actions you want Notes to perform on the documents it has selected. Do you want Notes to move them to a folder, summarize them in a newsletter that it mails to you, mark them as read, or delete them from the database entirely? Don't worry for now if you don't know precisely what actions will accomplish what you want, but try to describe the effect you are seeking.

> **NOTE** Personal agents can only perform the same range of actions that you could perform yourself as a database user. This means, for instance, that an agent can only modify documents if you have Editor-level or higher access to the database.

Once you have your agent planned, there are three ways you can create it. The simplest option is to copy and adapt an agent that already exists in the database. If there's no suitable agent already in the database, you can copy one you've found in another database and modify it if necessary. If the task you need to perform isn't covered by any existing agent, you can always create your own agent from scratch.

The next two brief sections cover the processes of copying an agent from the same database or a different one. The section that follows, "Creating an Agent from Scratch," deals with creating and modifying agents, covering all the options available in the Agent Builder.

> **WARNING** Agents can do a lot of work very quickly; equally they can do a lot of damage. If you started mistakenly deleting documents from a database yourself, you'd quickly realize what was happening, but an improperly constructed agent could delete hundreds of documents before you found the mistake. If you plan to construct an agent to work on a shared database, you would be wise to test it first on a local copy of the database before building it in the real database. Obviously, the importance of testing your agent on a dummy database depends on the value of the data with which it will be working and on the complexity of the actions the agent must perform.

To Copy an Agent from the Same Database

1. Use View ➤ Agents to display the database's list of agents.
2. Highlight the agent you want to copy.
3. Use Edit ➤ Copy, Ctrl+C, or click on the Edit Copy SmartIcon to place the agent on the Clipboard.
4. Use Edit ➤ Paste, Ctrl+V, or click on the Edit Paste SmartIcon.
5. If the database inherits its design from a design template, Notes will ask you whether you want the agent to be updated automatically when the template changes. Because you are making a copy of this agent in order to modify it, you are unlikely to want Notes to reverse your modifications when the template changes, so you should answer No.
6. Notes adds a new agent to the list. Its name is the same as the one you copied, but is preceded by "Copy Of...".
7. Follow the instructions in the section "Creating an Agent from Scratch" to modify the agent you have copied.

To Copy an Agent from Another Database

1. Open the database that contains the agent you want to copy.

2.   Use View ➤ Agents to display the database's list of agents.
3.   Highlight the agent you want to copy.
4.   Use Edit ➤ Copy, Ctrl+C, or click on the Edit Copy SmartIcon to place the agent on the Clipboard.
5.   Close the database.
6.   Open the database in which you want to place your copied agent.
7.   Use View ➤ Agents to display the database's list of agents.
8.   Use Edit ➤ Paste, Ctrl+V, or click on the Edit Paste SmartIcon.

9.   If the database inherits its design from a design template, Notes will ask you whether or not you want the agent to be updated automatically when the template changes. If you know that you will not need to modify the agent you are copying, you should probably choose to have Notes update the agent automatically. If you are going to modify the agent you are copying, choose No.
10.   Notes adds a new agent to the list. Its name is the same as the one you copied, except that it is preceded by "Copy Of... ".
11.   If necessary, use the instructions in the following section to modify the agent.

Creating an Agent from Scratch

If you can't find an agent to copy that performs the actions you want, you'll have to create one from scratch with the Agent Builder. You'll also have to use the Agent Builder if you need to modify a copied agent. Don't be intimidated, though; the process is really quite comprehensible.

To open a new agent in the Agent Builder, choose Create ➤ Agent. To edit an existing agent, double-click on its entry in the agent list. You'll see an Agent Builder screen similar to the one shown in Figure 16.2. For existing agents, Notes displays the agent's current structure; for new agents Notes provides default values.

Your first task is to name your agent. Agents you've copied from elsewhere will initially be named "Copy Of..."; new agents will be named "Untitled." Choose a brief name that reflects what the agent does. If you plan to run the agent by choosing its name from the Action menu, it's particularly important to choose a concise and descriptive name.

> **TIP**
> To place a manually run agent on a submenu of the main Actions menu, include a backslash character (\) in its name. For example, you could run an agent named *Filing Agents\Status Reports* by choosing Actions ➤ Filing Agents ➤ Status Reports. You can't use more than one level of submenus.

> **TIP**
> If you feel your agent has a special need for explanation, click on the Options button to find a field in which you can write a summary of its purpose and action. This text appears under the agent's name in the agent list.

If you have at least Designer-level access to the database, Notes displays a box that you can check to make your agent a shared agent that's accessible to all users of the database.

Choosing When the Agent Should Run

The first major question to answer in the Agent Builder is, "When should this agent run?" Your 10 choices are divided equally into five scheduled and five event-driven options.

Scheduled Agents

Scheduling is a good choice for maintenance agents. If you design an agent that automatically files messages from your Inbox based on their contents, you might want to run it once a day or once a week. Scheduled agents run in the background: You can work as normal while Notes performs the actions defined by the agent.

Your scheduling choices are On Schedule Hourly, On Schedule Daily, On Schedule Weekly, and On Schedule Monthly. With each type of scheduled agent, you can click on the Schedule button to specify the schedule in more detail. The name "hourly scheduled agent" is only a general description; you can actually choose to run this type of agent every 30 minutes, hour, two hours, four hours, or eight hours. By default, the agent runs on this schedule all the time, but you can choose a start time and stop time if you want.

Daily scheduled agents run by default at 1 A.M., weekly agents at 2 A.M. each Sunday, and monthly agents at 2 A.M. on the first day of each month. All of these defaults can be adjusted by clicking on the Schedule button. For all types of scheduled agents, you can also choose to have an agent not start operation until a particular date, and also to have it stop on a particular date. Hourly and daily agents can also be set not to run on weekends.

Finally, you can choose a server or workstation on which to run the agent. You will usually want to accept Notes' default suggestion, which is the same server or workstation as the one on which the database is stored. If you like, you can defer choosing a server until you enable the agent. To run scheduled agents locally, you must check the option Enable Scheduled Local Agents in your user preferences (see Chapter 14).

NOTE   **There is one more type of scheduled agent. The setting On Schedule Never is reserved for a particular class of agents created with Notes 3. When you upgrade to Notes 4.5 you should edit these agents and choose a different schedule setting.**

Event-Driven Agents

The other five options for when your agent should run are all *event-driven*. This means that the agent runs when something happens in the database or when you perform a particular action in Notes.

The first two event-driven options are to run your agent manually from either the Actions menu or the agent list. You would use one of these options when you want to run the agent by conscious choice rather than by triggering it automatically.

- The setting Manually from Actions Menu makes the agent a little more high-profile. Choosing a menu option will launch agents of this sort.
- Choosing Manually from Agent List means that to use your agent you will have to choose View ➤ Agents to display the agent list, highlight the agent's name, and then choose Actions ➤ Run. In the agent list, Notes describes these agents as Hidden, but they're just a little more difficult to launch. This option is good for infrequently used agents that might do harm if selected by accident, such as an agent that manipulates document fields. Use this option also when you want the agent to be launched by another agent.

The three remaining options trigger your agent based on events within the database.

- Choose the option If New Mail Has Arrived to have Notes trigger the agent when you receive messages. This is a common choice for use in mail database agents that are intended to automatically file incoming mail.
- The option If Documents Have Been Created or Modified triggers the agent every time a document is altered or added to the database. This is the only type of event-driven agent that accepts a limited schedule. You can specify start and stop dates, whether the agent should run on weekends, and the name of the server on which to run the agent.
- The option If Documents Have Been Pasted is useful in the particular circumstance where you are often pasting documents into a database using the document cut, copy, and paste techniques described in "Selecting Documents in a View" in Chapter 14. You might find that particular fields in these documents need manipulating and you could set up an agent to do this automatically.

Choosing Which Documents the Agent Should Act On

Question number two is "Which document(s) should it act on?" You'll be glad to know that certain choices of when your agent should operate limit your choice of which documents it should act on. Specifically, if you choose to have your agent triggered when new mail arrives, when documents are created or modified, or when documents are pasted, then the agent will only act on documents of those types.

If you choose a scheduled agent, your choices are to run the agent either on every document in the database or only on those that have been added or modified since the last time the agent was run.

Manual agents offer the widest choice. As well as the two options available for scheduled agents, you can also choose to run your manual agent on every document in the current view, on every unread document in the view, and on all selected documents (displayed in the current view or not).

Your final choice for a manual agent is Run Once (@Commands may be used). This type of agent operates either on the open document (in read-only or edit mode) or on whichever document is highlighted in a view. The @Commands referred to are a special class of Notes functions that duplicate the choices you can make in Notes menus.

> **TIP** If you want to run your agent on all documents in the database or on all documents in the view, the database must have a full-text index. Other document selection options don't have this limitation.

Refining Your Selection with a Search

If you wish, you can further restrict your selection of documents by specifying search criteria that the document must meet in order to be processed by the agent. You can add a search to all document selection options except for the Run Once option.

The way you construct this search is very similar to the full-text search process described in Chapter 15. You can type words to search for in the empty box below your initial document selection choice. If necessary you can use wildcards and search operators such as AND, OR, and near.

For more sophisticated searches, you can click on Add Search to have Notes display a Search Builder dialog box. This is almost identical to the one you would use to add a condition to a full-text search. The only difference is the new option In Folder. If you choose this search condition from the list at the top of the dialog box, Notes displays the same graphical hierarchy of folders and views that you see in the database's Navigation Pane. Here you can select a folder or view from which the agent will draw the documents on which it acts.

When you click on OK, Notes places a search token representing the condition in the search box. Unfortunately, Notes won't allow you to use search operators to combine multiple In Folder searches. For a full description of the other types of searches possible in Search Builder, read the section "Using Search Builder for More Complex Searches" in Chapter 15.

If you think you might want to use the same search criteria for full-text searching, you can choose to have Notes display the search on the Options menu on the full-text Search Bar as it does with saved full-text searches. To do this, click on the Options button at the top-right of the Agent Builder, check the box marked Show Search in Search Bar Menu, and click on OK.

Choosing What Action the Agent Should Perform

The third question that the Agent Builder asks you, "What should this agent do?" is probably the most crucial. Answers to this question are almost limitless, as Notes gives you three different languages in which to express them:

Simple Action(s) This is the option you'll choose most of the time, especially while you're new to creating agents. Notes provides 14 common actions that you can use separately or in combination. Dialog boxes prompt you for any necessary parameters to tell the action how to do its job. The effect of each of these actions is described in the section that follows.

Formula Choose this option to create actions that use the 190 Notes @Functions. These let you perform more detailed operations than the simple actions, but they are less user friendly. If you chose a Run Once agent, you can also use here the 358 Notes @Commands, which duplicate menu choices.

Script Scripts are the most flexible way of specifying an agent's actions. Scripts are programs written in a powerful language called LotusScript that can be used in many Lotus programs.

To select a language for Notes to use, click on the appropriate radio button.

> **NOTE** Reference documentation for **@Functions, @Commands, and LotusScript is available in the Contents ➤ Scripts & Formulas view of the Notes Help database. See the LotusScript and Notes Formula Language Overview for a general introduction. Notes also provides A-Z guides to the use and syntax of each element.**

Using Simple Actions

When you choose to express what an agent does in terms of simple actions, your tools are a large white text box in which to place your actions and an Add Action button that lets you choose the actions to use.

You can select one or more actions in any combination. Notes takes each document that your selection criteria have identified and applies in order the actions you specify. The only proviso is that Notes will always execute the action Delete from Database after any others you have included.

The following list details the parameters you must supply for each action and defines the action's effect where this is not self-explanatory. The phrase "selected documents" in these descriptions means those documents on which you chose to have the agent act, as refined by any search criteria you specified. It does not mean the documents checkmarked in any view unless you specifically chose to have Notes act on selected documents.

Copy to Database Choose this action to copy the selected documents to the database of your choice. If you choose the same database as the one in which the documents are currently stored, Notes duplicates the documents.

Copy to Folder This action places the selected documents in the folder you specify. Documents also remain in any folders in which they are currently filed.

Delete from Database Use this action to have Notes remove all the selected documents from the database. As noted previously, Notes performs this action after all others.

Mark Document Read This action marks every selected document to say that you have read it. The two field-modification actions automatically mark documents as unread; you can use this action to mark them read again.

Mark Document Unread This action marks every selected document to say that you have *not* read it.

Modify Field This is one of the most flexible of Notes' simple actions. Choose the name of a field from the list of all fields available in the database. Then enter a new value for the field in the box below. For plain text, keyword, and name fields, Notes lets you choose whether to replace the field's existing contents or to append the value you specify to any text the field already contains. For other field types, you can only replace the existing contents. Notes automatically marks each document as unread.

Modify Fields by Form This action lets you adjust Notes fields without knowing the fields' names. It also provides an easy means to alter several fields at the same time. Setting up the action works similarly to setting up a full-text search by form—Notes displays a replica form inside the Add Action dialog box. You can use the Form drop-down list to select the form that Notes displays. Where you want Notes to replace a particular field's contents, type the new value in the field. This action cannot append values to fields. Again, Notes automatically marks the selected documents as unread.

Move to Folder Use this action to move all the selected documents to a folder that you specify. Documents are removed from any folders they currently inhabit.

Remove from Folder This action removes all the selected documents from a folder that you specify. Any documents that are also filed in other folders will not be removed from those other folders.

Reply to Sender Use this action to send a reply to a memo or any other Notes document with a name in the From or $UpdatedBy fields. You can choose to reply to just the sender or to all other addressees. Type the body of the reply that you wish to send. Then you can choose to include a copy of the original document (like a Reply with History) and to reply just once per person (if the agent finds another document from the same person, it won't reply).

Run Agent This action allows you to link a series of agents together. Reasons for doing this include linking together agents that use LotusScript programs and @Functions, and helping in the construction of more complex manipulations. You can only chain together agents in the same database. Also, the only selection criteria that are effective are those of the first agent. After that, each successive agent just works with the documents that the first agent selected.

Send Document Use this action to mail the current document to one or more Notes users. The document must already have a SendTo field containing the recipients' names. (Most mail database documents will already have this field.) If the document has entries in the fields CopyTo and BlindCopyTo, Notes will add these recipients in the correct place.

Send Mail Message This action is a little more malleable than the previous one. Notes gives you fields in the Add Action dialog box in which you can type the addressee's name, a message subject, and a message body. As with Reply to Sender, you can include a copy of the original document, but you can also choose to send a DocLink instead (or, for overkill, in addition). You can click on the blue silhouette button to search the address book for names, or click on More to specify To, cc, bcc, and Subject fields in terms of either text or Notes @Functions.

Send Newsletter Summary This useful action allows you to quickly summarize all the selected documents. You have the same recipient, subject, and body text options as with sending a mail message, but this time you can check a box to have Notes add a summary of the selected documents below the body text you provide. You also must choose the name of a view in the database, from which Notes can draw text to annotate the DocLinks it includes in the summary. A final option lets you specify a minimum number of selected documents below which Notes will not mail a summary.

Your final option in the Add Action dialog box is labeled @Function Formula. This is duplicated on the simple action list to allow you to more easily combine @Functions with simple actions.

Testing Your Agent

 Once you've specified the when, which, and what of your agent, you can choose File ➤ Save, press Ctrl+S, or click on the File Save SmartIcon to save your new agent.

You may want to check that your agent is going to behave the way it should. Notes 4.5 offers a simulation function to help you do this. To test an agent, select its name in the agent list and choose Actions ➤ Test. Notes will run the agent, but without changing any documents.

Once the agent has finished operation, Notes displays a Test Run Agent Log dialog box with such information as the times at which the agent started and finished running, the number of documents that were processed, and any actions that would have been taken had you been running the agent for real. This information can help you decide whether your agent is working as intended or whether you need to make modifications.

Because you must choose Actions ➤ Test from the agent list, you can't test agents that use such selection criteria as All Documents in View and Selected Documents.

After testing your agent successfully, you can run it for real. If you want to run a scheduled agent without waiting for its schedule to trigger it, you can select the agent in the agent list and choose Actions ➤ Run.

You can check the progress of an agent at any time by selecting its name in the agent list and choosing Agent ➤ Log. Notes displays the agent log it recorded the last time the agent was run, containing the same sort of information as if you had tested the agent. If the agent has not been run since the last time it was modified, Notes displays a dialog box to tell you so.

NOTE

The Notes Help database contains a number of step-by-step examples of both personal and shared agents that you can create for various needs. To find these examples, choose Contents ➤ How Do I? from Help's navigator. Then open Do Everyday Tasks ➤ 11 Use Agents to Automate Tasks in the View Pane and browse the 15 topics titled Making an Agent That… or Making a … Agent. Most of these topics contain links to practical examples of how you might use each type of agent.

Looking at how to automate tasks with agents is about as deep as this book can get into Notes programming and database development without straying beyond its scope as a guide for beginning and intermediate Notes users. If you want more guidance on using Notes formulas, you should take a look at *Mastering Lotus Notes 4.5 and Domino*, also from Sybex. The remaining two chapters in this book return to a very familiar subject, your Notes mail database, to look at some more advanced mail functions.

Chapter 17

DOING MORE WITH TASKS AND THE CALENDAR

FEATURING

- **Managing your work with tasks**
- **The To Do view**
- **Finding free time for a meeting**
- **Booking rooms and resources**
- **Advanced scheduling functions**
- **Sharing your calendar**

As you and your colleagues become more familiar with Notes' calendaring and scheduling features, you will come to incorporate them more into your working routine. Soon you may find that you rely on Notes as the primary means of managing your calendar and scheduling meetings. By this point you are ready to put a few more scheduling and time management tools to good use.

This chapter looks at two related areas of your mail database: Task documents let you manage your workload in concert with your calendar, and advanced scheduling functions add extra sophistication to the basic invitation process you saw in Chapter 4.

Working with Tasks and Your To Do List

It's helpful to be able to organize messages in your mailbox into folders, but sometimes you also need to keep track of the actions you must take as a result of messages you've received. Notes lets you create Task records in your mail database to manage your time and workload.

How useful you find Notes tasks depends on the kind of job you do and how you like to organize your work. Take a look at this feature, try it out, and see if it's for you.

Converting a Message into a Task

Perhaps you opened your mailbox this morning and found five messages waiting for you. Two were just routine notifications that you filed away in appropriate folders. The remaining three messages all contained information you need to follow up on. One is really important, something you need to do right away. The other two are fairly important and you would like to complete them by the end of the day.

While you are reading these three messages, you can choose Actions ➤ Convert to Task to convert them to the form shown in Figure 17.1.

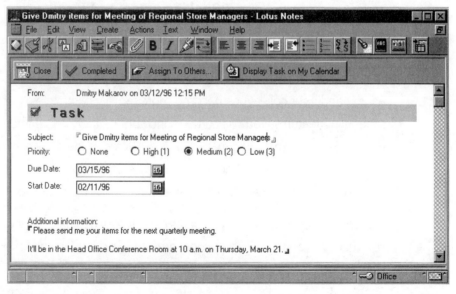

FIGURE 17.1: Converting a message into a task lets you set a due date and assign it to yourself or a colleague.

Notes takes the Subject line from the original message as the new task's title and places the body field under the heading Additional Information. You can edit either of these fields to better suit the message's new role as a task.

You can also select a priority for the task, the date by which it should be completed, and the date on which work should start. Tasks you create in this way don't have to just be items on your own To Do list; you can click on the Assign to Others button on the Action Bar to send the task to someone else. If you do choose Assign to Others, Notes adds two new fields, as shown in Figure 17.2, to let you name the person or people who should have responsibility for the task and any others who should receive a copy of your notification.

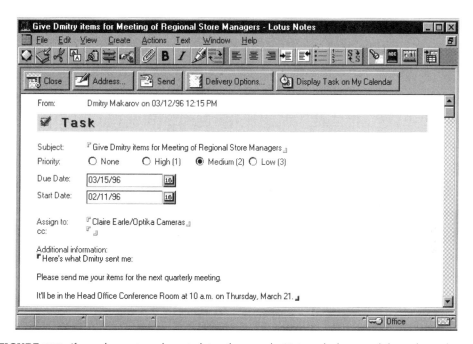

FIGURE 17.2: If you choose to assign a task to other people, Notes asks for more information so it can inform them.

If you would like Notes to include this task in your calendar, click on the Display Task on My Calendar button. Of course, you must enter a due date or a start date for Notes to be able to put the task on your calendar.

Once you've entered the requisite information for the new task, you can click on Close to save a task you've kept for yourself, or click on Send to notify those to whom you've delegated responsibility.

| TIP | When you choose to convert a message into a task, Notes automatically removes it from the Inbox and places it in the To Do view. |

Creating a Task from Scratch

As well as metamorphosing messages into tasks, you can also create new tasks from scratch using the New Task button at the top of the To Do view or by choosing Create ➤ Task. Again, you can either take responsibility for a new task yourself or you can assign it to one or more of your colleagues, who will receive notifications in their Notes mailboxes.

Dealing with Tasks Assigned to You

You have seen how you can choose to assign tasks to other Notes users, so you shouldn't be too surprised that they can also assign tasks to you. If someone does assign you the responsibility for a task, you will receive a mail message as notification. By default, Notes assumes that you will accept this assignment. If you prefer to decline it, click on the Please Reassign button. Notes then lets you include comments with your reply to the person who assigned you this task. After you have entered any comments you want to make, Notes sends off a reassignment message and places the task in the Rejected category of your To Do view.

Using the To Do View

Notes displays tasks you create from messages or from scratch in the To Do view of your mail file, an example of which is shown in Figure 17.3.

The To Do view categorizes your tasks by their status as follows:

- *Overdue* tasks are those whose due dates have passed but which are not yet complete.
- *Current* tasks haven't yet reached their due dates but have passed their start dates. Notes also lists tasks without assigned due dates under this category.
- *Future* tasks haven't yet reached their start dates.
- *Rejected* tasks are of two sorts: those that others assigned to you but that you rejected; and those that you assigned to other people but that they rejected.
- *Completed* tasks are those that you or others have reported as complete. If you assign a task to several people, Notes doesn't place it in this category until all those people report it as complete.

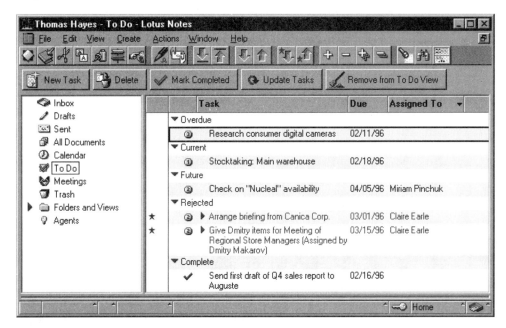

FIGURE 17.3: Your mail database's To Do view categorizes all your tasks and any that you've assigned to others.

Completed tasks display a checkmark; others show a numbered blob corresponding to the priority you assigned the task. As well as your tasks and those you've assigned to others, the To Do view also shows messages you've received that ask for a response by a particular date (see the "Special Options" section in Chapter 18 for more details).

Viewing Tasks on the Calendar

You can choose to display tasks alongside Calendar Entries in the Calendar view of your mail database. To do this, click on the Display Task on My Calendar button. If you later decide that you don't want to display a particular task on the calendar, open the Task document and click on the Remove Task from Calendar button.

Most tasks are indicated on your calendar (and in other mail database views) by a yellow checkmark icon like the one next to this paragraph.

Completed tasks are shown in views with a green checkmark icon.

If you have delegated a task to someone who has then declined it, or if you have declined a task delegated to you, Notes indicates this with a red cross icon in the view.

If you provided both a due date and a start date for the task, Notes displays the task on the start date on the calendar. If you gave only one date, Notes displays the task on that date. If you entered neither date, Notes will not be able to put the task on your calendar.

Tracking and Updating Tasks

Notes uses a number of hidden fields in each Task document to track the task's progress. To get a completely accurate picture of your To Do list, you need to run a special agent to update these fields. To run the agent manually, click on the Update Tasks button at the top of the To Do view.

> **TIP**
>
> You can also set up Notes to run this agent automatically on a schedule. You'll need access to run agents on your mail server (check with your Notes administrator if you're unsure whether you have this access). To set the agent to run automatically, open the Agents list in your mail database and check the box next to the "Update Tasks" agent. You may then have to provide the name of your mail server. By default, the agent runs every night at 1:00 A.M.

As you finish tasks on your To Do list, use the Mark Completed button to check them off the list. Notes moves these tasks to the Completed category at the bottom of the list. People to whom you've assigned tasks should also use Mark Completed when they are finished with their portion, and you will then receive a notification.

If you need to change the due date, start date, or priority for a task, you can edit the Task document to reflect this. If you assigned the task to others, send them copies to let them know of the change.

As completed tasks begin to accumulate at the bottom of the To Do view, you can use the Remove from To Do View button to help you focus on those that still need attention.

Advanced Calendar Functions

Back in Chapter 4, you learned all the workaday calendar functions of your mail database. Notes also offers a number of more sophisticated functions to make scheduling more powerful and flexible for you and your workgroup. The rest of this chapter looks at the more advanced functions that help you schedule meetings and reply to meeting invitations, work with other people's calendars, and configure your own calendar so that it works in the way that suits you best.

Setting Your Calendar Profile

When you are using your Notes calendar regularly, you may want to make a few adjustments so that it works in the way that best suits you. Notes keeps a Calendar Profile for each user; this profile allows you to customize how the calendar works. To open the Calendar Profile, choose Actions ➤ Calendar Tools ➤ Calendar Profile and you'll see a screen like the one in Figure 17.4.

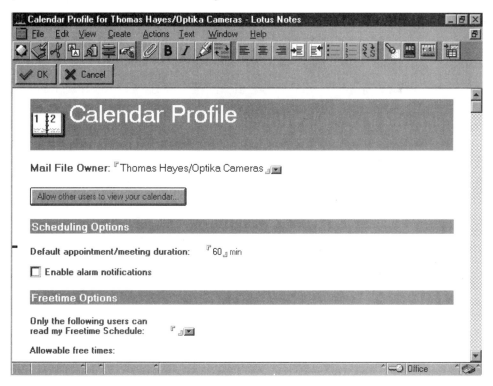

FIGURE 17.4: The Calendar Profile lets you customize Notes' calendar functions.

NOTE You may also have been prompted to fill out a Calendar Profile when you first opened your mail database.

The first field on this screen tells Notes which user is responsible for this mail file and should already have your own name in it. You should not need to change this field. Below it, the button marked Allow Other Users to View Your Calendar opens your Delegation Profile. If you want to let other people read your calendar or mail, read the section "Setting Your Delegation Profile" later in this chapter.

Scheduling Options

Back in the Calendar Profile, the first field in the Scheduling Options section lets you set the default length of time that Notes uses when composing new appointments and meetings.

Check the Enable Alarm Notifications box to have the ability to set alarms to remind you of your appointments and meetings. (This feature is turned off by default, but Notes gives you the option to turn it on the first time you try to set an alarm.)

If you do choose to enable alarm notifications, Notes gives you another option, which allows you to automatically set alarms for any combination of four categories of Calendar Entries: appointments and meetings, reminders, events, and anniversaries. For events and anniversaries, you choose the number of days in advance you want to be warned; for the other categories, choose the number of minutes. The alternative to automatic alarms is to set alarms individually for each Calendar Entry you create.

Freetime Options

The next section of options in the Calendar Profile deals with your Freetime Schedule (in Notesspeak, Freetime is a single word). Your Freetime Schedule allows Notes to tell other people when you are available for meetings. You tell Notes which times on which days you are normally available. Notes then looks at any items already booked on your calendar and combines the two sets of information when it reports your free time to other Notes users.

Notes assumes initially that you don't mind your Freetime Schedule being available for anyone to read. This is very different from allowing someone to read your calendar (an option you can choose in the Delegation Profile)—people reading your Freetime

Schedule can only tell what times you are available and unavailable, not what you are doing at those times. Nevertheless, if you want to restrict access to your Freetime Schedule to a select group of your most trusted henchpeople, Notes gives you a field in which you can specify their names.

> **TIP**
>
> **To let anyone find out when you are free, leave the list of users blank. To allow *no one* that privilege, enter only your own name in the field.**

Next comes the essential part of this section—listing the days and times you are available. Check the boxes for all the days of the week on which you normally work. Then edit the time range in each field to match the hours you are available. You don't have to stick to a single pair of times for each day; you can use commas to list as many time ranges as you want. For instance, the following entry would represent a 9 A.M. to 6 P.M. workday with a one-hour break and a half-hour break: **9:00 AM—12:30 PM, 1:30 PM— 4:00 PM, 4:30 PM—6:00 PM**.

> **NOTE**
>
> **To change the first day of your work week, see "Changing Your User Preferences" in Chapter 14.**

Advanced Calendar Options

At the bottom of the Calendar Profile is an expandable section of Advanced Calendar Options. The first two checkboxes let you automate certain calendar functions.

If you check the Meetings box, Notes will automatically accept any meeting invitations you are sent, as long as the time is marked as free in your Freetime Schedule. If the time is not free, Notes prefaces the invitation's subject as shown in your Inbox with "(Time Conflict)" and lets you respond yourself. If you want to automatically accept invitations from certain people only, Notes lets you list them by name.

If you choose to auto-process meetings, Notes will also automatically add to your calendar any broadcast invitations (invitations that don't require a response) that you receive.

> **NOTE** You must have Designer-level access to your mail database to choose to auto-process meetings (most users have sufficient access by default). When you close the Calendar Options window, Notes will ask you to choose a server on which to run the auto-processing agent; you should select your mail server.

You can also check a box to have Notes automatically take invitations out of your Inbox after you respond to them (or, in the case of broadcast invitations, after you add them to your calendar). You can still see these invitations listed in the Calendar and Meetings views.

The remaining section of Advanced Calendar Options lets you fine-tune how Notes behaves when you create new Calendar Entries. You can choose which of the five types of Calendar Entry you want Notes to use as the default. A checkbox tells Notes to hide each new Calendar Entry from other Notes users who can read your calendar (until you choose to make the entry public).

Finally you can turn on and off Notes' conflict-checking procedures for three classes of Calendar Entries: appointments and meetings, anniversaries, and events. When you subsequently create one of these types of Calendar Entry, Notes checks to see whether any other scheduled Calendar Entry overlaps. If there is a conflict, Notes warns you and lets you choose whether to add the new entry to your calendar.

To confirm any changes you have made to your Calendar Profile, click on the OK button on the Action Bar. Clicking on the Cancel button will leave the profile the way it was before you started meddling.

Setting Your Delegation Profile

The Delegation Profile lets you tell Notes who can read and manage your calendar, and who can read, edit, and send mail on your behalf. To edit your Delegation Profile, choose Actions ➤ Mail Tools ➤ Delegation Profile, or click on the button marked Allow Other Users to View Your Calendar on your Calendar Profile. Notes will display a screen like the one shown in Figure 17.5.

Calendar Access

The first section on this form lets you choose who can read and who can add items to your calendar. Initially, Notes is set not to give these forms of access to anyone. If you choose to, you can allow any other Notes user to read your calendar, and (separately) to create and edit calendar items on your behalf (this is what the confusing phrase "manage my calendar" means).

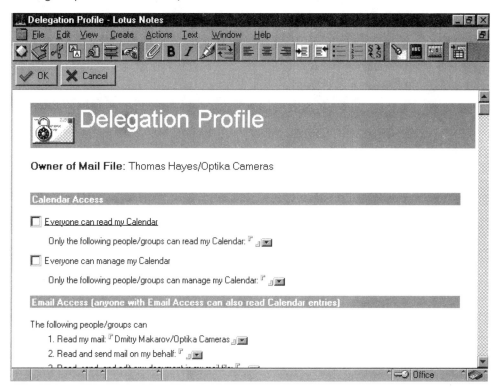

FIGURE 17.5: Your Delegation Profile lets you choose who can read and work with your calendar and mailbox.

More likely, you will only want to delegate this type of responsibility to certain named people—a secretary or administrative assistant, perhaps. Notes gives you two fields in which to confer each type of calendar access on other named Notes users:

- People whom you let read your calendar are given access only to Calendar views and Calendar Entry documents.
- People whom you let manage your calendar can read, edit , create, and delete Calendar Entries, and use Calendar views.

> **TIP**
>
> If you choose to let other people read your calendar, you can keep certain Calendar Entries private by selecting the Not for Public Viewing option. However, if you choose to allow some people to read your mail file, they can see all documents in the database, including those marked Not for Public Viewing. Also, people you allow to manage your calendar cannot select the Not for Public Viewing option when they create Calendar Entries on your behalf.

E-Mail Access

The second section lets you name people who should be given each of four levels of access to your mail file. The aim of these options is to allow you to delegate the responsibility to write mail in your name or respond to mail on your behalf. You can let other Notes users:

- Read your mail
- Create, send, read, and delete mail (but not edit existing messages)
- Create, send, edit, read, or delete any document in your mail database
- Delete mail

Any people you name in one of the first three categories will automatically be able to see your calendar, too.

Once you have the Delegation Profile as you would like it, click on OK to store it; if you goofed, click on Cancel.

Converting a Message into a Calendar Entry

As well as converting a mail message into a task, as you learned at the beginning of this chapter, you can also take a message you receive and create a Calendar Entry from it. Simply choose Actions ➤ Create Calendar Entry. Notes creates a new Reminder entry, placing the message subject in the brief description field, and the message body in the detailed description field.

Functions for Booking Meetings

In Chapter 4, we looked at how to send out invitations for a basic meeting, when you don't need to book a room, reserve special equipment, or juggle other people's schedules to find the best time. But often things aren't that straightforward, which is why Notes offers a variety of functions aimed at easing the bureaucratic nightmare of booking meetings for busy people.

Finding Free Time

One of the most tiresome aspects of booking meetings in the conventional way—with a desk diary and a phone, and perhaps some walking from one office to the next—is trying to find a time when everyone you want to attend is free. Finding a free time using Notes is a whole lot easier:

1. In your new Calendar Entry, make sure to do the following:

    - Specify a tentative date and time.
    - Name the people you want to invite to your meeting in the Send Invitations To and Optional Invitees fields.
    - Select any rooms or resources you want to book (see "Booking Rooms and Resources" later in this chapter).

2. Click on the Find Free Time button. Notes displays the Free Time dialog box, as shown in Figure 17.6.

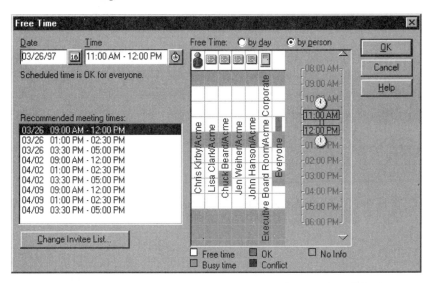

FIGURE 17.6: Find the most convenient time for your meeting in the Free Time dialog box.

WARNING Notes will not let you search for free time if you are editing a repeating meeting entry. How to reschedule repeating meetings is explained in Chapter 4.

3. If the time you suggested is free for all the attendees you named, Notes lets you know. If the time is not free for everyone, Notes displays the message "Scheduled time is NOT OK for everyone" and attempts to find other suitable times within a three-week period. Notes lists any alternatives it finds in the Recommended Meeting Times box.

4. If the time you suggested was free for all, you can click on OK to return to the Calendar Entry. If you want to take up one of Notes' recommendations, select the time in the Recommended Meeting Times box and click on OK. If Notes can't find any alternative times, or if the alternatives it offers don't suit you, you can search for a free time in any of the following ways:

- Use the By Person view of the free time grid to find a time when all or most of the invitees are available. Click on the By Person radio button to switch to this view if it is not already displayed. Use the time selection box in the same way as you would in a Calendar Entry to select a suitable time. Use the grid and the legend below to work out who is available when.

- Use the By Day view of the free time grid to find a suitable time for the meeting. Click on the By Day radio button to switch to this view if it is not already displayed. This view shows the collective free time of all the invitees over several days rather than showing individuals' schedules in separate columns.

- Click on Change Invitee List to add or remove people from the list you specified earlier. Notes displays the Change Invitees dialog box, with Notes users listed at the left and your invitee list at the right. To remove an invitee, select the person's name in the box on the right and click on Remove. To add an invitee, select a name on the left and click on either Required or Optional. To change the status of an invitee, you must first remove his or her name and then add it again from the box on the left. The Remove All button lets you start the invitation process afresh.

- Change the suggested Date and Time in the fields at the top left of the Free Time dialog box. Notes then recalculates its meeting time suggestions based on the new information.

5. Once you find a time that accommodates all or most of the invitees, click on OK to return to the Calendar Entry.

Tips on Finding Free Time   When Notes looks for meeting times to recommend, it first tries to find a time that is free for everyone you want to invite. If Notes can't find a time that suits everyone, it then gives preference to the people you named as required invitees. If Notes can find a time that suits all or most of these people, the program will recommend that time, regardless of whether your optional invitees are free.

If your suggested date and time are within the next seven days, Notes looks for alternative times within the next three weeks. If, however, you were trying to schedule a meeting eight or more days in advance, Notes looks for free times within the week before and two weeks after the date you suggested. Notes changes this three-week range to match any changes you make to the date and time listed in the Free Time dialog box.

When Notes suggests a block of free time in the Recommended Meeting Times field, some may be longer than the length you have specified for your meeting. For example, Notes may suggest 08:00 AM–11:30 AM as a possible time for a meeting that you have specified as an hour long. If you select this entry in the Recommended Meeting Times field, Notes assumes that you want your hour-long meeting to begin at the start of the available time (and so changes the meeting time to 08:00 AM– 09:00 AM). To select a different time within the available range, enter this directly in the Time field (09:30 AM–10:30 AM, for example), or click on the stopwatch icon to the right of the field to select it.

When you show the free time grid by person, Notes lists your free time in the first column in the grid, followed by the schedules of all the required attendees and then any optional invitees you have named. After the columns for people, Notes also represents the availability of any rooms or resources you want to book for the meeting (see the next section, "Booking Rooms and Resources").

If the Freetime Schedule of anyone you have invited is not available, Notes displays a gray bar for their entry in the free time grid. Notes also displays a message telling you, for example, "8 of 10 schedules available."

NOTE   Notes tells when you are free based on your Freetime Schedule as modified by the items already on your calendar. To change your Freetime Schedule or restrict who can read it, see the "Setting Your Calendar Profile" section earlier in this chapter.

> **TIP**
>
> If you are an exceptionally busy person, you may even want to use the Freetime Schedule to find out when you are available yourself! Notes only displays the Find Free Time button on Calendar Entries you have defined as invitations, so start off your new Calendar Entry as an invitation and enter a suggested date and time. Click on Find Free Time and use the functions of the Free Time dialog box to find a suitable block of time for your appointment or other event. When you return to the new document, select the type of Calendar Entry you want.

Booking Rooms and Resources

The scheduling functions introduced in Notes 4.5 are integrated with a special database that sorts out the muddle of booking rooms and equipment for a Notes-using workgroup, department, or company. If booking a conference room has involved multiple frustrating calls to a central facilities or administrative group (or if you are an administrator tired of resolving competing bookings for equipment and rooms), this database could make your life a lot simpler.

The Resource Reservations database can handle bookings for both rooms and other "resources." Resources could include computers, displays, overhead projectors, whiteboards, and anything else that might need to be booked for meetings. The database takes a little planning and configuration, and although most Notes-using companies will probably choose to use it, you may find that it hasn't yet been fully implemented where you work.

The database is described in more detail in Chapter 10. You can reserve rooms and resources from within a Calendar Entry, or directly from the Resource Reservations database. Making bookings from a Calendar Entry has the advantage that Notes automatically changes or cancels the booking if you reschedule or cancel the meeting. The sections that follow look briefly at how to make and break reservations from within an invitation.

Booking a Specific Room   If you know *where* you want to hold your meeting and just need to find an available time:

1. Specify the date and time of your meeting.
2. Expand the Reservations section at the bottom of the Calendar Entry form and click on Reserve Specific Room.
3. Notes displays a list of available rooms from which you can make your selection. Do so and click on OK.
4. If you now choose to use the Find Free Time option, Notes includes the room's booking schedule in the free time grid.
5. When you close and save the Calendar Entry, Notes places a request with the Resource Reservations database for the room and time you have specified.

    - If the room is free, Notes reserves it for you and sends you a notification.
    - If the room is unavailable, Notes sends you a message telling you that it couldn't make the booking. In this case, you can either open the original Calendar Entry and change your booking, or book the room directly in the Resource Reservations database (see Chapter 10).

Finding an Available Room   If you know *when* you want to hold your meeting, but are flexible about where to meet:

1. Specify the date and time of your meeting, and list all the required and optional invitees (so that Notes knows how large a room you will need).
2. Expand the Reservations section at the bottom of the Calendar Entry form and click on Find Available Room.
3. Notes lists a number of sites at which you can book rooms. Select a site for your meeting and click on OK.
4. When you close and save the Calendar Entry, Notes places a request with the Resource Reservations database for the site and time you have specified.

    - If there is a suitable free room, Notes reserves it for you and sends you a notification.
    - If no room is available, Notes tells you that it couldn't make the booking. In this case, you can either open the original Calendar Entry and change your booking, or book a room directly in the Resource Reservations database (see Chapter 10).

Booking a Resource   To book one or more resources for your meeting:

1. Specify the date and time of your meeting.
2. Expand the Reservations section at the bottom of the Calendar Entry form and click on Reserve Resources.
3. Notes displays a list of available resources; select one or more of them and click on OK.
4. If you now use the Find Free Time option, Notes includes the booking schedules for these resources in the free time grid.
5. When you close and save the Calendar Entry, Notes places a request with the Resource Reservations database for the resource and time you have specified.

    - If the resource is free, Notes reserves it for you and sends you a notification.
    - If the resource is unavailable, Notes sends you a message telling you that it couldn't make the booking. In this case, you can either open the original Calendar Entry and change your booking, or book the resource directly in the Resource Reservations database (see Chapter 10).

Changing and Canceling Resource Reservations   If you need to reschedule your meeting, Notes automatically cancels your old room and resource reservations and sends new requests to the Resource Reservations database.

> **NOTE**   Remember, as well as entering a new date or time for your meeting, you can reschedule it by dragging it to a different place on the calendar. See "Rescheduling with Drag-and-Drop" in Chapter 4 for full instructions.

You can cancel a room or resource that you have reserved for a particular meeting by opening the Calendar Entry and choosing the menu option Actions ➤ Remove ➤ Rooms & Resources. Select one or more rooms or resources whose bookings you want to cancel from the list that Notes displays and click on OK. You can then click on the appropriate buttons to reserve a different room or resource if you so choose.

NOTE
If you change or cancel a *room* reservation for a particular meeting, Notes sends out new invitations to inform the attendees. If you decide that, after all, you don't need an overhead projector, you'll be glad to know that Notes doesn't bother issuing new invitations for a changed or canceled *resource* reservation.

Tracking Responses to a Meeting

Once you have put together your meeting invitation, Notes sends it off to all your invitees, along with any booking requests for rooms and resources. As people respond to the invitation and Notes checks for conflicting resource bookings, you will receive notifications by Notes mail. These arrive in your Inbox and, if you switch to the Meetings view, you can also see them indented under the meeting's main entry.

You can also choose to see these responses listed in the Calendar Entry document you created:

1. Open the Calendar Entry.
2. Click on the Display Invitee Responses button in the Reservations section.

NOTE
Notes usually does not display this button for repeating meetings, or if you checked the box *I don't want responses from the invitees*. However, you will see this button if you chose to reserve a room or resource.

3. Notes opens an Invitee Responses dialog box, listing the names of people who have accepted, declined, or delegated your invitation; those who have yet to reply; those who suggested a different date, time, or place; the names of any people to whom attendance has been delegated; and the details of rooms and resource reservations that have been booked, turned down, or not yet confirmed. Luckily, you will not usually get responses in all of these categories.

> **TIP** Choosing *not* to receive responses from invitees (and to issue a broadcast invitation instead) can make sense for large meetings (a whole company meeting, for example), which will go ahead whether or not everyone can attend. When you create repeating meetings, Notes issues broadcast invitations by default.

Accepting/Declining a Proposed Meeting Change   If one of the people you invited to your meeting wants to suggest a different date, time, or place, Notes sends you a counterproposal message. Your choices are quite simple: Notes gives you an Accept Counter Proposal button and a Decline Counter Proposal button. If you accept, Notes sends out new invitations and makes new resource requests, if needed. If you decline, Notes sends an explanatory reply to the person who suggested the change.

Changing an Invitee's Response to Accepted   Imagine this scenario: You are trying to arrange an important meeting and a few recalcitrant colleagues refuse to reply to your invitations. Perhaps they do reply, but always decline even though their Freetime Schedules show them as available. You still have one card up your sleeve: As chairperson of the meeting, you can require that they attend. Here's how:

1. Open the meeting entry.
2. Choose Actions ➤ Change Status to Accepted. Notes opens a dialog box listing the names of invitees who have not yet succumbed to your polite entreaties.
3. Select the names of anyone whose attendance you are going to require and click on OK.
4. Notes sends messages to these people saying they are required to attend this meeting. When the invitee opens the message, Notes adds the meeting automatically to the person's calendar and marks the time busy in his or her Freetime Schedule.

As you can probably imagine, frequent use of this option is unlikely to endear you to your colleagues.

Removing an Invitee from the List

If you change your mind about some of the people you have invited, you can cancel the invitation on an individual basis. Open the meeting entry and choose Actions ➤ Remove ➤ Invitees. Choose one or more names from the list and click on OK. Notes sends these people a message informing them that they are no longer required to attend. When the invitee opens the message, Notes removes the meeting from his or her calendar.

Confirming a Meeting

If you arranged a meeting far in advance, or if it is particularly important that people attend, you can click on the Send Confirmation button on the Action Bar above a meeting entry to have Notes send a confirmation message to each invitee.

Canceling a Meeting

To cancel a meeting entirely, open the meeting entry and choose Actions ➤ Cancel Meeting. If the meeting is one in a series of repeating meetings, you can choose to cancel just this occurrence, all previous or all future occurrences, or the entire series. You can also use Actions ➤ Calendar Tools ➤ Delete Repeating Appointment(s) to remove repeating meetings.

Notes cancels any rooms or resources you booked and sends out a cancellation message to each invitee. When the message is opened, Notes removes the meeting(s) from the invitee's calendar.

> **NOTE** Remember to cancel separately any room or reservation bookings you made in the Resource Reservations database if you delete the repeating meeting to which they related. Notes can't cancel these automatically.

> **NOTE** If you delete the parent entry (shown in the Meetings view) for a series of repeating meetings, Notes converts each meeting in the series into a separate, nonrepeating meeting.

Reading Someone Else's Calendar

If your job involves administering schedules for other people, you may have been given access to one or more people's calendars or mail files. If this applies to you, here is how you can display *their* calendars on *your* computer:

1. Open your mail database, or select its icon in the workspace.
2. Choose Action ➤ Calendar Tools ➤ Open Another Calendar. Notes opens a small address selection dialog box.
3. Choose the Notes user's name from the list and click on OK. If necessary, change to a different address book to find the right person.
4. Notes opens the other user's calendar for you to browse. If you have been given access to read only the user's calendar, you are restricted to the Calendar and Meetings views. If at first Notes doesn't display other views, drag the left border of the View Pane to the right to reveal the Navigation Pane, from which you can switch to other views.
5. Read, edit, create, and delete Calendar Entries according to your needs and the level of access you have been assigned.
6. When you have finished, close the Calendar view window as normal (by pressing Esc, for example) to leave the other person's mail database.

> **NOTE**   Read "Setting Your Delegation Profile," earlier in this chapter, to find out more about working with other users' mailboxes and calendars.

That's the last of the advanced calendaring functions in your mail database, but there are still a few special functions that you can use on the e-mail side of things. Chapter 18 looks at these remaining mail functions, which range from the undeniably valuable (sending Internet mail) to the less-than-mission-critical (mood stamps, for example).

Chapter 18

THE WIDER WORLD OF NOTES MAIL

- **Delivery and receipt reports**
- **Signing and encrypting mail**
- **Special mail forms**
- **Stationery and letterheads**
- **Mail archiving**
- **Sending mail to the Internet and other mail systems**
- **Your Personal Name & Address Book**

By now you're comfortable with sending Notes messages to the members of the company softball team. You've used your company's Public Name & Address Book several times to address messages to people who don't even work in the same state as you do. But you know there's more.

Your friend across the aisle says he had Notes give him a confirmation of receipt when he mailed his quarterly report to the vice president. He's also using the Internet to keep in touch with other companies (and *their* softball teams). How does he do it? This chapter shows you how.

Delivery Options

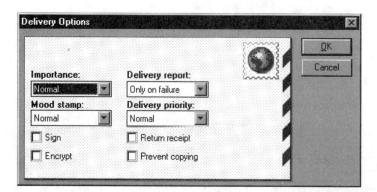

You probably already noticed the Delivery Options button that appears on the Action Bar when you create a new memo. Clicking on this button, or choosing Actions ➤ Delivery Options, opens the Delivery Options dialog box shown in Figure 18.1.

FIGURE 18.1:
The Delivery Options dialog box lets you alter a number of settings that determine how Notes treats your message.

The options you can set here are quite varied: Some affect how your message is delivered, others are more informational—the recipients of your message can use Actions ➤ Delivery Information to see the options you chose. The following sections describe what the settings do and how to use them.

Telling Recipients How Important Your Message Is

If you'd like to convey the importance of your message to its recipients, you can choose to assign it High or Low importance, instead of the default of Normal.

High-importance messages are marked with a red exclamation point in the recipient's mail database. In your own mail file, they are marked with a red envelope icon. Low-importance messages are not specially marked—your recipient has to choose Actions ➤ Delivery Information to find out that your message isn't very important.

NOTE Setting an importance for your message does not affect the speed with which it is delivered. For that, see the section "Assigning a Delivery Priority" later in this chapter.

Setting the Mood

New in Notes 4.*x* is the ability to choose a "mood stamp" for Notes to use for your memo. This lets your recipients know how the message is intended to be taken, by placing an icon next to the message in their mailbox views and adding an identifying graphic above the body field in the memo.

Apart from Normal, which doesn't display any special icon or graphic, Notes gives you 10 moods to use for memos. Three (personal, confidential, and private) help you convey the confidentiality of a message. The remainder are for special types of messages, such as questions, reminders, and thank-you notes. The icon for a private message is shown here.

Requesting a Delivery Report

When you go to the post office to mail a package, you can pay extra to have a postcard sent back confirming that your package was delivered. You can do something similar in Notes. You don't have to pay extra, but it probably costs your company as much as sending the original message did.

You have four choices for your Delivery Report:

Only on Failure This is the default option. With this setting, Notes only tells you if the message didn't get through. Otherwise, you can assume it reached its destination.

Confirm Delivery If you choose to Confirm Delivery, Notes sends you a message confirming that your memo was delivered. If your memo was addressed to 17 people, you'll get 17 confirmations. The confirmation doesn't tell you if the memo has been read, just that it has been placed in the recipient's mail file.

Trace Entire Path This is a new option in Notes 4.*x*. It works the same way as having Notes confirm delivery, except that you receive one report from each server through which the memo passes on its route to the recipient. Finally, you'll get a report telling you that the memo has been delivered.

None If you choose none, Notes doesn't even tell you if it couldn't deliver the message. If you're constantly sending messages to large groups of people and the Non-Delivery Reports you get back from some of them are bugging you, you might consider this option.

NOTE If you want to find out when the recipient opens your memo, ask for a Receipt Report, described later in this chapter.

Assigning a Delivery Priority

The main thing to know about the Delivery Priority setting is that it only affects mail that you send to people who use a server on a *different* "Notes network." Your company may have decided to have all its servers in the same network or to divide them into any number of smaller networks.

A good rule of thumb is that the Delivery Priority setting will definitely have no effect on messages you send to people who use the same Notes server as you, and it will probably have no effect if the recipients work in the same building as you do.

TIP If you want to know for sure whether someone uses the same Notes network as you, here's how. Check what server the person uses by looking at his or her record in your company's Public Name & Address Book. The name of the server is listed next to the label Mail Server. Then check what network that server uses by looking at the Server ➤ Networks view of the Public Name & Address Book. If the network has a different name than the one your server uses, the Delivery Priority setting *will* have an effect on how quickly your message is delivered. If the network is the same, setting Delivery Priority has no effect.

When you send mail to people who use the same Notes network as you do, Notes transfers the mail almost instantaneously from your mail file on the server to the recipient's mail file on the same server or a connected server. The next time the recipient's workstation checks for mail, your message will be there. Of course, the recipient may choose not to read it for a while or may be on vacation and won't look at his or her Notes mail for two weeks. But changing the delivery priority won't affect this.

What the delivery priority does affect is mail that Notes has to send to someone who uses a Notes server on a different Notes network. To send mail to another network, Notes has to make the equivalent of a toll call. Sometimes it really is making a toll call, but often it's quite a bit more expensive than that. The three options you have in the Delivery Priority field affect when Notes makes that call:

Normal Normal-priority mail is sent the next time Notes is scheduled to make a call. That might be very soon, but could be several hours away. At worst, your Notes server will connect once a day.

High High-priority Notes mail is sent right away, regardless of cost. In essence, you're telling your Notes server, "Drop everything and make a call to the other coast! No, I don't care what time of day it is there or how expensive the call might be."

Low Low-priority Notes mail is held until it is least expensive to transmit. By default, this is between midnight and 6 a.m., but your Notes administrator may have changed this setting.

How do you decide which priority to use? First of all, there may be some kind of policy at your company that says, for example, "Only the president may send high-priority mail." If your company has not set a policy, here are some guidelines:

- Stick to normal priority nine times out of ten. If it doesn't immediately strike you that a message is urgent or very large, normal priority is your best choice.
- If it's important that a message not be delayed an hour or two, consider sending it high priority. Certainly if people are waiting for something you're sending, don't make them fret for the sake of a few pennies in telecommunications costs.
- If you're sending a really big message (usually this means one with a large file or many files attached) that can wait for delivery until the evening, consider using low priority. Two other factors favoring low priority are if a lot of recipients are listed and if the message will be sent to Notes users overseas.

Signing and Encrypting Mail

You might already have wondered, "What if someone has been intercepting the e-mail I've been sending?" or, "How do the people who receive my messages know that it's me sending them and not just someone pretending to be me?"

In general, you can be fairly sure that no one is intercepting the messages you send and that no one else is sending messages in your name. Notes' built-in security makes it a lot harder to read a message *en route* than to pull a paper memo out of the interoffice mail, take a quick peek, and slip it back in. Similarly, someone can more easily fake a paper memo with your signature than pretend to send an electronic message in your name.

But if it's important that a message be secure or guaranteed to come from you, then Notes does offer mechanisms to do these things:

- *Signing* a message tells Notes to attach an electronic authentication so that the person receiving a document knows who really sent it. When the recipient opens your message, Notes checks the authentication attached to the message against a list of authorities it trusts to authenticate documents. It's a bit like producing a picture ID. If Notes trusts the authenticity of the document, it displays a message such as "Signed by Thomas Hayes on 02/01/96 17:02:23, according to Optika Cameras" on the status bar. If Notes doesn't trust the authenticity of a signed document, it tells you so.
- *Encryption* means to scramble the body of a message so that anyone who intercepts it in transit will just see gobbledygook. Notes automatically unscrambles encrypted messages when they reach their destinations. Only the body is scrambled because Notes needs to use the other fields to work out where, how, and when to send messages. If you have a color monitor, look at the L-shaped angle brackets around each field in a document. If they are shown in red, this means Notes can encrypt the information in that field.

You can choose either or both of these options by checking the appropriate box in the Delivery Options dialog box. If you'd like to automatically sign or encrypt every memo you send, or if you'd like to encrypt your stored mail, you can set this in your user preferences. Changing these settings is described in Chapter 14.

Encryption and signatures are only as good as your own security. If you let others know your Notes password, they can read your mail and send signed and encrypted messages in your name.

NOTE If you positively *want* people (such as secretaries and administrative assistants) to be able to send messages in your name, read the section "Setting Your Delegation Profile" in Chapter 17.

Requesting a Receipt Report

Asking for a Delivery Report lets you know when your message has been placed in the recipient's mail file, but you still don't know that it has been read yet. If you ask for a Receipt Report with your mail, Notes sends you a message when the recipient actually opens it. But this still isn't a guarantee that the person actually read your message. He or she might never have gotten beyond your first line. As with Delivery Reports, if your message went out to 17 people, you'll (eventually) get 17 Receipt Reports.

Preventing Others from Copying Your Mail

If you are sending a sensitive message through Notes, you may worry that you can't control what the recipient does with it. He or she might forward it to a competitor, or, worse still, to the company president.

One way you can make this more difficult is to check the box marked Prevent Copying. Then, Notes won't let the recipient copy any part of the message via the Clipboard, forward it, create a Reply with History based on it, or even print it.

You shouldn't rely on this option to wholly eliminate the risk of your message being passed on, as there are ways to get around it. But for most Notes users, this should be a sufficient way to prevent copying.

Special Options

As well as the regular message delivery options we've looked at, Notes also offers a few extra choices. You can open the Special Options dialog box by choosing Actions ➤ Special Options.

Setting an expiration date for your message lets the recipient know that it's not of value after a certain date. Then he or she can archive the message, save it, or delete it as appropriate. You can also ask recipients of your message to reply by a particular date. Notes will then place the message automatically in the To Do view of their mailbox (see Chapter 17). You can tell Notes that it should deliver any replies to your message to someone else's address. This way, when recipients choose a Reply or Reply with History, the other person's address will automatically be provided.

The final two settings in this dialog box let you fine-tune how this message is delivered via the Internet. Usually, if you send a message via the Internet (see later in this chapter for information on doing this), Notes converts the whole message into plain ASCII text. However, it's possible that your recipient also has Notes. If that's the case, you can check a box here to have Notes attempt to preserve as much of the document structure as it can for your recipient.

You can also choose how Notes should deal with message attachments you want to send via the Internet. The Internet was originally devised to handle text, and a number of conversion methods have since been invented to allow people to exchange nontext files. Normally, you should leave this option set to use the method your Notes administrator prefers. However, if you know a particular recipient prefers files encoded in a certain format, you can adjust this setting.

Special Notes Mail Forms

When choosing an item from the Create menu to begin a new message, reply, or task, you may have noticed the option Create ➤ Special. This opens a submenu with five forms for special circumstances. Whether and how much you use these forms will depend on the nature of your job. Read the descriptions that follow to see if any might be useful to you.

> **TIP**
>
> If your mail file is open or its icon is highlighted in the workspace, then these five forms will appear on the Create ➤ Special submenu. If you're *not* currently using your mail file, you can find them on the Create ➤ Mail ➤ Special submenu.

As well as the five forms described in the following sections, your company may also have made available other special forms that you can use by choosing Create ➤ Mail ➤ Other and selecting the form's name from the list that appears.

Bookmark

The Bookmark form offers you a convenient way to send a Notes-using colleague a link to any document in any Notes database. When you encounter a document you think someone should know about, choose Create ➤ Mail ➤ Special ➤ Bookmark to open a new Bookmark document, like the one in Figure 18.2, with a DocLink to the document at which you were looking.

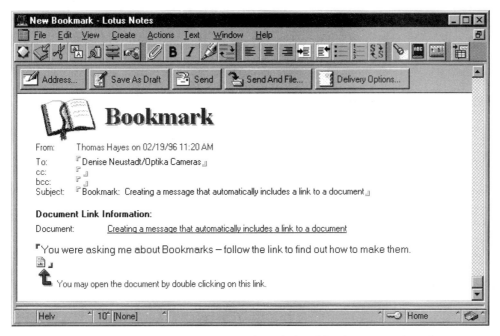

FIGURE 18.2: This Bookmark points to a Notes Help topic describing the process of creating a Bookmark.

You could achieve the same results by using Edit ➤ Copy As Link to put a link on the Clipboard and then pasting the link into a new memo. However, making a Bookmark takes fewer steps and makes the link more obvious to your message's recipient.

> **NOTE** In order to use the DocLink, your recipient must have access to the database that contains it. Also, you can't automatically create Bookmarks that use View or Database Links, although you can paste these links in yourself.

Phone Message

If your job involves taking calls for other people, you may find the Phone Message form to be useful. You can send a phone message just like a memo, except that it contains extra information about the call.

The Phone Message form may reduce the number of sticky notes you have to place on your colleagues' desks. Of course, sending a phone message via Notes is only useful if the recipient checks his or her Notes mail regularly.

Serial Route Memo

The unappealingly named Serial Route Memo lets you send a message that goes from one person to the next in a list of names that you specify. It's the electronic equivalent of a routing slip.

The Serial Route Memo form gives you just one Route To field in place of a normal memo's three address fields. Here you type in order the names of the people on your routing list, each separated from the previous one by a comma. You can't list groups here because the memo only goes to one person at a time, in the order you specify.

Write the subject and contents of your memo as you would normally and then choose whether you want Notes to send you a notification at each step of the memo's route. Click on Send to Next Person to start the memo on its travels.

Recipients of your memo will see their own names next to the label Current Person in Route; those who have yet to receive the memo will see their names next to Remaining Route List. If appropriate, they can edit the memo to add comments or change any delivery options before clicking on Send to Next Person to pass the message along.

Temporary Export Certificate

This form, new in Notes 4.5, will provide hours of endless amusement on your next overseas trip. The cryptographic algorithms that let you sign and encrypt your mail are classified as weapons systems by the U.S. State Department.

In theory, you need an export license to take the North American version of Notes out of North America. In practice, you need only complete the few fields on this form and obey some simple rules to be in compliance:

- Keep your notebook computer with you at all times.
- Don't try to sell Notes to anyone.
- Don't travel to any country under U.N. embargo or on the State Department's ever-changing list of terrorism sponsors.

The form itself provides full legal details.

Memo to Database Manager

You may find the Memo to Database Manager form in other databases as well as your mail database. It's a regular memo form that automatically fills in the name of the manager(s) of the Notes database you are using.

Who is this person, the Notes database manager? He or she has ultimate control over the database. Database managers can add and remove people from the list of users who have access to the database, and they can change what level of access you and other users have. So this sounds like a useful form, since it lets you get in touch with someone who can change the database. Well, there are a few snags that mean that you probably will hardly ever use this form.

Several people may have Manager-level access to the database. One of them may actually know something about it. The others might be just listed as backups. When you compose a Memo to Database Manager, Notes addresses it to all these people and you have no way of telling who's the right one to contact.

Furthermore, it's quite common for Notes servers and all sorts of other groups also to have Manager-level access to the database so that they can transfer information back and forth. Notes lists all of these other servers and groups in the address field, which makes things even more confusing.

If you have a question about how to use a database, the manager may not even be the right person to ask. Often managers just control who has access to a database that is created and maintained by someone who has *Designer-level* access.

Finally, the Memo to Database Manager form in your own mail database is even less useful than ones you might see in other databases. Usually, the managers of your own mail database are you and your Notes administrator. If you start sending mail to yourself, you know it's time to take a break.

If you have questions about a database, better ways to find out who to contact are to look at the database's policy documents (Help ➤ About and Help ➤ Using), or to look in the database. These features are described in Chapter 9.

Using Mail Stationery and Letterheads

Stationery and letterheads add the kind of flexibility to Notes e-mail that you would have with paper and a typewriter. Changing the letterhead simply alters the graphic that appears at the top of your mail message. Creating stationery lets you save a message template, complete with distribution list, full or partial contents, and even header and footer information.

Choosing a Letterhead

If you would like to vary the graphic that appears at the top of your messages, choose Actions ➤ Mail Tools ➤ Choose Letterhead from a mailbox view.

Notes displays a list of 30 letterheads for you to preview. As you select each name in the list box, Notes displays an example of the letterhead below it. By default, Notes uses the Pencil and Grid letterhead; some of the examples in Chapters 7 and 8 use the letterhead From the Desk. If you don't want to use a letterhead, choose the option Plain Text. Notes uses the letterhead you select for any subsequent messages.

Using Stationery

If you frequently have to recreate the same basic message, either by typing it from scratch or copying it from one you sent before, then you may well find Notes stationery useful.

Creating Stationery

Creating stationery lets you save certain elements of a message to use as the basis for later messages. First create a Notes message that contains the elements you want to store. If you'll usually be sending these messages to a particular group of people, you can enter their names in the address fields. If there are elements of the message contents (such as text, graphics, or hotspots) that will usually be the same, place these in position.

When your template is ready, choose Actions ➤ Save As Stationery. Notes asks you to name the stationery you've created and then tells you that it will store the document in your Drafts view and create a new message each time you open it.

Customizing Stationery

If you would like to go further than just storing default addresses and body text, Notes also lets you create stationery with a customized header and footer. Choose Actions ➤ Mail Tools ➤ Create Stationery to display the Create Stationery dialog box. To create stationery with a customized header and footer, choose the option Personal Stationery. Choosing the Memo option here is an alternative to Actions ➤ Save As Stationery as a way to create regular stationery.

When you choose Personal Stationery, Notes shows you a stripped-down version of a memo form. The address, subject, and body fields in the center of the memo work as normal. You can enter defaults here in the same way as you do when you create regular stationery.

The fields at the top and bottom of the document are for you to enter text or graphics you'd like to appear on the stationery. For example, you could place a corporate or departmental logo in the header field and contact details in the footer. You can copy graphics into these fields via the Clipboard or import from a file on disk. Once you have the stationery designed to your liking, click on the Close button, choose to save your new stationery, and enter a name for it.

Using Stationery for a Message

Any stationery you create is displayed in the Stationery category of your Drafts view. Notes uses an icon of several sheets of paper to identify stationery you have created. To create a message that uses this stationery, either double-click on the name of the stationery you want to use or highlight the name and click on Use Stationery.

You don't have to keep any of the defaults that the stationery provides for you. You can change the addressees, subject, body, or delivery options for the message. If you are using stationery with a customized header or footer, you can change or remove these.

When you are content with the form of your message, save it or send it as you would normally. The original stationery remains unaltered in your Drafts view.

Editing, Renaming, and Deleting Stationery

To edit stationery you have already created, highlight it in your Drafts view and click on Edit Document. Notes asks you whether you want to edit this stationery or just create a new message with it—you answer that you want to edit it. Then you can edit the stationery and save it as you would normally.

You can change the name of a piece of stationery by highlighting it in your Drafts view and clicking on Rename Stationery. You can delete an item of stationery as you would any other document.

Letting People Know When You Are Away

Notes offers a neat way to automatically reply to people who send you e-mail while you are out of the office. Notes lets you create a profile that lists when you will leave and return and what message to send to which people. However, there is one caveat: To use this feature you need to have access to run agents on the Notes server on which your mail file is stored. If you aren't sure whether you have this sort of access, ask your Notes administrator.

For those who do have this level of access, here's how to notify people that for the next two weeks you'll be on the beach and not taking their calls:

1. In your mail database choose Actions ➤ Mail Tools ➤ Out of Office. Notes opens a document titled Out of Office Profile.
2. Type in the dates on which you expect to leave and to return.
3. Following this, there are three sections that let you tailor your replies. You need only complete as many sections as suit your circumstances.

   - The first section is for the message that Notes will send to most people who send you e-mail while you're out. Here you can supply a subject and message text for Notes to send in reply; you may want to edit Notes' fairly curt suggestions to make them a little friendlier.
   - The second section lets you specify an alternative reply for Notes to send to people included on a list of names that you specify. This lets you give more specific details, such as contact information, perhaps, to people or groups that you choose.
   - The final section lets you name people or groups that should receive no messages about your absence. You'll have your own reasons for using this option, and I won't speculate on them!

4. To put the profile into effect, click on Enable Out of Office Agent. If Notes asks you to name a server for the agent to run on, choose your mail server.

Between the dates you specify, Notes will field your mail and send out messages with the details you provided. Notes sends a maximum of one message per person, no matter how many messages that person sends you.

On the day you said you would return to the office, Notes sends you a message titled Welcome Back, listing all the people it notified while you were out of the office.

Choose Actions ➤ Mail Tools ➤ Out of Office and click on I Have Returned to the Office to stop Notes answering your mail for you. If you forget to tell Notes that you've returned, Notes will continue to send you Welcome Back messages. If you return to the office earlier than you planned, just click on I Have Returned to the Office to stop mail notification.

Cutting Your Mail File Down to Size

Even if you don't keep every message you receive, your Notes mail database can get big fast. Your company may have a policy on how big they'll let it get. Big mail databases work very slowly and consume a lot of storage space on Notes servers that other people might like to use.

You can do four things to help keep down the size of a mailbox:

- Don't save messages (sent and received) that you *know* you'll never need to look at again. If you mail your friend a lunch invitation, are you really going to need to refer to it in six months' time?
- Don't duplicate attached files that you have stored somewhere else. Attached files take up *lots* of space. You can detach a file to your hard disk with the instructions in Chapter 7. Then remove it from the memo as follows:

    1. Put the memo in edit mode.
    2. Select the attachment.
    3. Press Delete or choose Edit ➤ Clear.
    4. Type a couple of words to say that you detached the file, what its name was, and where you stored it.
    5. Close the document, choosing Save but not Send.

- If your mailbox starts to fill up with old messages that you'd like to keep but that you don't need to read at the click of a mouse button, you can have Notes archive your mail. Follow the directions in the next section, "Archiving Your Mail".
- Compact your mail database regularly. When you delete documents, Notes keeps the free space on hand to use for storing new documents. As a result, the database takes up more space than it really needs. Notes lets you remove these empty spaces; follow the directions in the "Compacting Databases" section later in this chapter.

None of this should prompt you to get rid of any documents you think you might need later. It's always better to keep the text of a 20-page annual report stored somewhere than to have to recreate it from scratch.

> **TIP**
>
> Don't get so concerned about the size of your mail file that you feel obliged to print out old messages to save them. This is *not* a good solution. The disk space to store a single-page text message costs about $1/20$¢ at today's hardware prices. So printing out that message and filing it is clearly a false economy.

Archiving Your Mail

Notes provides an easy way to archive documents from your mail file. You set up a profile that tells Notes what kind of documents to archive, and then Notes automatically moves documents that meet your criteria to an archive database on your computer or a Notes server.

Creating an Archive Profile

1. Open the Archiving view in your mail database and click on the Setup Archive button. Notes opens an Archive Profile document.
2. You have two options for telling Notes which documents it should archive, and you can use either or both.

    - If you choose to archive expired documents, Notes transfers to the archive documents with defined expiration dates once the documents have exceeded their expiration date by a number of days that you specify. However, few of the messages you receive will have expiration dates, and this option is unlikely to remove many documents from your mail file.
    - If you choose to archive inactive documents, Notes transfers to the archive any documents that you haven't opened within a period of time that you specify.

3. Your next choice is whether to have Notes create an archive log each time it archives documents. This is a special document that appears in your Archiving view to show which messages Notes archived.
4. You can also have Notes automatically place DocLinks to the archived messages in the archive log. Notes lets you specify who can edit this archive profile in the future.
5. If other people have access to your mail database, you can decide whether to allow them to modify your archive profile.

6. Your final choice is where to place the archive database. Click on the Specify Archive Location button to open a dialog box that lets you select a location and filename for the archive. If you choose to store it locally, Notes places it by default in the Notes data directory on your computer. To store the archive database on a Notes server, you'll need to have access to create databases on that server. You can also change Notes' suggestion of a filename for the archive database.

7. Once the profile is complete, click on Save Profile to have Notes store your settings and create the archive database. When the database has been created, click on Close to return to the Archiving view.

8. Next, you need to do something a little strange—switch to another view of your mail file and then back to the Archiving view.

NOTE The reason for this chicanery is that the archive process is partly dependent on a variable that is stored in your NOTES.INI file. The buttons available to you on the Action Bar depend on the setting of this variable, but Notes only checks this setting when it enters the view. Therefore, you have to leave and re-enter the view to get Notes to display the correct buttons.

9. Now you can click on Enable Scheduled Archiving to prime the archive process.

If at any time you need to change the archiving criteria, just click on Setup Archive to edit the archive profile.

Sending Documents to the Archive

By default, the archive process checks your mail file and transfers documents once a week, at 2 A.M. on a Sunday. If you want to run the process without waiting for the schedule, click on the Archive Now button. After you confirm that you really want to do this, Notes starts archiving.

You can also manually archive documents to which you feel you no longer need immediate access, even if they don't match the archive profile you set up. Just select the documents in any view or folder and choose Actions ➤ Mail Tools ➤ Archive Selected Documents.

Reading Documents in the Archive

The archive database that Notes created for you uses the standard Notes mail template. You can open the database and browse the archived documents by clicking on the Open Archive Db button. If you chose to have Notes include DocLinks in archive logs, then you can also view documents in your archive by opening the archive logs listed in the Archiving view of your mailbox and clicking on the appropriate DocLink.

Compacting Databases

You can compact any database by opening its Database Properties InfoBox, selecting the Information tab, and clicking on the Compact button. Click on the % Used button to have Notes display how much of the database's space is in use for storing documents. Lotus recommends compacting a database when its space in use falls below 90 percent.

Notes uses your computer to compact local databases (stored on your hard disk or on a file server). However, the task of compacting is carried out in the background, so you can still use other parts of Notes at the same time. For shared databases (including mail files stored on servers), the task of compacting is handled by the server. Either way, you will have to wait a few minutes before you can use the database again.

> **NOTE**
>
> You don't need any special access level to compact a database. However, you should probably just stick to compacting your mail file and any local databases you have. You're unlikely to need to compact a shared database, as your Notes administrator probably has developed a schedule on which shared databases are automatically compacted.

Communicating with Other E-Mail Systems

The time will come when you want to send an e-mail message to someone other than a Notes user at your company. With the rapid proliferation of Internet e-mail accounts, that time may already have come. Notes can connect to just about any other type of e-mail system, but whether you personally can send messages to a particular e-mail address depends a lot on what types of connections your company has judged important.

As well as sending and receiving messages from other e-mail systems, Notes can also communicate by fax, pager, and telephone. Making these connections is similar to sending messages to different e-mail systems, and so we'll also look at communicating by fax, pager, and telephone in this part of the chapter.

You can send four basic types of "external" messages:

- Messages to other people at your company who use a different e-mail system (say cc:Mail or IBM PROFS)
- Messages to people who use Notes at other companies
- Messages to people on the Internet and other public networks
- Non-e-mail messages (fax, pager, etc.)

Because there are many different ways to connect Notes to other e-mail systems, this chapter can't give you step-by-step instructions on how to send mail to each different type of e-mail service. What it will do is give you some general pointers and tell you what's out there, and then say, "Go ask your Notes administrator." He or she is the person who can tell you exactly which e-mail systems you can connect to and exactly how to address your messages to make sure they get through.

Addressing Messages to Other E-Mail Systems

You might be thinking, "Why would my company not want me communicating with people who use the Snappy Brand mail system?" The two main reasons have to do with cost. For each different type of e-mail system to which your company connects Notes, your company has to buy a piece of software called a *mail gateway* and connect it to a Notes server. Most gateways cost quite a bit of money. To send and receive messages via the gateway, your company also has to pay, whether it's in the form of the phone bill or a subscription to a commercial e-mail service.

For each gateway your company decides to set up, it has to think up a *domain name*. This is just a name that Notes users in your company can use to tell Notes where they want their mail to go. In general, you address mail to someone on another e-mail system using this format:

```
<e-mail address> @ Domain
```

where *<e-mail address>* is the person's address on the other e-mail system and *Domain* is the domain name of the appropriate mail gateway. Sometimes, the mail gateway you need to use is connected a bit more indirectly, and you need to use several domain names. Then, the address you enter might look like:

```
<e-mail address> @ Domain3 @ Domain2 @ Domain1
```

Exact information on how to address your messages should be available from your Notes administrator. Perhaps someone in your company has written an explanation of how to use whatever gateways are available. If your company offers its own shared database of information for Notes users, you may find an explanation there.

You usually have to be quite precise about typing in e-mail addresses for other systems. While Notes can often figure out that Tom Hayes and Thomas Hayes are the same person (or at least ask for clarification), other e-mail systems can be flummoxed by a single misplaced period or space (in fact, most e-mail addressing schemes don't allow spaces). So copy addresses carefully! As long as you use the correct address format for each recipient, you can include any combination of recipients in your message.

When you start sending messages beyond Notes, you are bound to make a few mistakes. It's a good idea to ask for at least a basic Delivery Report (the Only on Failure option). That way, Notes will tell you if it can't deliver your message.

When a Message Doesn't Arrive

If Notes does run into problems, you will receive a Delivery Failure Report that looks something like the one in Figure 18.3. You'll get one report for each copy of your message that Notes couldn't figure out how to send.

The most common problem with external messages is that Notes doesn't recognize the domain name you used. If you can find out what needs to be changed, you can click on the Resend button on the Action Bar, or choose Actions ➤ Resend, to see the Mail Resend dialog box. From there, you can correct the address and try again. If it isn't immediately obvious how to fix the address, talk to your Notes administrator.

Even if your message successfully leaves Notes, it may still run into problems. Sometimes, the receiving mail system can't work out to whom to send your message. If this happens, some mail systems send you a note advising you of the problem. Others are more "passive-aggressive," and you can only tell there's a problem because your messages never arrive.

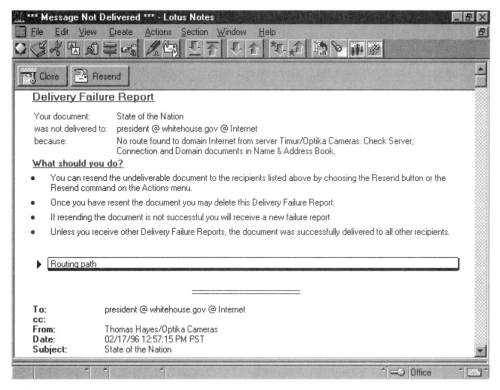

FIGURE 18.3: If Notes can't get your message to its destination, it will send you a Delivery Failure Report.

It's a good idea when you send a message to someone on a new system to ask the person to send you a reply. If you don't get anything back within a reasonable length of time, follow up with a phone call. Receiving a Delivery Report after sending an external message does not guarantee that the message reached its destination, because the report is sent back to you as soon as the message leaves Notes. Some other mail systems support Receipt Reports—receiving one of these reports *does* indicate that your message was received.

What You Can Send to Other Systems

Often, an entire message can't be accurately reproduced in another e-mail system. Many e-mail systems use text only. In systems like these, messages are reproduced without graphics and without italicized text, bold text, and other font attributes. The degree of support that other e-mail systems provide for attached files also varies. Ask your Notes administrator and perhaps experiment with the help of a cooperative recipient to find out exactly what kinds of attached files you can transfer.

> **NOTE** You may need to use a particular method of encoding attachments to send them to certain other e-mail systems. See the "Special Options" section, earlier in this chapter.

If you use the Internet to send a message to someone at another company who also happens to use Notes, you can have Notes try to preserve the message's structure. To do this, choose Actions ➤ Special Options while you are creating the message. Notes opens a dialog box that lets you alter certain less frequently used settings. Check the box marked *I am sending this Notes document to other Notes mail user(s) through the Internet*. Then click on OK.

Notes will do what it can to preserve the Notes-specific elements of the message. In some cases, the varied nature of the equipment that carries Internet transmissions may mean that Notes can only deliver a text message.

Sending Messages to Other E-Mail Systems in Your Company

If other parts of your company use a different type of e-mail system, it usually makes sense to provide a connection between the two systems somehow. Mail gateways are available that can link Notes to popular e-mail systems such as Banyan Systems BeyondMail, DaVinci eMAIL, DEC VAX/VMS Mail, Lotus cc:Mail, Microsoft Exchange, IBM PROFS, and WordPerfect Office.

Some of these gateways are sold by Lotus. Others are sold by third parties. One of the most commonly used gateways is the Lotus Notes cc:Mail Messaging Transfer Agent, a separate product that Lotus offers to connect Notes and cc:Mail. We'll take a look at this product as an example of how to send mail to other e-mail systems.

Once your company has installed the gateway, it decides on a domain name. If this is your company's only gateway to cc:Mail, the domain might be called something sensible, like *ccMail*. But it doesn't matter if it is called *Mephistopheles*, as long as you know the name. You also need to know the name of the cc:Mail user you're sending your message to and the name of the cc:Mail *post office* the recipient uses. Post offices are to cc:Mail what Domino servers are to Notes.

Say your message is going to Amy Hagopian who uses the Accounting post office, and say some joker *did* name the cc:Mail domain Mephistopheles. The correct way to address messages to Amy would be:

```
Amy Hagopian at Accounting @ Mephistopheles
```

Note that you have to use the word *at* in one place and the "at" symbol (@) in another. If you are lucky, your company will have chosen to add Amy's name to the Public Name & Address Book, either by typing in her name and her e-mail address or by having cc:Mail and Notes exchange address information automatically. If Amy's name is in the Public Name & Address Book, you can almost forget that Amy uses a different mail system at all. To send her a message, simply type her name.

Sending Messages to Notes Users at Other Companies

If two companies that use Notes do a lot of work with each other, they can link their Notes networks to some degree. One advantage of linking your company's Notes network to another's is that you can share as many or as few databases as you want with whichever employees of the other company you choose. You can also let some or all of your Notes users send mail to some or all of the other company's Notes users. The mail you send can contain all the features of the Notes messages that are sent within your company. You don't need any special gateway software to accomplish this.

The only disadvantages are that it takes a little planning to set up the link and that, if the link isn't set up carefully, you might give people at the other company access to more of your Notes network than you meant to. As companies often keep a lot of sensitive information in Notes, they tend to be cautious about linking their networks to other companies' networks.

If you do have a link to another company's Notes network, your Notes administrator can tell you the right domain name to use when addressing mail.

If you want to send a message to someone who uses Notes at a different company and you don't have a Notes-to-Notes link, you have to find an external service that you both have access to and pass the message that way. A good bet is the Internet. The "What You Can Send to Other Systems" section, earlier in this chapter, explains how to tell Notes to try to preserve special features of your message when sending it via the Internet to another Notes user.

Sending Messages to the Internet and Other Public Networks

If your company has the correct mail gateways installed, you can send e-mail to millions of people worldwide who use many different public e-mail systems. Of course, if you really do send e-mail to millions of people, your employer isn't going to thank you for it.

Direct Connections to Public Mail Networks

Gateways are available that connect Notes directly to some public mail networks. Here are some of the public networks to which your company might connect directly:

The Internet In case you tuned out all the "information superhighway" hype, the Internet is a global computer network with literally millions of users. It offers a variety of nifty services (see also the description of the Web Navigator in Chapters 11 and 12), but Internet e-mail is the easiest to connect to and therefore the most ubiquitous.

X.400 This is an international standard for exchanging and addressing electronic messages. If your company has an X.400 gateway for Notes, you can send messages to any other company with an X.400 gateway.

MCI Mail This is a commercial e-mail service provided by the telecommunications company MCI Corp.

Generally, if your company has a gateway to one of these public services, you need to use a domain name (see the cc:Mail example in "Sending Messages to Other E-Mail Systems in Your Company," earlier this chapter) to send mail to people who use the service. If you're lucky, a sensible domain name will have been chosen and you can address your outgoing mail to an Internet address, for example, in the form:

```
ahagopian@another.company.com @ Internet
```

Ask your Notes administrator what the proper address format is for any gateways you have to public networks.

Indirect Connections to Public Mail Networks

With other public networks such as America Online and Prodigy, your company probably hasn't set up a gateway. Instead, you can send mail to these networks via a public network for which you *do* have a gateway. Often, this means the Internet. You address your message so that Notes sends it out onto the Internet, which delivers it to America Online or Prodigy, which delivers it to your recipient.

To communicate with someone on one of these networks, you need to know his or her *user name* or *account name.* These terms refer to a short pseudo-word that identifies the person with whom you want to communicate. User names often have some relation to the person's actual name, but not always. For example, Jim Simpson's user name on America Online might be *jsimpson* or *jims* or *js52d*.

If the user name you obtain is in the internal format of the particular network, you may need to make some changes to make it into an Internet address. Table 18.1 explains the formats for common public network services.

TABLE 18.1: Address Formats for Common Public Network Services

Network	Network Address	Internet Address	Comments
America Online	jsimpson	jsimpson@aol.com	
AT&T Mail	jsimpson	jsimpson@attmail.com	
CompuServe	76543,210	76543.210@compuserve.com	The comma in the CompuServe address becomes a period in the Internet address.
Delphi	jsimpson	jsimpson@delphi.com	
eWorld	jsimpson	jsimpson@eworld.com	
Genie	jsimpson	jsimpson@genie.geis.com	
MCI Mail	555-1212	5551212@mcimail.com	MCI Mail user names are usually structured like telephone numbers. You need to omit the hyphen when converting to an Internet address.
	jsimpson	jsimpson@mcimail.com	MCI Mail has also added more conventional user names. Use this form if the user name does not look like a phone number.
Microsoft Network	jsimpson	jsimpson@msn.com	
Prodigy	jsimpson	jsimpson@prodigy.com	

Sending Fax, Telex, and Other Messages

In addition to mail gateways, there are a number of gateways available for sending and receiving Notes messages via fax and telex, and sending messages to a radio pager. Often there are separate products for each direction of communication. For example, Lotus sells both inbound and outbound fax gateways.

Sending mail to an outbound gateway that your company has installed works very similarly to using an e-mail gateway. For example, you might address a fax message to:

```
(708) 555-1212 @ FaxGate
```

Depending on the type of phone line your company has installed, inbound fax gateways may or may not be able to route a fax directly to your Notes mailbox. If your company's phone line won't allow faxes to be sent straight to you, a fax administrator reviews each fax that arrives through the gateway and forwards it to the appropriate person. Again, the best source of information on what resources are available to you is your Notes administrator.

Lotus also has developed a technology called Phone Notes that other companies have used as the basis for telephone-to-Notes products. These products can place voicemail messages as part of Notes documents and read your Notes mail to you over the phone. They are not gateways as such, but do offer yet another way to access the information in Notes.

Receiving Messages from Other E-Mail Systems

As with sending messages beyond Notes, how you receive messages from other e-mail systems varies depending on the mail gateway you use and how it is configured. You won't be surprised to read that your Notes administrator is the authority to consult when you want to find out how other people can send you e-mail.

If your company has an Internet mail gateway for Notes, this means that you already have an Internet mail address (which your Notes administrator can tell you). Assuming your company is happy about your being accessible via the Internet, you can distribute your Internet address like you would your phone number as a way for people to contact you.

Often, if you send a message to someone who uses a different e-mail system, the message includes your address. The recipient can just write your address down and use it to send mail back to you. Even if your address isn't included, the recipient may have the option of replying to your message automatically. In these cases, the recipient's e-mail system figures out how to get the reply back to you.

As an example, here's how Amy, the cc:Mail user, might send mail to your Notes mailbox via the Lotus Notes cc:Mail Messaging Transfer Agent.

Amy looks in the cc:Mail directory for the post office that connects to Notes (its name is listed as part of your address in your message to her). Post offices are listed in red in the cc:Mail address book. Once she selects the post office, cc:Mail lets her enter your Notes mail address. Most of the time, the address consists of just your name, but if several people have the same name or if there are many steps between the gateway and your Notes server, the address might be a little more complex than just a name.

Again, your company may have chosen to have some or all Notes users listed in the cc:Mail address list. If that's the case, Amy can address messages to you just as she would to anyone using cc:Mail.

More Uses for the Personal Name & Address Book

Now you are thoroughly conversant with the ins and outs of sending mail to other e-mail systems. But you're getting very tired of the long addresses you have to type in order to send mail. Even typing your boss' name has become a chore—you'd like to use a shortcut if possible. And you've noticed that you often send messages to the same group of people. Is there an easy way to address messages?

The solutions to all three of these problems—long addresses, finding shortcuts for addresses, and addressing groups—can be found in the same place, your own Personal Name & Address Book. Your address book works a lot like your company's Public Name & Address Book, which we looked at in Chapter 3. However, it is specific to you and is a place where you can record name and address information about people and groups with whom you frequently correspond.

In general, the structure of your Personal Name & Address Book is a simplified version of your company's Public Name & Address Book. This means that things usually work the same way in each. The icon for your Personal Name & Address Book will look like the one shown here. As with any Notes database, to open it you just double-click on the icon.

When you open your Personal Name & Address Book for the first time, you will probably see an empty view. This is actually a view of the Person documents in your address book, but since you haven't yet entered any information about people into the address book, the People view is blank.

Keeping Track of Addresses on Other Mail Systems

To solve our first problem, the need to type long addresses for people on other e-mail systems, we are going to use the Person document. To start a new Person document, you can click on the Add Person button, or you can play at being Dr. Frankenstein by choosing the menu option Create ➤ Person.

Notes looks at the Person documents in your Personal Name & Address Book each time it sends a message. If it looks in the address book and finds the name of the person to whom you addressed your message, it can put that person's e-mail address in place of his or her name. Figure 18.4 shows the Person document for Mary Chou, a sales representative with Nikus Camera Corp.

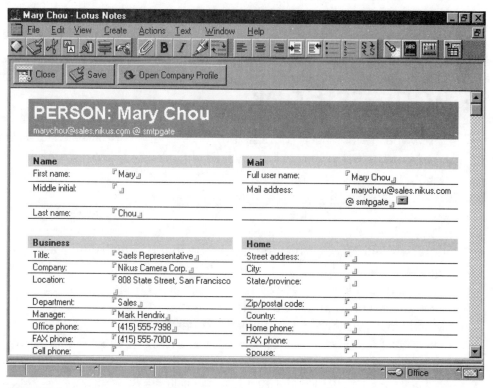

FIGURE 18.4: Creating a Person document can speed up addressing messages to people on other e-mail systems to whom you regularly write.

The only information you have to enter in a Person document is a last name—the rest is optional. To make the document useful to you for sending messages to people who don't use Notes, you want to provide a first name, a last name, and a mail address. The mail address contains the full address you need to use to send e-mail to this person from your Notes mailbox. Notes provides a Mail Address Assistant to help you construct addresses for certain types of mail systems.

Click on the arrow button next to the Mail Address field and Notes will present a dialog box that lets you choose the person's mail system. You can choose Fax, Internet Mail, Lotus cc:Mail, Lotus Notes, X.400 Mail, or Other. Each option presents a different dialog box in which you can enter details to compose the address. Most are a simple matter of entering a user name, a gateway name, and perhaps one other parameter. However, for the international mail standard X.400, you can enter up to 18 parameters!

The Person document also has fields for a whole host of other personal details. If you want to use your Personal Name & Address Book as your primary source of contact and address information, then you'll probably enter lots of information here. If you just use the database as a place to store e-mail addresses, then you really don't need to enter the names of each person's spouse and children.

Once you've saved a Person document, you can type the person's name—Mary Chou, in our example—in an address field and Notes will substitute the full e-mail address when you send your message.

You can save even more typing by providing a short name for a person. In the Advanced section at the bottom of the person document, you'll find a field labeled Short Name. Enter an abbreviation or nickname here and in the future you can just type the short name when addressing messages. In the example in Figure 18.4, you might type **mc**, Mary Chou's initials. Then you would only need to type these two letters to address a memo to her.

Automatically Adding Address Book Entries

You don't have to add each person's name to your Personal Name & Address Book manually. Notes provides a quick way to automatically add names.

Say you receive a message from someone via the Internet. You want to put the person's e-mail address in your address book so that you can more easily send him or her messages in the future. While reading the message, you can choose Actions ➤ Mail Tools ➤ Add Sender to Address Book. Notes runs an agent that automatically creates a Person document for the person who sent you the message. If your address book already contains an entry for someone with this name, Notes will ask you if you really want to add a new one. You can also use this agent at the view level to create Person documents for the senders of the highlighted or selected messages.

Making Your Own Mailing Lists

In Chapter 3, we saw how to address memos to groups named in your company's Public Name & Address Book. But what if certain combinations of people to whom you frequently send messages don't fit in one of the companywide groups?

If you are sure that other Notes users in your company need to address the same group of people, ask your Notes administrator to add the group to the Public Name & Address Book. But if you suspect that it's just you who needs the group, the place for it is in your Personal Name & Address Book.

Choosing Create ➤ Group opens a new Group document. Defining a group is quite straightforward. A brief name is best for the group, because you have to type this name exactly each time you address a message to the group. You probably won't need to change the Group Type setting from Multi-purpose. Type a few words of description to remind yourself what the purpose of the group is. Then enter the names or e-mail addresses of all the people you want to include in the group.

Separate each member from the next with a comma or semicolon, or press Enter after the name to put each member on a separate line. If the person uses Notes or has a Person document in either your own or your company's Name & Address Book, you only need to include his or her name. Otherwise, you have to include a full e-mail address.

In fact, you don't have to stop at people's e-mail addresses. If your company has an outbound fax gateway for Notes, you can include fax numbers. You can also include the names of other groups that are listed in either your private or public Name & Address Book. For example, you could have a Sales Department group whose members are the groups Sales Managers and Sales Representatives.

> **TIP**
>
> If your organization has a well-defined structure, it's good to make your groups match this structure, with big groups made up of little groups. However, when Notes tries to send a message to a group that has another group as its member, it has to stop and look up the membership of the second group. Therefore, groups can only be "nested" five levels deep. If you try to send a message to a group that has more than five subgroup levels beneath it, Notes gives you an error message.

NOTE One drawback of using a personal group is that the information about who is a member of the group is only available to you. This means that recipients of your memo who try to reply to the whole group will not be able to do so. This is an advantage in some situations, but in most cases it is an unanticipated side effect of using a personal group.

Recording Shortcuts for People's Names

If it really is too much trouble to type your boss' whole first *and* last name each time you send her a Notes message, you can invest a few keystrokes now to save yourself some in the future.

To make shortcuts for any Notes user, you can create a minigroup in your Personal Name & Address Book that contains just that one person's name. Give the group a very short name—your boss' initials perhaps—and in future this is all you need to type to address messages to her.

You may wonder why you create a Group document and not a Person document. The reason is that you shouldn't create Person documents in your Personal Name & Address Book when those people already have entries in the Public Name & Address Book. If you did have one Person entry in each, Notes would get confused as to which to use. To get around that, you can use a group with just one member.

Other Forms and Views

If you use your Personal Name & Address Book heavily, you may want to keep details about companies separate from details about their employees. Notes lets you create Company documents that store some basic details about each firm. Clicking on the Open Company Profile button at the top of a Person document takes you automatically to the appropriate Company document.

Your Personal Name & Address Book is also the place Notes keeps the Location documents that tell it how to connect to your company's Notes network when you are at the office, at home, or on the road. Notes uses Location documents for every user, but most desk-bound Notes users will never need to change the default settings established when Notes was installed. Mobile Notes users may need to know a little more about Location documents, and so the subject is dealt with in more depth in Chapter 13.

Notes stores two other kinds of documents in your Personal Name & Address Book. Server Connection documents tell Notes how to connect to a particular server. Again, they are mentioned in the discussion of mobile Notes in Chapter 13. Server Certificates authorize you to use Notes servers at a different company, for instance. You are unlikely to need to deal with these yourself.

That's just about everything the average Notes user could need to know. If you need more information, here's where to turn:

- If you are unsure about a Notes term, flip to the glossary (Appendix C) for a quick explanation.
- If you have to install or set up Notes yourself, you'll find full details in Appendices A and B.
- If your work calls for you to need very detailed information on a particular facet of Notes, take a look at the Notes Help database.
- If you want to parlay your newly acquired Notes knowledge into a database development position, read Sybex's *Mastering Lotus Notes 4.5 and Domino*. If you need to know about administering a Notes network, read *Lotus Notes 4.5 Administrator's Guide*, also from Sybex.

Part 5

Appendices

Appendix A

INSTALLING LOTUS NOTES, NOTES MAIL, OR NOTES DESKTOP

Many users of Lotus Notes will find that their copy of the program has already been installed and set up by their Notes administrator. If this is the case, your administrator has made sure that everything is working correctly, and you are not obliged to learn procedures that you would only need to use once.

But this isn't always the case. Sometimes *you* need to set up Notes so it knows who you are, and sometimes you have to install the software as well. Appendices A and B guide you through the process in straightforward terms.

This appendix covers the installation process, which entails telling Notes how to place its program files on your computer or to use files that already exist on a network server. This appendix explains how to install the Notes Workstation software (sometimes called the Notes Client). If you yourself are a Notes administrator who needs to install the Domino Server software, you should follow the instructions that come with the installation disks.

Appendix B deals with Notes setup. It explains how to tell Notes who you are and how you want to use the program.

NOTE The procedures for installing and setting up Notes Mail and Notes Desktop are almost identical to the procedure for setting up Notes. All three packages use the same program files. The different capabilities provided in each are determined by the User ID file, which identifies each user to Notes (see Appendix B for a little more information on User ID files). To install Notes Mail or Notes Desk-top, follow the instructions for installing the full version of Notes.

NOTE The versions of Notes for Unix operating systems support concurrent installation on multiple hosts, which means that many users of Notes for Unix will find that their system administrator has already installed the software for them. For this reason, and because the Unix installation procedure bears little similarity to that of other operating systems, it is not covered here. If you need to install Notes on a Unix workstation, follow the printed installation instructions provided with the software, or use a workstation with Notes already installed to follow the instructions in the Install Guide for Workstations database.

Before You Install Notes

Before you start installing Notes, you need to find out a number of things from your Notes administrator:

1.   Will you be installing Notes from a set of 3.5" floppy disks, from a CD-ROM, or from a set of installation files stored on a file server? If you are installing Notes from floppy disks or a CD-ROM, you need to get your hands on the appropriate disks. If you are installing from a file server (or a CD-ROM drive connected to a file server), you need to know the location of the Notes installation files.

2. Will you be installing your own copies of Notes' program files on your computer's hard disk or using shared program files stored on a file server? If you're going to use shared files on a server, you need to know the location of those program files.

3. Which, if any, of the following items will you need to install for yourself (often these files are available on your Domino server or a file server):

- Database templates
- Documentation databases
- The Notes Help or Help Lite database
- Domino.Action templates

 NOTE You also need information from your Notes administrator to set up your workstation once you've installed the files, so you can save yourself time by finding out the answers now to the questions at the beginning of Appendix B.

You should make sure to close any other software applications running on your computer before starting to install Notes. This is particularly important for other Lotus applications, which may use shared files that the installation process needs to update.

If You Are Upgrading from an Earlier Version

If you are an existing Notes user upgrading to Release 4.5, you should back up or rename certain files before you start the upgrade process.

Make copies of the following files in your Notes data directory or Notes Preferences folder: NOTES.INI (Windows users can find this in the Windows directory), DESK-TOP.DSK, NAMES.NSF, and your user ID file, which will be named something like THAYES.ID. These copies should use a different extension, such as NOTES.BAK.

If you have customized certain types of files, you should either rename the files until you have completed the installation or back them up to a different directory. Notes automatically overwrites these files during the installation process. The types of files to protect are: database templates (.NTF), modem command files (.MDM), and scripts (.SCR). Additionally, Windows and OS/2 users should also protect any customized files of the following types in the Notes data directory: bitmaps (.BMP), macros (.MAC), and SmartIcons (.SMI and .TBL).

Doing the Installation

Installing Notes shouldn't cause you any lost sleep. The basic procedure is that Notes presents options on the screen along with short descriptions. These descriptions and the more detailed explanations provided in this appendix help you choose the option appropriate for you. Once Notes has found out how you want to install the program, it copies the appropriate files automatically and returns you to your operating system. Then, you can proceed to start Notes for the first time and set up the program to meet your personal preferences (see Appendix B).

For Windows and OS/2 users, these instructions are written on the assumption that drive A is a floppy disk drive, drive C a hard disk drive, drive E a CD-ROM drive, and drive N a network drive. If your computer and network are configured differently, just substitute the appropriate letters. For example, if you were installing from network installation files located in the directory X:\PROGRAMS\NOTES, you would use X:\PROGRAMS\NOTES\INSTALL to launch the installation program.

If you are installing Notes for Windows NT, follow the instructions given in this chapter for Windows 95. The procedure is the same.

> **NOTE** You may encounter slightly different file specifications for CD-ROM installation to those given in this chapter. If the exact path specified is not available on the CD you are using, use File Manager or Explorer to look for the file INSTALL.EXE for Windows installations and the file INSTPM.EXE for OS/2 installations. Windows 95 files will usually be in a directory named W32INTEL. Windows 3.1 files will be in the directory WIN16.

Starting the Installation Program

If you are installing from a set of floppy disks, place the first Notes Install disk in your floppy disk drive. If you are installing from a CD-ROM, place the Lotus Notes CD in the CD-ROM drive.

If you need more information at any point in the installation process, you can click on the Help buttons, which are available on every screen. If you are using Windows, you can also press F1 at any time to get help.

In Windows

In Windows 3.1, Windows for Workgroups 3.11, and Windows NT 3.51, select File ➤ Run from the menu in Program Manager. In Windows 95 and Windows NT 4.0, select Start ➤ Run from the Taskbar. Then:

- Type **A:\INSTALL** to install from floppy disks.
- Type **E:\WIN16\INSTALL\INSTALL** to install from CD-ROM for Windows 3.1 and Windows for Workgroups 3.11.
- Type **E:\W32INTEL\INSTALL\INSTALL** to install from CD-ROM for Windows 95 and Windows NT.
- Type **N:\INSTALL** to install from files stored on a server.

Notes displays a lengthy software agreement for you to read. Once you have done so, confirm your agreement with the licensing conditions.

Notes asks you to wait while the install program copies its temporary files to your hard disk and then tells you that it is searching your hard disk for any Lotus applications already installed. Then you will see a screen like the one in Figure A.1. Enter your name and your company's name and click on Next. Do not select Install on a File Server. Notes asks you whether the names you just entered are correct. If you made a mistake, click on No; otherwise click on Yes to confirm them.

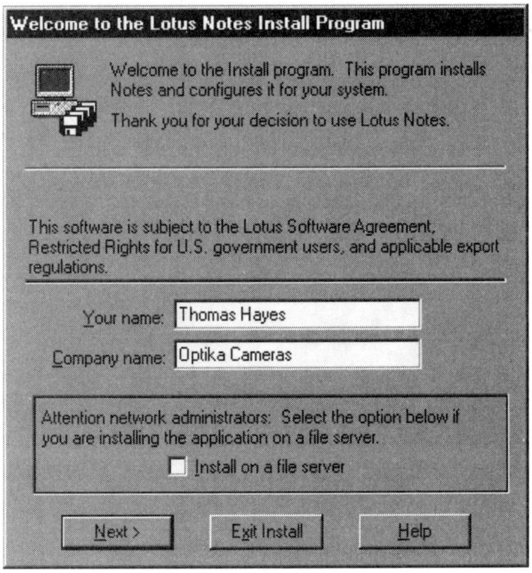

FIGURE A.1:
Tell Notes your name and that of your employer.

> **NOTE**
>
> If you are going to be running the Windows version of Notes from shared program files stored on a server, you can skip a large chunk of the installation procedure and start reading again at the section "Installing the Files," toward the end of the chapter.

If you are upgrading to Notes 4.5, Notes will warn you that it has found an existing copy of Notes on your hard disk and will recommend that you install the new copy in the same directory. Click on Next once you have read the warning.

If you are using Windows 95, you will need to choose a location for your Main Lotus Directory. The default location is C:\LOTUS\.

Notes now displays the Install Options dialog box, shown in Figure A.2.

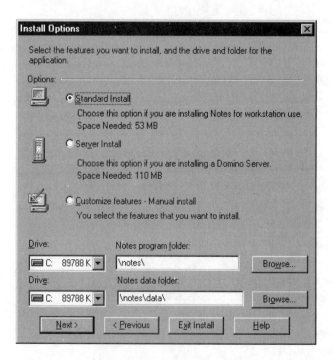

FIGURE A.2:
The Install Options dialog box lets you choose what type of installation you want and where to install it.

First, specify the drive and directory in which you want Notes to install both its program files and its data files. By default, Notes stores program files in C:\NOTES\ and data files in C:\NOTES\DATA\. If you are already a user of Lotus SmartSuite, the installation program will suggest a NOTES subdirectory within your main SMARTSUITE directory. Notes shows you the amount of space available on each drive (in Kbytes). Do not use more than eight characters for either directory name, even in Windows 95 and Windows NT.

Then choose the type of installation you want. You have three choices:

Standard Install This installs Notes in the most commonly used configuration. You don't need to decide which components to add and which to leave out. To choose this option, select its radio button and click on Next. Then skip the next main section in this appendix and start reading again at "Installing the Files."

Server Install This option allows Notes administrators to install Domino server software. If this describes what you are doing, you should read the *Lotus Notes Install Guide for Servers*. If you are installing Notes for Windows 3.1 or Windows for Workgroups, you will not see this option.

Customize Features - Manual Install This lets you choose which combination of Notes components to install. Read the next main section, "Choosing Which Features to Install," to decide what combination you need.

In OS/2

In OS/2, open an OS/2 window from the Workplace Shell.

- If you are installing from floppy disks, go to the A: prompt and type **INSTPM**. Then press Enter.
- If you are installing from a CD-ROM, go to the OS2\INSTALL directory on the CD and type **INSTPM**. Then press Enter.
- If you are installing from a file server, go to the OS2\INSTALL directory on the file server and type **INSTPM**. Then press Enter.
- If you will be using shared program files, go to the shared copy of Notes and type **EPFIDLDS.EXE**. Then press Enter.

Alternatively, you can select File ➤ Run from the File Manager window, type the appropriate filename, including the full path, and click on Run. Notes asks you to choose the type of installation you want. You have three choices:

Standard Installation This lets you choose which combination of Notes components to install. You should select this option unless you have been told you will be using shared program files.

Server Installation This option allows Notes administrators to install Domino server software. If this describes what you are doing, you should read the *Lotus Notes Install Guide for Servers*.

Shared Installation Choose this option *only* if you have been told you will be using shared program files.

Read the instructions that Notes displays and then click on Continue. Check the Update CONFIG.SYS box to have Notes update this OS/2 system file with path information.

WARNING If you are upgrading from a previous copy of Notes, make sure to check the Overwrite Files box. If you do not, Notes will ask you for confirmation each time during the installation process that it needs to replace an existing file with a newer one. This will mean that installation takes much longer, and that you will have to stay at your computer the whole time. You also risk receiving a non-functional installation of Notes if any of the earlier files remain.

Click on OK to close this dialog box. Now read the next main section, "Choosing Which Features to Install," to decide what combination of features you want.

On the Mac

On the Macintosh, the procedure differs a little depending on the location of your Notes installation folder. If you are installing from files stored on a file server, follow these steps:

1. Select the Chooser from the Apple menu.
2. Click on the AppleShare icon.
3. Make sure that AppleTalk is active and then choose the AppleTalk zone for the file server to which you want to connect.
4. Choose the server that contains the Notes Install Disk folder and click on OK.
5. Enter any name and password information that you need to provide to connect to the server.
6. Choose the volume that contains the Notes Install Disk folder and click on OK. An icon for this volume appears on your desktop.
7. Close the Chooser dialog box.
8. Double-click on the icon for the server volume.
9. Double-click on the folder that contains the Notes Install disks.
10. Double-click on the Notes Install Disk folder.

11. Double-click on the Installer icon.
12. When the Lotus Notes screen appears, click on OK.
13. Notes offers you three options:

> **Easy Install** This installs Notes in the most commonly used configuration. You don't need to decide which components to add and which to leave out. If you choose this option, you can skip the next section and start reading again at "Installing the Files."

> **Custom Install** This lets you choose which combination of Notes components to install. Read the next section, "Choosing Which Features to Install," to decide what combination you need.

> **Custom Remove** If you have already installed Notes 4.5, you can use this option to selectively delete components without completely removing Notes.

If you are installing your copy of Notes for Macintosh from a CD-ROM, double-click on the icon for the CD-ROM on the desktop. Double-click on the Lotus Notes folder and then follow the instructions from step 10 in the network installation steps given above.

If you are installing from floppy disks, place the first Notes Install Disk in the drive and begin with step 11 in the network installation steps listed above.

Choosing Which Features to Install

Your choices of which Notes features to install are quite similar whether you are installing Notes on a Macintosh or on a workstation running OS/2 or some variant of Windows. For Windows and Macintosh installations, you have a Standard Installation or Easy Install option that chooses the most common set of features automatically. If you chose this option you can skip this section.

If you are installing on an OS/2 computer, or chose Customize Features in Windows or Custom Install on the Mac, you'll see a Customize dialog box something like the one shown in Figure A.3. The exact details of the options available to you depend on which operating system you are using.

NOTE If you are an OS/2 user who will be using shared program files, you can click on the Select All button to tell Notes that you want to install everything, and then skip to the next section in this appendix, "Installing the Files."

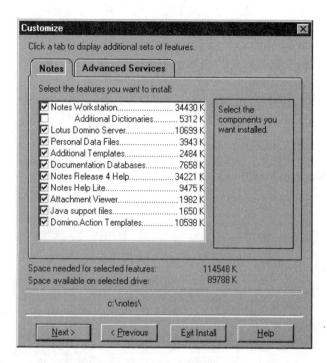

FIGURE A.3:
This dialog box lets you choose exactly which Notes components to install.

You should place checkmarks next to the options you wish to install and remove the checkmarks from options you don't want. Notes displays a brief description of the highlighted option to help you decide (on the Macintosh, click the "i" icon next to each item). This is what each option does:

Notes Workstation These are the main Notes program and data files. Without them, there's no Notes. If you use a Macintosh, this option may be named simply Lotus Notes. *You must select this option.*

Additional Dictionaries If you expect to be communicating in other languages, check this option to have Notes install foreign-language dictionaries. This option is not available on the Macintosh.

Lotus Domino Server Windows 95 and NT users may see this option. Make sure this box is not checked.

Personal Data Files These files contain various settings specific to how you run Notes on your computer. OS/2 users may see this option labeled Notes Data. Macintosh users may not see these files listed separately. *If this option is available, you must select it to run Notes properly.*

Set Notes Preferred Memory to 4MB This option is only displayed for Macintosh users. Select this option if you are using an older Macintosh and want to change the preferred memory size for Notes applications from 2.7MB to 4MB (recommended if you have sufficient RAM).

Additional Templates Macintosh users may see this entry listed as Notes Template Applications. These are the standard database templates that Notes offers as a basis for new databases you create. These files are usually available on your Domino server, so you should deselect this option if you don't expect to design a lot of Notes databases. If you're going to use Lotus Notes Mail or Lotus Notes Desktop, definitely deselect this option. If you're going to design databases on a remote computer (such as a notebook or home computer), leave this option checked.

Documentation Databases Again, these databases are usually available on your Domino server. You may want to install your own copy of these databases if you are putting Notes on a remote computer with a large amount of disk space (not a notebook). Macintosh users will see this option labeled Notes Documentation Databases.

Notes Release 4 Help This is the main Notes Help database. It is generally available on your Domino server. On the Macintosh, this option is just labeled Notes Help. If you are using a remote computer with plenty of hard disk space, you might want to install your own copy of the Help database. Notes Help Lite is a slimmer version of the same database. You should not install both.

Notes Help Lite This is a reduced-calorie Notes Help database, specially designed for storage-constrained notebook users. Install this if you are a notebook user. Do not install both Help and Help Lite.

Attachment Viewer This lets you see the contents of attached files in Notes. The viewer is comparatively small and is recommended unless you are *very* short on disk space. OS/2 and Macintosh users will see this option labeled Notes Viewers.

Java Support Files These files enable Windows 95 and NT users of the Web Navigators to run Java applets. Install them if you expect to use either version of the Web Navigator.

Domino.Action Templates If you are a Windows 95 or NT user planning to develop your own dynamic Web sites from Notes databases, you may want to install these files, although they are probably on your Domino server. Most users won't need these files.

Microsoft OLE Extensions This option lets Macintosh users use Microsoft Object Linking and Embedding 2.07 to place objects in Notes documents.

Apple XTND Translation System This option lets Macintosh users import and export certain types of files.

If you are installing the Windows version of Notes, you may see a tab labeled Advanced Services. You can safely ignore the two installation options on it unless you are a Notes administrator.

Installing the Files

NOTE This is the point at which Windows users who chose the Standard installation, Macintosh users who chose Easy Install, and all users of shared program files rejoin the rest of us. You don't have to choose which Notes components you want installed, but you still need to decide where Notes should place its files. If you are going to be using shared program files, the only location you need to specify is for Notes personal data files.

OS/2 users should now select a drive and directory in which to store the Notes files. Notes displays the amount of disk space it needs for the features it is going to install and the amount available on the drive you have selected. If you chose a customized installation, the disk space figure will change as you select and deselect options from the list.

If you do not have sufficient disk space on the drive you have chosen, you can change to a drive with more space:

- In Windows, click on Previous. Notes takes you back to the Install Options dialog box where you can specify a new drive and directory for the Notes program and data folders.
- In OS/2, click on Disk Space. Choose a drive that has sufficient free space. Select Change Directories to Selected Drive. Click on OK.
- On the Mac, click on Select Folder. Choose Desktop or Hard Disk for the location of the new installation folder and select the folder's name. To create a new folder, click on New, type the folder's name, and click on Create. Click on the button labeled Select <folder name>.

Don't try to fit Notes onto a disk with barely enough room, because Notes will need more space later to store your work. If you enter the name of a directory that does not yet exist, Notes creates it during installation.

To proceed with the installation, click on Next in Windows, or click on Install in OS/2 or on the Mac.

If you are upgrading from an earlier release, Notes may ask you to confirm that it should delete obsolete files. Click on Select All and then on Next to proceed.

Windows users must tolerate an extra dialog box like the one shown in Figure A.4. Here you choose a program group or program folder in which Notes will place your Notes program icon. If necessary, you can create a new folder. When you are happy with your choice, click on Next.

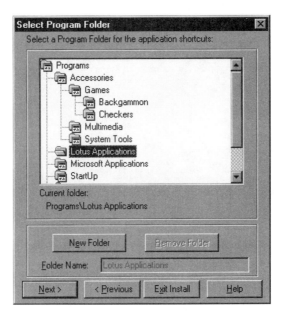

FIGURE A.4:
If you are using Windows, tell Notes where you want it to place your program icon.

You may then see a message asking if you *really* want to start copying files to your hard disk now. Double-check that you don't have any other applications open. If you do, you should switch to each application and close it down before returning to the Notes installation program. (Switching between applications is explained in the section "Keeping Notes Running While You Use Other Software" at the end of Chapter 1.) Then click on Yes to have Notes start copying.

As Notes copies files, it displays an on-screen bar to show you how the installation is progressing. If you are installing from a network drive or CD-ROM, this process is relatively quick; the floppy disk installation takes quite a while. Also, if you are installing from floppy disks, you need to remain at your computer to change disks every so often.

Notes also shows a series of graphics that explain some of the benefits of Notes 4.5. Once the files have all been copied, your options depend on the type of computer you are using. Windows users should click on Done to return to Windows. OS/2 users should click on OK and then Exit. Macintosh users have the option to Restart the computer or to Quit and go back to the Desktop.

Your next task is to set up Notes to know who you are and what you want to do. If you have the answers to the questions at the beginning of Appendix B, go ahead and launch Notes; you're obviously on a roll and you might as well get everything set up right away. If you need more information before you set up Notes, or if you just need a break, you can leave setting up Notes until later.

Appendix B

SETTING UP LOTUS NOTES, NOTES MAIL, OR NOTES DESKTOP

Most Notes users have their copies of the software installed and set up for them by their Notes administrators. These lucky people don't need to concern themselves with the information in either of these appendices. If you know for a fact that Notes files haven't been installed on your system, you need to read Appendix A first. If you have already followed the instructions in Appendix A, or if you know your administrator installed the Notes files but didn't set up Notes for you, this appendix is the place to be.

If you don't know what your administrator did and he or she isn't around to ask, look on your desktop for an icon like the one shown here. If you can't find this icon and you don't have a group or folder named Lotus Applications or Lotus Notes on your system, chances are that Notes hasn't been installed at all; begin with Appendix A. If you do have a Notes icon, the instructions in the section "Starting Notes," later in this appendix, will help you to work out whether you need to go through the setup procedure.

Why Do I Have to Set Up Notes?

Installing most software is a matter of popping the disks in your disk drive and answering two or three questions. Installing Notes works pretty much the same way, and either you or your Notes administrator has already been through this process to get Notes' files installed on your computer.

However, Notes also requires you to go through a setup process the first time you use the program. The reason is to let Notes know who you are, how you will communicate with other Notes users, and how you will use shared resources.

Obviously, it's a lot more important for your e-mail software to know what your full name is and how to exchange information with your colleagues than it is for your spreadsheet software to know that information. So persevere a little longer while we go through Notes setup—you'll only need to do this once.

Before You Set Up Notes

Before you set up Notes, you need to find out a number of things from your Notes administrator:

- What type of connection will I have to my home Domino server? The choices are: a direct network connection, a remote (modem) connection, both network and remote connections, or no connection.
- Will my user ID be supplied on a disk (either on a floppy disk or stored on a network hard disk), or will I get it from the company's Public Name & Address Book? If it's on a disk, what is its location and filename?
- What is my user name? (Make sure to get the precise form that Notes will use, such as *Thomas Hayes/Optika Cameras*.)
- What is my home server's name?
- What is the password for my user ID? (You need to pay attention to capitalization, spaces, and punctuation marks.)
- If I have a network connection to my home server, what type of network do we use, and what is the name and location of my mail database on the server?
- If I have a remote connection to my home server, what is the phone number for my home server, what type of modem will I be using, and to what port is it connected?
- If I have both network *and* remote connections, I need answers to both the previous questions.

- What time zone am I in and do we follow Daylight Savings Time? (You might just know the answers to these two already.)

Starting Notes

You start Notes by clicking on an icon like the one shown here. The group or folder containing the icon may have any name—try looking for Lotus Notes, Lotus Applications, or Main. When Notes starts up, you briefly see a "splash screen" while Notes gets the program ready for operation.

Then, you will see one of two screens. If you see the dialog box shown in Figure B.1, you need to set up Notes to know who you are and how you will use the program, following the instructions in the rest of this appendix. If you see a regular Notes workspace, then Notes has already been set up for you. You can skip the rest of this appendix.

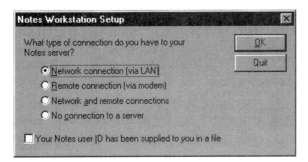

FIGURE B.1: Notes needs to know how you're going to connect to your home server and where to find your user ID.

Telling Notes How You're Going to Connect

Notes uses the Notes Workstation Setup dialog box (shown in Figure B.1) to find out how you are going to communicate with your home Domino server (to send and receive mail and use shared information). Your choices are:

- A network connection for office computers that are wired directly to a local area network (LAN).
- A remote connection for notebook computers, home computers, and any other computer that connects to Notes via a modem.

- Both network and remote connections for, say, a notebook that is sometimes used in a network-connected docking station.
- No connection. With this option, you can't use Notes mail or share information with your Notes-using colleagues.

The second question in this box relates to your user ID file, a small file that tells Notes who you are and the organization to which you belong. Before you can use Notes, your Notes administrator has to create your user ID file. Then, he or she can either put it on a floppy disk or network hard disk for you, in which case you should check the box provided, or store it in Notes alongside your entry in your company's Public Name & Address Book. Here you're telling Notes which option your administrator chose, so that it knows where to look.

When you've told Notes how you're going to connect to your home Domino server and where to find your user ID, click on OK. If your user ID is on a disk, Notes will display a standard file selection dialog box that lets you tell the program where to find your ID file. You should select the appropriate floppy disk drive or enter the location of an ID file stored on a network drive. Notes may next ask if you want it to copy the user ID file to your Notes data directory; click on Yes.

Your user ID will probably be password-protected, so next you'll see a dialog box asking you to supply your password. Notes displays *X*s as you type in your password to prevent others from reading it over your shoulder. Be careful to type the password in the correct combination of upper- and lower-case letters; Notes passwords are case-sensitive.

> **NOTE** For more information on Notes passwords, see Chapter 1.

Telling Notes about Yourself and Your Computer

Once you've told Notes where to find your user ID file and have provided a password, you will see one of the dialog boxes shown in Figures B.2 through B.5. Why am I being so vague? Well, the dialog box you see depends on your choice in Figure B.1. There's a different box for each of the four types of possible connections to a Domino server.

Read the appropriate set of instructions below to find out how to fill in the blanks in the dialog box on *your* screen.

If You Have a Network Connection

If you told Notes that you have a network connection to your home server, you see the dialog box in Figure B.2. If your user ID was supplied on a disk, Notes automatically fills in your name from the ID you chose. Enter the name of your home Domino server and select the type of network your company uses. A Setup button lets you configure the network settings more precisely. However, if your network settings are incorrect, you should probably enlist the help of your Notes administrator before trying to change them.

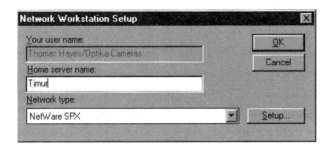

FIGURE B.2:
A network Notes user needs to supply a user name, server name, and network type.

If You Have a Remote Connection

If you told Notes that you're going to have a remote connection to your home server, you see the dialog box in Figure B.3. If your user ID was supplied on a disk, Notes automatically fills in your name from the ID you chose. Enter the name of your home Domino server and its phone number.

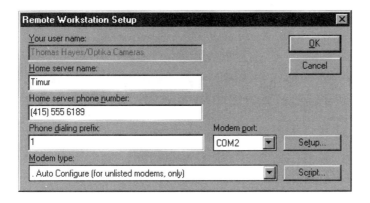

FIGURE B.3:
A remote Notes user needs to supply a user name, server name, and phone number, and also identify a modem and the port that it uses.

You also need to select the type of modem you will be using from the list provided. If your modem is not listed, select the Auto Configure option (toward the bottom of the list). Once you have identified your modem, you need to tell Notes which port to use to communicate with it.

> **NOTE**
>
> **The Setup button next to the modem port number lets you set several detailed modem parameters. Most users do not need to alter these parameters at this point. If you experience trouble connecting, read about modem settings in Chapter 13, which deals with mobile Notes use. If you still can't connect, contact your Notes administrator.**

If You Have Both Network and Remote Connections

If you told Notes that you're going to use both network and remote connections between your computer and your home Domino server, you see the dialog box in Figure B.4. If your user ID was supplied on a disk, Notes automatically fills in your name from the ID you chose. Enter the name of your home Domino server and its phone number.

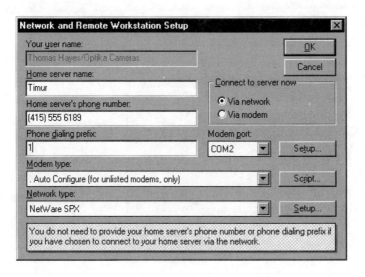

FIGURE B.4:
Choose both types of connections and you have to answer both types of questions.

Select the type of modem you will use from the list provided. If your modem is not listed, select the Auto Configure option (toward the bottom of the list). Once you have identified your modem, you need to tell Notes which port to use to communicate with it.

> **NOTE**
>
> The Setup button next to the modem port number lets you set several detailed modem parameters. Most users do not need to alter these parameters at this point. If you experience trouble connecting, read about modem settings in Chapter 13, which deals with mobile Notes use. If you still can't connect, contact your Notes administrator.

Then, you must select the type of network your workgroup uses from the list. Clicking on the Setup button next to the Network Type field lets you change more detailed network settings. However, if the default network settings do not work, you should probably enlist the help of your Notes administrator before trying to change them.

Finally, choose which method you want to use to connect to your Domino server at this time. If you can use either method, a Network connection is preferable. If you do choose a network connection, you aren't compelled to provide a phone number or dialing prefix right now, but enter that information if you have it.

If You Have No Connection to a Domino Server

Although not having a means of connecting to a Domino server leaves you without Notes mail or the ability to share databases with your coworkers, at least you don't have to answer too many questions. The dialog box you'll see next is shown in Figure B.5.

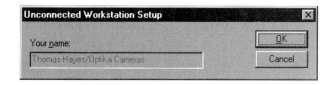

FIGURE B.5:
Unconnected Notes users just need to remember their own names.

Your one question (so don't blow it) is "What is your name?" If your user ID was supplied on a disk, Notes will even automatically fill it in for you.

Telling Notes What Time Zone You're In

Once you've entered the myriad details about your connection to your home Domino server, click on OK. Now you get to watch another little bar move across the screen while Notes creates some of your personal effects.

WARNING

If Notes runs into problems with the network you specified, it may ask you for additional information, such as a LAN Unit Number. Your first response should be to click on Cancel to go back and double-check the network settings you supplied. If that doesn't resolve the problem, call your trusty Notes administrator—you don't want to be mucking around with LAN Unit Numbers on your own.

When Notes finishes configuring itself with your settings and personal information, it needs to find out the time zone in the region in which you work. Most Notes users just need to select the appropriate time zone here. If you live in a city such as Indianapolis that doesn't observe Daylight Savings Time, or overseas in a country that doesn't set the clocks forward once and back once each year, then you need to deselect the DST option.

Notes takes you to the Notes workspace, where you will *probably* have three sparkling new icons. However, you shouldn't be disappointed if you have fewer icons; it just means that your administrator has set up Notes a little differently at your company. If you have more icons, you can celebrate. Your friendly Notes administrator has set up Notes to provide you with icons for some commonly used Notes databases.

Whatever icons you see, your next step, if you've set up your own copy of Notes, should be to proceed to Chapter 1 to start using Notes mail.

NOTE

If you are upgrading to Notes 4.5 and made backup copies of customized SmartIcon sets, modem files, etc. before you started installation, now is the time to rename these files or copy them back into the appropriate locations in your Notes data directory.

Appendix C

GLOSSARY OF TERMS

This glossary provides a brief definition of terms you may encounter in using Notes, other programs, and the Internet. Words in *italics* are used to point to other glossary definitions of particular relevance.

About document   A special Notes document that tells you the purpose of a database. Notes displays the About document automatically the first time you open a database. To see it again, choose Help ➤ About This Database.

access control list (ACL)   A list of database users that specifies what rights each has to read, create, modify, and delete documents, views, and other features of a database.

access level   The rights that a user has been given to work with a particular database. The seven basic access levels are Manager, Designer, Editor, Author, Reader, Depositor, and No Access.

Action Bar   A row of labeled buttons that is displayed in many forms and views above the main panes and below the *SmartIcons*. Clicking on an Action Bar button performs a simple function, such as creating a new document or moving an existing one to a folder.

agent   A stored set of actions that performs automatic tasks on one or more documents. Each agent consists of a document selection formula, a trigger, and one or more actions.

attachment   A computer file placed within a rich-text field in a Notes document. The file can later be detached, launched, viewed, or printed (by the recipient of a mail message, for example).

Author-level access   A database access level that allows the user to create new documents in a database, and to read but not modify documents that others have created. Authors can also read the contents of database views.

Bookmark   A favorite Web page stored in the *Web Navigator*'s Bookmarks folder for easy access. Also, a special mail form used to draw attention to a *DocLink*.

browser   See *Web browser.*

bullet   A small, black circle used to identify each item in a list. Notes provides a simple function to create bulleted lists in your documents.

button   A labeled gray rectangle in a form or document that performs an action when clicked. Buttons are commonly used to help users navigate through a workflow database or to automate certain tasks.

categorized view   A view in which document entries are grouped according to the contents of one or more fields.

Category field   A field provided specifically to allow users to provide their own document categorization.

cell   The smallest unit of a table, where a single row and column meet.

checkbox   A graphical means of making a selection in which the available options are not mutually exclusive. Compare with *radio button*.

Clipboard   A part of your computer's operating system that acts as a temporary storeroom for information, allowing you to transfer text, graphics, and other information between documents, between databases, or even between separate programs.

collapsible section   One or more paragraphs of a document that can be reduced to a title to make it easier to navigate a large document.

database   A self-contained collection of documents, forms, views, and folders. The documents hold the actual data; the forms, views, and folders tell Notes how to present the data to you. Databases are represented by labeled icons in your Notes workspace.

database catalog   A special Notes database that provides basic information on all or many databases stored on a Domino server, a group of servers, or all the servers in a domain.

database icon   One of many square buttons displayed on the tabbed pages of the Notes workspace. Database icons are the principal point of access for Notes databases. The icon displays a graphic and the database's name. It can also show the database's filename, the server on which it is stored, and the number of unread documents.

database library   A special Notes database that provides detailed information on selected databases available to a workgroup.

database replication   See *replication*.

DDE   Abbreviation for Dynamic Data Exchange, a method of sharing data between programs that is available in Windows and OS/2.

Depositor-level access   A database access level that allows the user to create new documents in a database, but not to read documents that others have created. Depositors cannot even see database views.

Designer-level access   A database access level that allows the user to modify the forms, views, and other structural components of a database, but not to change the access control list. Designers have the same document-creation and editing rights as editors.

design pane   A special portion of the window in which you can enter formulas for such features as *agents*, *buttons*, and *hotspots*.

desktop   The main screen of your computer's operating system, usually obscured by windows for the programs you are running. Also, an alternative name for the Notes *workspace*.

dialog box   Any type of window smaller than the full screen used to provide or solicit information. *Buttons* allow you to close the dialog box and perform various other functions. You will see dialog boxes displayed by Notes, your computer's operating system, and other programs you use.

dial-up Notes   See *mobile Notes*.

dial-up server   A *Domino server* equipped with *modems* and a telephone connection to provide a point of access for *mobile Notes* users. Also called a dial-in server.

DocLink   An icon that, when clicked, takes you to another Notes document.

document   The general name for anything you or someone else creates with a Notes form. Each form creates a different type of document, such as a memo, reply, or address entry.

document preview pane   See *Preview Pane*.

Domino   A Notes function that translates Notes databases into linked Web pages and vice versa. Domino also allows users of *Web browsers* to interact with Notes databases while maintaining Notes' access controls. See also *Domino server*.

Domino server   A powerful computer running special software to perform Notes housekeeping tasks such as transferring mail and retrieving pages from the Internet. It stores shared Notes databases and communicates through a computer network. Some Domino servers also communicate by modem with mobile Notes users. Prior to Notes 4.5, Domino servers were called Notes servers.

edit mode   A mode in which you can modify a document. The opposite of *read-only mode*.

Editor-level access   A database access level that allows the user to modify and delete documents that others have created in a database, as well as to create, modify, and delete documents of his or her own.

e-mail   Abbreviation for electronic mail, which describes any software that allows computer users to exchange text messages and other information.

embedding   One technique for placing data from another program in a Notes document. Embedded data remains the same even if the source file from which it came is modified or deleted. The data can be edited in Notes without access to the source file. See also *linking* and *subscribing*.

encryption   The process of encoding part of a document so that only users who have been given a secret encryption key can read it.

field   A named area on a form for entering a single type of information, such as a document title, a date, a price, or the text of a report. A field is the smallest entity in Notes. See also *rich text* and *plain text*.

file attachment   See *attachment*.

file server   A computer that provides a central access point for files, programs, and printers. Compare with *Domino server*.

folder   A place you can put Notes documents to organize them in your own way. Folders look a lot like views but contain only what is put in them. With some special folders, such as the Inbox, Notes also adds and removes documents itself.

font   The style of print used for a particular piece of text. Common font families include Times, Helvetica, and Courier.

footer   The text displayed along the bottom margin of a document.

form   The "template" for a document. Notes forms differ from Notes documents in much the same way that paper forms differ from paper documents. Forms store the information you need to make sense of Notes documents, such as the labels next to the fields, and any buttons and graphics.

formula   An expression used to program Notes to perform a series of actions. Formulas are employed mostly by database designers, but you may come across some limited uses of them in *agents*, *buttons*, and *hotspots*.

forwarding   Sending a copy of a mail message or other document to one or more other Notes users.

FTP   Abbreviation for file transfer protocol, the standard format for sending and receiving binary files (files other than unformatted text) over the Internet.

full-text searching   A sophisticated feature that lets you search a Notes database for words and phrases, as well as perform more complex searches using wildcards and logical operators. To perform a full-text search, the database you want to search must have a full-text index—a special file that lets Notes perform searches within seconds.

gateway   See *mail gateway*.

Gopher   A once-popular Internet application that uses a menu system to allow users to search for and download information.

group   A special document in a *Name & Address Book* that simplifies sending a message to many people at once. Also called a user group or mailing list.

groupware   Software that helps people work collaboratively. The ability to automate workflow and display timely progress information is usually seen as a key feature. Other important elements include: integrated electronic mail, shared reference information, electronic discussion forums, integrated scheduling, and support for multiple types of computer hardware, software, and networks.

header   The text displayed along the top margin of a document.

hierarchical view   A view in which responses are grouped beneath the main document to which they relate. Also, any similarly structured view such as one where prior versions of a document are listed as subordinate to the most recent version.

home page   The highest-level Web page at a Web site, providing a point of access for the other Web pages. A Web site's home page is often analogous to the contents page of a magazine.

home server   The Domino server on which your Notes mail file is stored.

horizontal scroll bar   An optional feature (View ➤ Show ➤ Horizontal Scroll Bar) that allows you to see a document or view that is too wide to fit on screen at once.

hotspot   A special region in a document or form that, when clicked, pops up text, performs an action, or allows you to follow a link to a Web page or another Notes document, view, or database.

HTML   Abbreviation for Hypertext Markup Language, the standard way of encoding Web pages.

HTTP   Abbreviation for Hypertext Transfer Protocol, the standard protocol for transferring Web pages to Web browsers. Often seen in lower-case form as http.

hunt group   A group of *dial-up servers* accessible via a single telephone number. Companies with many Notes users can use hunt groups to spread the communications workload among several servers.

hypertext   The concept of linked electronic documents where selecting a graphic or piece of highlighted text displays a second document. Hypertext systems include Web pages, Notes documents, and most multimedia systems. The term "hypermedia" is sometimes used for hypertext systems that have been extended to incorporate audio and video components.

icon   Any small picture used to communicate the purpose of an element on a computer screen. Notes uses several different types of icons. The most important are *database icons*, used as basic access points for Notes databases. Notes can also display icons in the columns of a database view to signify that a document has an attached file, for example. Icons are also used to provide quick access to Notes features (*SmartIcons*) and special database features (on the *Action Bar*). Finally, you may well start Notes by clicking on an icon in your computer's operating system.

InfoBox   A special type of dialog box that lets users of Notes and other Lotus software view changes to a document or other program element as they are being made. For example, you can experiment with fonts and colors in the Text Properties InfoBox and watch the effect of your changes on the text in your document.

Internet   The collective name for a large number of interconnected computer networks across the globe. The fastest-growing of the many Internet services is the *World Wide Web*.

InterNotes server   A Domino server that maintains a connection to the Internet, allowing Notes users to use the Server Web Navigator.

InterNotes Web Navigator   See *Server Web Navigator.*

ISP   Abbreviation for Internet Service Provider, a commercial organization that provides you with services to connect to the Internet.

keyword   One of several predefined choices in a field. A keyword can actually be one or more words. Sometimes keyword choices are set by the database designer; in other cases they can be added by database users. Keywords help to ensure that similar documents can be sorted properly in *categorized views*.

launching   The process of automatically opening an attached file, or a linked or embedded object, in the application that created it.

linking   One technique of placing data from another program in a Notes document. Linked data can be updated to reflect any changes made to the source file from which it came. Users with access to the source file and the creating application can edit linked data in Notes. See also *embedding* and *subscribing*.

links   Notes links let readers switch to another document, view, or database. *URL* links take the reader to a Web page. Links to other documents are known as *DocLinks*.

local database   A Notes database stored on your computer's hard disk, on a floppy disk, or on a *file server*.

Location document   A document in your *Personal Name & Address Book* that allows you to tell Notes how to connect to a server when you are using your computer in various circumstances. You can create several Location documents and specify a wide range of settings on each.

macro   See *agent*.

Mailbox database, MAIL.BOX   See *Outgoing Mail database*.

mail gateway   Software that lets you send mail to and receive mail from users of other electronic mail systems, such as cc:Mail and the Internet.

mailing list   See *group*.

Manager-level access   The highest level of database access. Managers can modify access control lists in addition to exercising all the rights of lower access levels.

memo   The basic type of Notes message. Reply and Reply with History are some other types of Notes messages.

menu bar   The thin row of words below the *title bar* and above the *SmartIcons* that provides the main access to Notes' functions. Click and hold down the cursor on one of the words to display a "menu" of options.

message   A *document* that has been (or will be) sent through Notes mail. In your mailbox, message and document mean the same thing. In other parts of Notes you use documents that you don't generally mail to other people, so they aren't usually called messages.

Microsoft Internet Explorer   A commercial *Web browser* that can be used as an alternative to the *Web Navigator* interface for accessing the World Wide Web.

mobile Notes   The process of using Notes without a direct network connection, connecting instead by dialing a *Domino server* with a *modem*. Mobile Notes users keep *replica* copies of Notes databases and use the *Replicator* to manage the synchronization process.

modem   A contraction of MOdulator/DEModulator. A modem is a telecommunications device that translates computer data into a form that can be sent over an ordinary telephone line. At the other end of the line, another modem translates this back to computer data so that the computer to which yours is "talking" can understand what your computer "said."

Name & Address Book   A special type of Notes database that stores information about users of Notes and other e-mail systems and how to contact them. It may also contain information on Domino servers and other parts of your Notes network's structure. You will see both *Personal Name & Address Books* and *Public Name & Address Books*.

Navigation Pane   One of three panes available in a Notes view. The Navigation Pane contains the active *navigator* and is always the pane nearest to the top left corner of the screen.

Navigational Bar   A special feature of the Notes workspace that can be displayed below the *SmartIcons* and above the *Action Bar* to help you control the *Web Navigator*. Clicking on the button at the left end of the Navigational Bar changes it to the *Search Bar*, which helps with full-text searching.

navigator   A graphical means of selecting views and documents in Notes. Each database has a standard hierarchical "Folders" navigator, and can also have simpler custom navigators. See also *Navigation Pane* and *Web Navigator*.

Netscape Navigator   A commercial *Web browser* that can be used as an alternative to the *Web Navigator* interface for accessing the World Wide Web.

Notes administrator   A network manager or systems administrator who has detailed knowledge of Notes and is assigned special access rights. Small organizations may only have a single Notes administrator; larger ones will probably have at least one at each workplace using Notes.

Notes client   See *Notes workstation*.

Notes database   See *database*.

Notes mail database   A special Notes database from which a user can send and receive mail. Your mail database is sometimes also called your Notes mail file or Notes mailbox. Although your mail database is stored on a *Domino server*, only you can open it. A *mobile Notes* user can keep a *replica* mail database on a notebook or home computer.

Notes server   See *Domino server.*

Notes workstation   A regular computer that runs Lotus Notes, like the one on your desk, or on your lap. The term *Notes client* is sometimes used instead.

OLE   Abbreviation for Object Linking and Embedding, a method of sharing data between programs that is available in Windows and on the Macintosh.

Outgoing Mail database   A local repository that stores the mail of a *mobile Notes* user until the user connects to a *dial-up server.* The Outgoing Mail database is sometimes called the Mailbox database, and always has the filename MAIL.BOX.

Page Minder   A *Personal Web Navigator* feature that alerts you when the content of one or more Web pages is changed.

Passthru server   A *dial-up server* that lets *mobile Notes* users connect indirectly to another *Domino server* that is not itself equipped as a dial-up server.

Permanent Pen   A special combination of font, color, and point size that lets you mark changes consistently when editing documents and adding comments.

Personal Name & Address Book   The version of the *Name & Address Book* that is for your own use. You can store details of e-mail addresses, create personal *groups* to use as mailing lists, and use *Location documents* to tell Notes to use different settings at different times.

Personal Web Navigator   A local database that allows a Notes user with a direct Internet connection to browse Web pages translated into Notes format. Compare with *Server Web Navigator.*

plain text   A type of Notes field that does not allow you to apply text formatting. The format of a plain-text field is set by the form's designer. Compare with *rich text.*

point size   The size of a particular font measured from the base of one line to the base of the next, in units of $1/72$".

pop-up   A highlighted word (usually indicated by a green rectangle) or graphic that, when clicked, "pops up" a rectangle containing a block of explanatory text. Pop-ups are often used to define technical terms.

posting   An article or response sent to an Internet newsgroup or Notes discussion database.

Preview Pane   An optional element of a view window that lets you see (and sometimes edit) the contents of the document highlighted in the *View Pane* without fully opening that document. The Preview Pane can also be used within a document to read the contents of another linked document.

private view   A view designed for individual use. Most users will only see private views when they have been specifically provided by the database designer. This type of view is called "private on first use," which means that it only becomes your private view when you first try to open it. Advanced users can use Notes database design skills to create their own private views of most databases.

Public Name & Address Book   The version of the *Name & Address Book* that is used by your whole company (or a large segment of it). It names all Notes users, details public *groups* you can use as mailing lists, and contains a large amount of other information that Notes needs to route mail and manage database access.

quick address   A clever feature that lets you type the first few letters of a Notes user's name into an address field and have Notes fill in the rest.

radio button   A graphical means of making a selection in which only one option is allowed from a series of choices. The name refers to older radios where pushing the button for one station made all the other buttons pop up. Compare with *checkbox*.

Reader-level access   A database access level that allows the user to read the contents of a database's views and documents, but not to create new documents or to modify or delete existing ones.

read-only mode   A mode in which you cannot modify a document, only read it. The opposite of *edit mode*.

Read Public Documents access An access level that allows the user to read documents within a database that have been specifically designated as public. This level can be used to allow limited access to another user's mail database, or to give Internet users restricted access to the Web version of a Notes database.

refresh You can refresh a view or document to reflect changes that have been made to it after editing or making deletions. Refreshing also recalculates computations in fields. To refresh, press F9 or choose View ➤ Refresh.

remote Notes See *mobile Notes*.

replica A special copy of a database that is updated by exchanging information, or "replicating," with the original database, either on a regular schedule or at will. See also *replication* and *stacked replica*.

replica stub A new database replica that has not yet been filled with documents.

replication A process by which two databases are updated so that each contains the same information. Replication can be performed between two servers, or between a server and a workstation. See also *mobile Notes*.

Replicator A special *workspace* tab that provides a simple interface to the *replication* process for *mobile Notes* users.

Response document A type of document, typically in a discussion database, that is created as a response to a main document. Further comments can be added with a Response to Response document. See also *hierarchical view*.

rich text A type of Notes field that allows text and paragraph formatting, tables, hotspots, embedded and linked objects, attached files, and many other Notes features. Compare with *plain text*.

scroll bar See *horizontal scroll bar*.

Search Bar   A special feature of the Notes workspace that can be displayed below the *SmartIcons* and above the *Action Bar* to help with *full-text searching*. Clicking on the button at the left end of the Search Bar changes it to the *Navigational Bar*, which helps you find your way around Web pages.

section   See *collapsible section*.

selective replication   *Replication* of only certain documents in a database, to reduce connection times and save disk space for *mobile Notes* users.

server   A reasonably powerful computer that provides services for users of other computers. See also *Domino server* and *file server*.

server database   See *shared database*.

Server Web Navigator   A shared database that allows Notes users without a direct Internet connection to browse Web pages retrieved by a *Domino server*. Also known as the InterNotes Web Navigator. Compare with *Personal Web Navigator*.

shared database   A Notes database that resides on a *Domino server*.

signature   An electronic code that authenticates a Notes document as having been written by the person named as its author.

SmartIcons   A row of customizable buttons displayed below the *menu bar* that provide a shortcut for performing certain Notes commands and actions.

stacked replica   A Notes *database icon* that shows multiple replicas of a single database on the same icon.

status bar   A thin bar at the bottom of the Notes window that Notes uses to display messages, access levels, and communications status. You can use it as a shortcut to format text, change locations, and access your mail database.

subscribing   A method of viewing data from Macintosh applications in a Notes document. The data can be automatically updated when the source file changes.

table An array of *cells* in rows and columns that can be placed in a rich-text field.

template A Notes database design that can be used as a starting point for a new database.

title bar The top line of the screen, providing a brief description of the open window.

trash folder The folder in your mail database or another database that contains documents you have chosen to delete. You can later confirm that you want to delete these documents or return them to the database.

unread mark An electronic tag on a document that tells Notes you have not yet read it. Many views display unread documents in red and marked with an asterisk in the margin. You can mark documents read or unread (regardless of whether you have actually read them) to make a view easier to scan.

URL Abbreviation for uniform resource locator, the formalized address that tells the Web Navigator and other browsers how to find information on the Internet. Two common types of URLs begin `http://` for Web pages and `ftp://` for files.

user group See *group*.

User ID A file that uniquely identifies each Notes user. Each Notes user must have his or her own User ID file.

Using document A special Notes document that tells you how to use a database. To see the Using document, choose Help ➤ Using This Database.

view A particular way of looking at the information in a Notes database. Views are always made up of rows, each giving information about a particular document. A view shows all the documents that match a certain criterion.

View Pane The primary pane of a Notes view, containing the listing of documents available in the database—that is, the pane that actually displays the view. The other panes are the *Navigation Pane* and the *Preview Pane*.

Web   The short name for the *World Wide Web*.

Web Ahead   A *Personal Web Navigator* feature that lets you tell Notes to preload all the links that stem from one or more *Web pages* to a depth of up to four subsequent pages.

Web browser   Any program that lets you view pages on the *World Wide Web*. Notes' *Personal Web Navigator* and *Server Web Navigator* are both Web browsers. Notes also allows you to use commercial browsers such as Netscape Navigator and Microsoft Internet Explorer if you prefer.

Web Navigator   Either of two databases (the *Server Web Navigator* and *Personal Web Navigator*) that let Notes users browse *Web pages*.

Web page   A single hyperlinked document on the *World Wide Web*, defined by its *URL*.

Web site   The set of pages that comprise a person or organization's presence on the Web.

workflow application   A Notes database or suite of interlinked databases designed to efficiently manage a core commercial process.

workgroup software   See *groupware*.

workspace   The Notes "desktop"—the entire assemblage of Notes windows, the tabbed pages where you display database icons, menus, SmartIcons, Action Bar, status bar, and title bar. Often the phrase is used more narrowly to refer just to the tabbed pages and database icons. You can organize your workspace by naming the tabbed pages and by adding, moving, and removing icons and tabs.

World Wide Web   A part of the Internet devoted to locating and displaying hypertext and hypermedia documents (*Web pages*). The Web, as it is generally known, is the primary cause for the explosion in interest in the Internet within the past few years. To access the Web, you use a *Web browser*.

Index

Note to the Reader: Main level entries are in **boldface**. **Boldface** page numbers indicate primary discussions of a topic. *Italic* page numbers indicate illustrations.

Quick Guide to Views

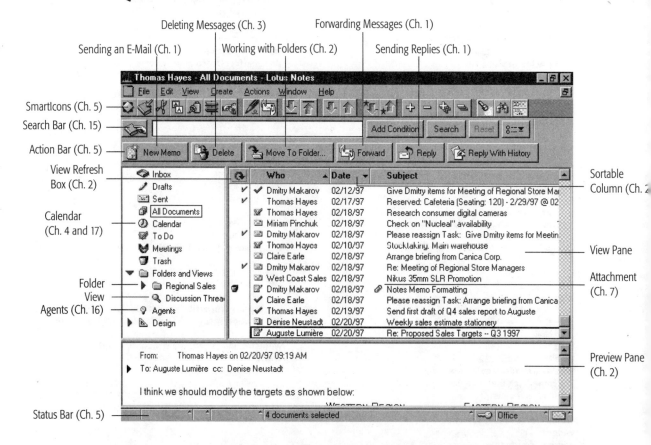

Deleting Messages (Ch. 3)
Forwarding Messages (Ch. 1)
Sending an E-Mail (Ch. 1)
Working with Folders (Ch. 2)
Sending Replies (Ch. 1)

SmartIcons (Ch. 5)
Search Bar (Ch. 15)
Action Bar (Ch. 5)
View Refresh Box (Ch. 2)
Calendar (Ch. 4 and 17)
Folder
View
Agents (Ch. 16)
Status Bar (Ch. 5)

Sortable Column (Ch. 2)
View Pane
Attachment (Ch. 7)
Preview Pane (Ch. 2)

Database Access Levels

Icon	Access Level	Icon	Access Level
none	No Access		
	Depositor or no database open		Editor
	Reader		Designer
	Author		Manager